WINGBEATS:

Exercises & Practice in Poetry

Edited by
Scott Wiggerman &
David Meischen

🐈 **Dos Gatos Press** 🐈

Austin, Texas

Wingbeats:
Exercises & Practice in Poetry
© 2011, Dos Gatos Press
ISBN–13: 978-09760051-9-3

The editors wish to thank Fred Courtright, Ann Farrar, and Kris Marshall for advice and assistance as regards permissions issues; Kristee Humphrey and Judy Jensen for critiquing our page layout during the early stages; Kathryn Rogers and Diane LaGrone for their meticulous attention during a final proofreading; the poets who generously allowed their poems to be used as examples in the *Wingbeats* exercises; and—most important—the teaching poets who submitted exercises for this book.

First Edition
10 11 12 13 5 4 3 2 1

Cover Design: Kristee Humphrey
Manufacturing: Morgan Printing Book Division of Ginny's Printing

Dos Gatos Press
1310 Crestwood Rd.
Austin, TX 78722
www.dosgatospress.org

WINGBEATS:

Exercises & Practice in Poetry

Imagination grows by exercise.

W. Somerset Maugham

I have no fancy ideas about poetry. It doesn't come to you on the wings of a dove. It's something you have to work hard at.

Louise Bogan

Preface

Each fall since 2005, we have hosted a series of readings that feature poets from the *Texas Poetry Calendar,* the initial impetus for the creation of Dos Gatos Press. After the first couple of years, everywhere we went, we recognized other poets and they recognized us; we realized that Dos Gatos Press was supporting a state-wide community of poets outside the enclaves of the Texas cities and towns where these poets resided. We also recognized in each other a hunger for poetry, a desire as writers to get better and better at our craft. Without fail, the poets we meet are eager to try new approaches to the written word.

A book of poetry writing exercises was a logical next step. We reached out to a network of poets all over the country: poets we'd met at various readings, conferences, and workshops; poets we'd read and admired in a variety of journals and anthologies; poets we'd encountered solely through social media and e-mail. We wrote to poets with advanced degrees who teach at colleges and universities, as well as poets, many self-taught, who teach poetic craft outside academia—journal editors, publishers, those involved with writers' and artists' organizations. A wonderfully diverse group replied in the affirmative, and by the fall of 2010, we had begun to assemble, edit, and organize a wide-ranging collection of exercises from teaching poets around the country.

The best compliment we could offer our contributors is that, over and over as the exercises arrived, we said to each other, "I can't wait to try this one." In fact, we did not wait! We tested a couple dozen of the exercises over the past year—and were delighted with the results. In workshops, Scott has used several already—with resounding success—with participants at various skill levels, from high school students to practiced poets. These include Ravi Shankar's infinitely adaptable "A Manipulated Fourteen-Line Poem," Abe Louise Young's collaborative "Birds in the Classroom," and Susan Terris' quick and enjoyable "Seven (or Ten) Line Poem." For those exercises we didn't have time to try, we often recruited other writers for test runs; several of the example poems found in this book are from our recruits, while others are from the poets who wrote the exercises—or from their students and acquaintances.

Wingbeats is founded on the belief that every practitioner of a craft needs regular exercise in that craft and that each of us has something to learn by trying the exercises others have discovered and refined. Not every exercise will lead to a finished poem, and some, like Annie Finch's "Compass of Poetics," are not meant to. No exercise is foolproof; what works for one person won't necessarily work for another. We have our favorites, and you'll soon have yours. But we do believe that you will gain *something* from each of these exercises—at a minimum, an appreciation for the numerous ways poems can be approached, developed, and shaped.

Turn the page, then, and browse our table of contents. It represents one set of categories, but keep in mind that many of the exercises could readily fall under more than one chapter heading. Most of them, for example, could have been placed in "Exploring the Senses," and there's often a fine line between "Chancing the Accidental" and "Complicating the Poem." With these issues in mind, we developed an alternate table of contents (page 298) to provide other ways of accessing the *Wingbeats* exercises.

Which exercise titles excite you? Turn to those pages. Browse some more. Try an exercise you can't resist: Jenny Browne's "Love Letter to a Stranger." Try something unusual, adventurous, outside your comfort zone: Bruce Covey's "Two Sides of the Same Coil: Blending Google Sculpting and Automatism." Try a collaboration with another poet or poets as outlined in Gretchen Fletcher's "Entering the Conversation of Poetry." Get out art supplies and try a hands-on exercise like Jane Hilberry's "Meeting Your Muse." Explore a new form, as Rosa Alcalá does in "A Walking Petrarchan Sonnet." Push yourself with Patricia Smith's powerful but disturbing "Dressing." Or try a new approach to revision, as Laurie Kutchins does in "Scissors & Gluesticks: Re-Visioning the Poem."

Make this book your own. Tweak. Adapt. Combine elements from two or more exercises: Naomi Shihab Nye's "New Combinations: Nouns and Verbs" with Andrea Hollander Budy's "The Postcard Poem" or Anne McCrady's "Speaking the Unspoken" with William Wenthe's "Stretching the Sentence." Most of all, have fun!

Scott Wiggerman and David Meischen

I. Springboards to Imagination

II. Exploring the Senses

III. Echoing the Familiar

VI. Going Difficult Places

VII. Complicating the Poem

Alternate Table of Contents

Acknowledgments

Index

Chapter I:
Springboards to Imagination

It's a very excruciating life facing that blank piece of paper every day and having to reach up somewhere into the clouds and bring something down out of them.

Truman Capote

Listing:
Side to Side, Top to Bottom

About nine years ago I embarked on a writing practice that has changed my life—not only when it comes to publishing, but even spiritually and emotionally. It started as a simple New Year's resolution among friends in a creative writing class. We decided to write a poem every day that year, no matter what. If we missed a day, we had to write two the next day. My friends gave up around April or May, and I . . . well, I'm the only idiot who's still doing it.

For the first two years or so, there were times when the exercise was quite painful. I either had no time to write, or worse, no material to write about—or so I believed. But over the years, I began to develop a side exercise that helped me tremendously when it came to the material part of the problem.

I began to create certain kinds of lists of possible topics to write about. And as they grew, these lists left me with no excuse when it came to that sit-down-and-do-it moment there in front of the coffee mug each morning. I could no longer play the "no inspiration" card. What I discovered along the way was that each time I would tackle some item from the list, it would spark the memory of one or two other items to add to the lists.

The short of it is that this exercise has resulted in seven books—six collections of poetry that are based on themes that arose from these lists, as well as a memoir that used the listing technique extensively.

But, as I mentioned earlier, there's more to it than the publications. This nine-year daily writing practice has saved my life in some ways. It has served as a good friend through some dark years. And in dealing with the mental and emotional health issues that resulted from those years, my daily sessions with a journal and pen also came to serve as a "data dump" for my brain—something akin to defragmenting the junky hard drive of my mind. I attribute much of who and what I am today to this wonderful, literary, healing exercise.

The Lists

Letters ones that need to be, or never got, written—whether the recipient is alive or no longer with us

Letters to the Editor topics and issues that matter to you (Well-written rants are still important to culture, society, and saving the world.)

The Great Family Stories the individual stories that define your life and your family's history . . . the ones that always get told, over and over, at Thanksgiving

Important Places your hometown, annual vacation spots, where you spent summers, where he/she asked you to marry him/her

Important Events and Dates the events and dates that remapped your world, changed the way you look at life, influenced the way you perceive time (Where were you when JFK was assassinated . . . when the Beatles landed . . . or when you learned of the 9/11 attacks?)

The Five Senses the sights, sounds, smells, tastes, and touches that shaped your life—from Hershey's chocolate to the squeak of Grandma's back screen door . . . from first kisses to the smell of early summer rain hitting warm pavement

Food and Drink These two play off of the "tastes" from the previous list, but food and drink play such a huge role in our lives that they really need to have their own list. (And whenever possible, recipes can be a wonderful addition to this list—even if they don't show up in the work, they can highly influence it.)

The Arts the books, movies, and music that have had a profound effect on your life

The Lost Arts the "good things" that we have lost, or are losing, in society and culture

Good Riddance the "not-so-good" things you're glad are gone

Characters the childhood/high school friends, relatives, and family members who always stood out in the crowd; the laughs, gaits, and quirky traits that left fingerprints on your life

Special Personal or Family Photographs the pictures that "speak." Writing in response to visual art—ekphrastic writing—has a long tradition. [See "The Question of Attraction: Ekphrasis," page 39.]

These lists are only meant to be launching pads. Other ideas for your own lists will get you into the swing of the practice.

The Ultimate List: The Timeline

An incredible complement to all the other lists—one that can spark an amazing number of things to write about in and of itself—is the timeline.

My friend and fellow professor here at the University of Oklahoma, Catherine L. Hobbs, suggests in her book, *The Elements of Autobiography and*

Life Narratives, that you keep/create two timelines: "one for . . . your 'private' life and one for your 'public' life."

> **The Private Timeline** What were the key, "close to home" moments in your personal life, or in the life of your family, that shaped you and your future? What events—big or little, profound or subtle—changed you?

> **The Public Timeline** What were the moments or events that shaped and changed the world?

Once you've created these two timelines, take a look at how the two mesh. As for me, I was shocked at how many "memories" and moments to write about rose up solely out of this particular aspect of the exercise. In fact, I'm still writing about the results of this encounter.

For a long time I've been mystified as to how a memoir would be pieced together. Where would a person begin? What would matter? And how should it be ordered or organized? Not to oversimplify, but I will say that when I took the twelve lists above and held them up next to—and then began to plug them into—the two timelines, the overwhelming prospect of memoir became much clearer . . . more possible to me.

Examples

I. Lists Below is one of my lists. There are small towns in three states, as well as a southwestern state capital, a place in the mountains, and two California beach towns. There are two international cities—one south of the border and the other separated from me by oceans, continents, and thousands of miles. There's even something called Blue Rock in a tiny Texas Hill Country town. Each one of these could spur a new poem—or a new list that might lead to several poems.

Important Places

1. Longview, Texas (hometown)
2. Cyril, Oklahoma (Dad's hometown)
3. Girard, Kansas (Mom's hometown)
4. Green Mountain Falls, Colorado
5. Santa Fe, New Mexico
6. Carmel, California
7. Redondo Beach, California
8. Blue Rock – Wimberly, Texas
9. Jerusalem, Israel
10. Tequila, Jalisco, Mexico

II. Poetry Finally, I offer a poem that I might not have written without my notebook and my lists.

1965

You can't write about your birth
without cheating. Memory
had no roots back then . . .
    hadn't become the endless
    falling off that it is now.

But the museum of America's mind
tells me that the Beatles had landed
at Kennedy Airport the year before
and injected something primal, feral even,
into the collective screams of teenaged girls . . .

    and that later, while I was learning
    to roll over, the movies were obsessed
    with beaches, surfboards, and bikinis . . .

    and that Sonny could sing to Cher
    "I Got You Babe" even though she
    was much taller and just about to dump 'im . . .

    and that Malcolm X would prove
    that white, Catholic presidents weren't
    the only candidates running for assassination.

And now, decades down the road from it all,
the nation somehow survived our stoned gazes
into the gooey bubbles and red glow of lava lamps
and the tens of thousands of sons and daughters
we shoved down the throat of a denuded Vietnam . . .
    let alone the even greater and unbearable number
    of Vietnamese we murdered in the gory process.

But we'll also have the softer memories
of granny glasses and green Gatorade . . .
    as well as the more hormonal reveries

of The Byrds singing "Turn! Turn! Turn!"
and the Stones screaming "I Can't Get No . . ."
and the Oldsmobile Toronado's 385 hp
engine and "split" automatic transmission.

Still, I wonder . . . Is there anything important
in the act of scrounging around in the airless attic
of the year I spilled into the mess of humanity?
Is it a foothold in climbing the Everest
of a fairly comfortable American life?

Well, of course I don't know. But maybe
it has something to do with the desire
that creeps over our mid-lives
that makes us want to jump
off the fast train of time
and slowly start walkin'
back down the tracks
the other way.

Nathan Brown is a musician, photographer, and poet from Norman, Oklahoma. He holds a Ph.D. in Creative and Professional Writing from the University of Oklahoma and teaches there as well. Mostly he travels now, performing readings and concerts as well as speaking and leading workshops on creativity, creative writing, and the need for readers not to give up on poetry. Brown has published six books: *My Sideways Heart; Two Tables Over,* winner of the 2009 Oklahoma Book Award; *Not Exactly Job,* finalist for the Oklahoma Book Award; *Ashes Over the Southwest; Suffer the Little Voices,* finalist for the Oklahoma Book Award; and *Hobson's Choice.* Just released in the spring of 2010, Nathan's new album, *Gypsy Moon,* is his first musical project in over a decade.

Meeting Your Muse

This is an exercise designed not to produce a piece of writing, but to give you a sense of what your very own personal creative energy is like and what feeds and inspires it. The exercise takes you and a partner through a series of steps that results in the naming of a "muse," by which I mean a source of energy that inspires artistic production. It can also—just as a fun bonus—be used to generate insight into specific problems.

I have found that there's a lot of energy in this exercise and that people are often startled at what emerges. Even writers who have been working a long time may discover things about their writing processes that they didn't know.

The exercise is based on the principles of Appreciative Inquiry, which, in a nutshell, means looking at what has worked well in the past and figuring out how you can do more of it (my apologies to the real practitioners of Appreciative Inquiry for that reductive summary).

The exercise may appear to be somewhat complex, but it is definitely worth the trouble. The exercise *must* be done with a partner. Do not attempt it alone; it won't work.

The Set-Up

I like to start by reading William Stafford's poem "When I Met My Muse," readily available online. If working with a class, you could have some discussion of conceptions of what the muse is, though I prefer students to suspend all preconceptions when they actually begin the exercise.

I tell them that the muse that emerges could be anything. Some examples from other students: an atom, foie gras, a woman with green eyes, a swirl of blue and purple, a certain lake, the Stanley Cup. I also ask students to trust their imaginations, no matter how strange their answers may seem.

What's interesting to me about this exercise is how *specific* the muses are about what they require. Some people need to work with shapes; some need color in their surroundings; some need to be located where they can observe people but not interact with them; some need to work with pre-existing materials; some need a clean house; some need chaos; some need to to be outdoors. The muses can also generate unexpected perspectives on a Life Question, a particular question to which you are seeking answers.

Procedure

Before starting, write down a question—a Life Question—with which you are wrestling. Think of an issue or challenge or question you're facing in your life right now, something you just haven't been able to solve or about which you're not sure how to proceed. (It need not be related to writing.)

Working in pairs, go through the *entire* sequence of questions outlined below for one person, then change roles and do the *entire* sequence for the second person. The partner will record the list.

Let's say that Lisa and I are partners and we're working first with Lisa's muse. I will go through the list below, asking Lisa each question and taking notes about what she says. I won't comment along the way; I'm just reading the questions and recording her answers. At Step 9, I can offer my thoughts. After we've finished the sequence with Lisa, she will ask me the questions and record my answers.

Meeting Your Muse Sequence

1. Describe a time or a couple of specific times when your creative energy was flowing. Note that "creativity" doesn't necessarily mean you were making paintings or writing poems. You might have been gardening, cooking, boxing, doing math or running a meeting—any activity in which you felt a heightened sense of energy. Be specific—e.g., "I was living in a house in Bloomington with my friend Jed when I was twenty-two and we didn't have any money but we decided we were going to decorate the house. . . ."

2. Analyze the factors that contributed to your creativity. Consider: Why were you especially creative then? What was going on in your life? What did the energy feel like?

3. If you were to recreate a set of circumstances that would foster such creativity now, what would you do?

4. Think for a minute about yourself and the quality of your energy when you're in a creative state. What is that energy like? Try to get a sense *in your body* of what the energy feels like and where you feel it most strongly.

5. Now imagine that energy as an entity in itself. This is your muse. Visualize that entity. See if it has a gender or a name or a hairstyle. It may be a non-human entity.

6. Ask your muse what would make him, her, or it happy. Don't censor and don't worry if it sounds odd. Is there a particular place or kind of place that makes your muse happy?

7. Can you commit to doing at least one of the things you named in step six during the next week?

8. Ask your muse for advice about your Life Question. Don't worry about whether the advice makes sense or is practical. Just listen.

9. Ask your partner for any connections she or he has made while listening to you.

10. Your partner will write up a quick summary of how to make your muse happy and give it to you to keep.

Variations

When I'm teaching this exercise, I bring in art supplies (pastels, watercolors, poster board, fabric, beads, a variety of papers, magazines to cut up, glue, scissors—any assortment of materials will work) and have each person make a visual representation of his or her muse. (I tell them it doesn't have to be "good" art and it doesn't have to be a literal representation.) Afterwards we put all the muses up on the wall and do a tour of the room; each person introduces his or her muse. In a workshop, members can support each other better if they know who/what their muses are, and it helps individual writers to keep that visual representation where they see it often. And although it may sound a bit goofy or grade-schoolish to bring in art supplies, people (from college students to corporate executives) generally love this part of the exercise.

This muse poster was created by Jane Hilberry's student Logan Johnston.

An Example

The muse exercise can also lead to muse poems. Here's mine:

My Muse Prefers

a five-star hotel with Jacuzzi and big bathrobes.
I always book a room with two beds,

one for her to lounge on. She eats both
of the mints on the pillows. She won't start the day

till we've read the morning news, and if the
croissants are stale, there's hell to pay. Sometimes

I look around to find she's disappeared,
gone off for a pedicure. She speaks to me

in languages I can't understand—she's pretending
to be in Paris, strolling the Champs-Elysées.

She drops allusions to works of art I haven't seen,
thinks I'm a bit of a rube. And maybe I am—

doing her work for her, following her every suggestion,
as if she were a goddess. She wants me to take her

to the Greek Isles; the air there will give her fresh ideas.
I know how it works: I'll be carrying the luggage

when she meets a Greek man with curly chest hair
and a deep tan. Then she'll be gone for good.

Jane Hilberry is a Professor of English at Colorado College, where she has taught Creative Writing for over twenty years. She also teaches arts-based Leadership Development courses for senior leaders at the Banff Centre and elsewhere. Hilberry has published poetry in journals including *The Hudson Review, The Virginia Quarterly Review,* and *The Women's Review of Books,* and her book of poems titled *Body Painting* won the 2005 Colorado Book Award for Poetry. Her latest book is a collaboration with her father, poet Conrad Hilberry, called *This Awkward Art: Poems by a Father and Daughter.*

Compass of Poetics

The overall goal of this exercise is to become more conscious of your un-examined poetic assumptions. You will be challenged either to push outward from your self-appointed boundaries or to explore more deeply within their confines. Or both.

Further, this exercise should:

- deepen your sense of your poetic roots
- help you discover new potential avenues for poetic influence
- freshen your awareness of your poetics and open opportunities for any needed change

You will need poetry anthologies, collections, and websites, as well as browsing time, from several hours to a week or more.

Procedure

The overall exercise has two steps—Touchstones and the Compass. Take as much time as you like between the two steps, years even. You may find that the Touchstones alone will give you plenty to think about for quite a while.

I. Touchstones

Print, photocopy, or copy out five pairs of poems, each pair written during a different century. One of each pair should be a poem you love and/or admire as a model for your poetry, and the other should be a poem you dislike and/or wouldn't consider as a model for your poetry. Unless you have very good reasons to do otherwise, make sure at least half of the ten poems were originally written in English.

Record the title and author of each poem, as well as the approximate date it was written. Read the poems aloud—several times each. On each poem, write a brief statement of the reasons for your choice. This statement can be a developed paragraph, but notes, either typed or handwritten, including underlines and circling, work fine too. Allow yourself to be as creative and subjective as you like in your explanations of why you like or don't like a poem.

When your packet of touchstones is complete, put it away—for a few hours if you are impatient, or as long as a month or two. Take it out when you have plenty of time, read through it, and write a meditation on what you find. What patterns do you see? Are there similarities in your likes and dislikes through the centuries? In addition to the basic yes/no contrast within each century, look for other contrasting pairs of poems that cross centuries.

Touchstones

21st century
Yea Cathy Park Hong, "Windowless House," 2007
Musical language, political/historical focus, high stakes, both in theme and narrative, inventive liberties with syntax
Nay Ai, "Disgrace," 2003
Narrower theme, focused on personal history and personal biases

20th century
Yea William Carlos Williams, "The Last Words of My English Grandmother," 1920
Gives other character a voice, polyphonic, dialectic, open to diversity
Nay T. S. Eliot, "Aunt Helen," 1917
Caricature, distant perspective, no interest in growth towards unity

19th century
Yea Walt Whitman, "Song of Myself," 1855
Mature strength and emotional resiliency, exuberant tone, rhythmic momentum, long poem length, boldness
Nay Alfred, Lord Tennyson, "If I were loved, as I desire to be," circa mid-1800s
Self-pitying, focused on desire

13th Century
Yea Rumi, "Love is Reckless," mid-1200s
Passion, risk-taking, facing fear
Nay Heinrich von Morungen, "The Wound of Love," early 1200s
Ennui, melodrama

8th Century
Yea Li Po, "Dialogue in the Mountains," circa mid-700s
Humorous tone, earthiness, simplicity of language
Nay Wang Wei, "Parting," circa mid-700s
Melancholic tone

This touchstones chart was created by Annie Finch's student Amy Alvarez.

II. The Compass

Draw a compass in the shape of a circle with these points. See the example on the facing page, created by Amy Alvarez from her Touchstones (page 13).

East Air/Thought—the theme, ideas, and intellectual content of a poem, including dialogue, statement, narrative, syntax, sentence length, and rhetoric

South Fire/Energy—the rhythmic push of lines, the crucible of structure, and the interplay of rhyme and word-music

West Water/Feeling—mood, including emotional tone of images, connotations of diction and vocabulary, and implied or direct statements of feeling

North Earth/Body—imagery, the concrete particulars and inhabiting world, including persona

Center Ether/Spirit—overall goal, inspiration, source, ground, or vision—political, spiritual, self-knowledge, entertainment, communication, and so on

For each point on the Compass, look over your touchstones and write a few words indicating what your chosen poems reveal about your poetic stance in that area.

Variations

Supplement/illustrate any of the poems with works of art from the same century in other aesthetic forms (images, music, etc.), noticing how they illuminate the same aspect of poetics you are focusing on in your contrast.

Follow-Up

Summarize what you have learned about your own poetics. How do you feel about what you have found? Which attitudes and assumptions about poetry feel most like your own, and which can you easily trace to others? Do any feel particularly stale, or particularly exciting? Look again at the "shadow" side of the compass, the poems you chose as negative examples for yourself. Do any of their qualities hold the attraction of the forbidden? Are there aspects of writing poetry you have been denying yourself and now want to explore, or familiar attitudes you are ready to outgrow? What directions would you like your poetics to take in the future? How can you best embody your ideal poetics in the poems you are writing now?

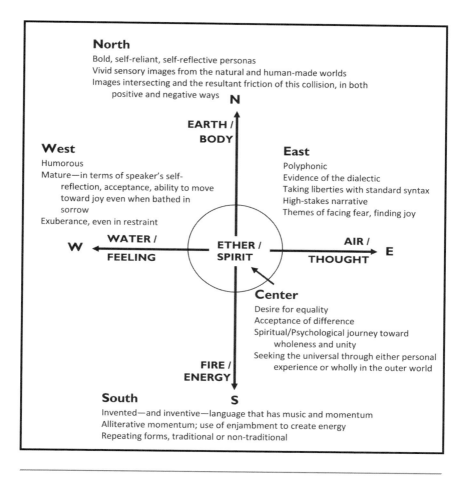

North
Bold, self-reliant, self-reflective personas
Vivid sensory images from the natural and human-made worlds
Images intersecting and the resultant friction of this collision, in both
positive and negative ways

N

EARTH /
BODY

West
Humorous
Mature—in terms of speaker's self-
reflection, acceptance, ability to move
toward joy even when bathed in
sorrow
Exuberance, even in restraint

WATER /
FEELING

W

ETHER /
SPIRIT

AIR /
THOUGHT

E

East
Polyphonic
Evidence of the dialectic
Taking liberties with standard syntax
High-stakes narrative
Themes of facing fear, finding joy

Center
Desire for equality
Acceptance of difference
Spiritual/Psychological journey toward
wholeness and unity
Seeking the universal through either personal
experience or wholly in the outer world

FIRE /
ENERGY

South

S

Invented—and inventive—language that has music and momentum
Alliterative momentum; use of enjambment to create energy
Repeating forms, traditional or non-traditional

Annie Finch is the author of *Spells: New and Selected Poems,* forthcoming from Wesleyan University Press; *Calendars,* finalist for the Forward Poetry Book of the Year Award; the long poem *The Encyclopedia of Scotland; Among the Goddesses: An Epic Libretto in Seven Dreams;* and *Eve,* recently selected for republication in Carnegie Mellon's Classic Contemporaries Poetry Series. Finch's other work includes a translation of the *Complete Poems* of Renaissance love poet Louise Labé, as well as books about poetry—including *A Formal Feeling Comes; An Exaltation of Forms,* with Kathrine Varnes; *The Body of Poetry: Essays on Women, Form, and the Poetic Self; Multiformalisms: Postmodern Poetics of Form,* with Susan M. Schultz; and the forthcoming *A Poet's Craft: A Complete Guide to Making and Sharing Your Poems.* Winner of a Black Earth fellowship and the Robert Fitzgerald Award, she is Director of the Stonecoast M.F.A. Program in Creative Writing at the University of Southern Maine.

Ellen Bass

The Word List: Your Assignment, Should You Choose to Accept It

I used to resist writing exercises. Or perhaps *resist* is the wrong word. Maybe it's truer to say that I just couldn't get inspired by them or even manage to use them, however clumsily, to construct poems. But some years back my friends, poets Dorianne Laux and Joe Millar, and I began writing together—giving each other assignments—and in that process I became a convert.

The exercises we devise are varied: we may require a particular poetic form, topic, technique, or the inclusion of a certain phrase or other elements, but we always include a word list as well, about ten words that we might use as we write our new poems.

Rationale

For a long time now, we've been giving these assignments to our students as well, and the results are remarkable. I think there are a number of reasons this kind of exercise is so successful. For one, including all the elements (or even some of them) occupies the conscious mind and allows the subconscious or deeper mind freer rein. The conscious mind is trying to solve the puzzle of fitting these words into the poem, somewhat like a person doing a jigsaw puzzle, freeing the less conscious mind to wander. Giving the conscious mind a task occupies the usual censors so that ideas and associations that have been previously inaccessible become almost miraculously available.

The word list functions as a path to unexpected places—places that the writer might not otherwise think to travel. Although some students excel in imaginative leaps, many find it hard to stretch out from their original idea, so the poem remains predictable, pedestrian. The word list can urge the poem into the unexpected, the strange. It can lead the poem into territory that the poet would not have intentionally chosen but that is more interesting, more evocative.

Another benefit of the word list is that it invites fresh language into the poet's habitual vocabulary. The given words may be more practical, earthy, mechanical, elegant, gorgeous, scientific, particular, or odd than the poet would ordinarily choose. And those new words may lead to startling, yet apt detail, description, images, and metaphors.

I've seen this exercise work well with both beginning and experienced poets, but it's useful to caution beginning students that the idea is not to write a nonsensical poem. Sometimes a zany, wonderful, tour de force may result, but you don't want to sacrifice meaning just to get in all the words.

Another important instruction for this exercise is that students needn't use all of the words or elements on the list. And sometimes they needn't use any of them. I've had students who were inspired simply by thinking about the list. The words led them to poems they wouldn't have written otherwise, but the poems didn't actually use any of the words. More often, students use just some of the words or elements. And, of course, during revision, words from the list might need to leave the poem. Once gone, though, they still may have served a function in having moved the poem forward.

I like to present this exercise as a "take it or leave it" choice. I find that beginning students can be intimidated if they feel they *must* not only write a poem, but a poem that includes this list of words. But if it's given as a suggestion they may or may not want to follow, they often find it makes writing the poem easier, rather than harder. It's as though some of the elements of the poem are given to them gratis and they don't have to come up with everything on their own. And for students who have been writing for a long time, the word list is a great way to break out of ruts and long-standing patterns and breathe new life into their poems.

Generating Word Lists

Word lists can be created from many sources. I like to skim through books of poetry, but you can also find great words in the vocabulary of crafts, the trades, cooking. Think of all the words involved in sewing, auto mechanics, astrophysics, or anatomy. Complex and unusual words are great, but very common words are useful too. If you give your students this exercise repeatedly, it's good to vary the way you gather the words.

Here are a few lists to get you started:

Word List I leaf, torn, ham, draft, sprawl, linen, leash, hay, thirst, Braille, search, why

Word List II magnify, whisker, wake, peel, bruise, angel, spool, bush, brush, stiff, listen, puzzle

Word List III, with a Twist our, shy, mantillas, dies, bake, shabby, vulgar, pebbled, prim, slug, chip, peck, fiddle. **Include** a character from literature, myth or legend.

Word List IV, with a Twist silt, resin, architect, drill, giddy, pilgrim, impossible, fuel, oyster, maul, plunge, defense, lobe. **Include** a food and a tool.

Word List V, with a Twist time, bridle, crest, tusk, erase, hush, ice, ghost, pouch, charred. **Include** a famous person and the name of a city, as well as a song title and/or a line from a famous poem.

Variations

The word-list exercise can be used in almost any setting. It works well in classes and with groups. It's fun to do with poet friends, either in person or via e-mail. In that case one person makes up the assignment and gives (or sends) it to the others. There's a designated amount of time given to write, which could be anything from half an hour to a week. Then the friends share their poems. The word-list approach is also something you can do for yourself in isolation. You can make up a word list on the spot and include other elements as well and then sit down and write. Or you can make up a number of lists (maybe ten or twenty) and put them in a hat and when you sit down to write, pull one out and that's your assignment.

An Example

For the poem that follows, I used a *long* word list and a twist:

heavens, crack, troubled, stung, duck, dog-eared, flame, bourbon, gangster, swagger, plum, coffee, wait, shedding, stone, honey, swollen, royal, release, dragon, breath, stub, confident, reckless, crush, obsession, blond, soaked, root. **Include** a famous person, a season, a time of day, and a color.

As you can see, I didn't use all the words or elements in the poem. But the words made it possible for me to write the final stanza, which without the list clearly would not have emerged as it did.

If You Knew

What if you knew you'd be the last
to touch someone?
If you were taking tickets, for example,
at the theater, tearing them,
giving back the ragged stubs,
you might take care to touch that palm,
brush your fingertips
along the life line's crease.

When a man pulls his wheeled suitcase
too slowly through the airport, when
the car in front of me doesn't signal,
when the clerk at the pharmacy
won't say *Thank you,* I don't remember
they're going to die.

A friend told me she'd been with her aunt.
They'd just had lunch and the waiter,
a young gay man with plum black eyes,
joked as he served the coffee, kissed
her aunt's powdered cheek when they left.
Then they walked half a block and her aunt
dropped dead on the sidewalk.

How close does the dragon's spume
have to come? How wide does the crack
in heaven have to split?
What would people look like
if we could see them as they are,
soaked in honey, stung and swollen,
reckless, pinned against time?

Ellen Bass has published several books of poetry, including *The Human Line* (Copper Canyon Press, 2007), which was named a Notable Book of 2007 by the *San Francisco Chronicle,* and *Mules of Love* (BOA, 2002) which won the Lambda Literary Award. She co-edited the groundbreaking *No More Masks! An Anthology of Poems by Women* (Doubleday, 1973). She has had work in *The Atlantic, The American Poetry Review, The New Republic,* and elsewhere. Her nonfiction books include *Free Your Mind: The Book for Gay, Lesbian and Bisexual Youth and Their Allies* (HarperCollins, 1996) and *The Courage to Heal: A Guide for Women Survivors of Child Sexual Abuse* (HarperCollins, 1988, 2008). She teaches in the low-residency M.F.A. writing program at Pacific University.

Dip the Ladle

The objective of this exercise is to create a work that unveils something about yourself that you were not completely aware of. What emerges will have passion and depth because it arose from an intuitive place, one that is so private you yourself were not conscious it existed.

Procedure

I. On a library or bookstore shelf, find a poetry collection that you have never read before. As your eye travels from one page to the next, stop at the first phrase that jumps out at you or otherwise gives you pause. Jot it verbatim on a clean sheet of paper. Do not continue reading; give your full attention to this particular array of words.

II. Write the words again, but this time in random order. Let your mind swell with associations. Then write that same phrase in a columnar format. What images crop up? Make a mental note of them. Next jot down each word of your phrase several times. Is a specific memory provoked? Sit with that memory but do not write about it; just let it fill you. If multiple associations or images bombard you, write down key elements, if you must, but don't get descriptive. Conversely, if nothing surfaces, trust that because you were snagged by this particular phrase, something about it resonated. There's a need to connect with that, and a potential poem lies in the making. Give yourself license to allow this to happen. Chances are you will be moved toward a past experience that you denied had a strong impact on you at the time, or one that affected you in a way you have put off acknowledging.

III. Once you have tapped into this racing river, dip your ladle and pour the contents onto a clean sheet of paper. Let your stream of consciousness flood in whichever direction it may go. You'll know when you have enough on paper, and that engulfed in this flood is a brand-new poem. At a later time, plan to work cooperatively with your instincts to fine-tune what you found, and stay in touch with those instincts as you work through the revision process.

Variations

You can do this exercise solo or with those you trust. If shared, read aloud the phrase that grabbed you, then your stream of words in response. Discuss why the phrase from the original poem had power over you. Once you've had the time to refine and revise your own piece, share that finished version as well.

An Example

"Unplanned Punctuation" was inspired by lines from Alison Townsend's poem, "What I Never Told You About the Abortion." Here is the phrase that caught me:

That I wished you'd said, "A baby? Let's do it!"
instead of "It's your body. You decide."

Unplanned Punctuation

Those five words could have implied
contradiction with a sigh seeping up
from the diaphragm to separate the second
from the third, a signal that if the heart
were only capable, it would declare
its muscle. Or an ellipsis—even an ellipsis
after that third word would have let me
taste your hesitation. Possibly a drop
in tone when you got to the fifth and final
word showing a lack of conviction in what
your tongue was doing. But these were
the words you thought I depended on
so you said them, and I couldn't tell

by your mouth, your brow or hands
whether you really owned them.
The absence of dashes, even the softening
by a comma where the first period was placed
would have propped the window sash—
but there was no wishbone or duet,
no shovel and matching pail, just a lone
shoehorn whipped out fast—too fast—
from a pocket like a relay race baton
I was to take without pause, no looking back,
no lingering with the flannel, just take it
and run. *It's your body.* You said. *You decide.*

When I read Townsend's poem, I was struck by the immense gap between "Let's do it!" and "It's your body. You decide." Those two responses were as wide apart as Mexico and Alaska—each leading to totally separate outcomes. I tried jotting, "It's your body. You decide" onto paper in various ways (as outlined in the exercise), then turned my attention to the punctuation. Clearly, it was the punctuation that had an effect on the message—as indicated in the poem that ensued. For example, take a look at what happens to that phrase with the use of alternate punctuation: "It's your body; you decide!" or "It's your body ... You decide. ..." I spent time writing out alternate options before beginning my own poem.

Shoshauna Shy has published poems in numerous journals and magazines, including *The Seattle Review, Cimarron Review, The Briar Cliff Review, Rattle, Rosebud,* and *Poetry Northwest.* One of her poems was selected for the Poetry 180 Library of Congress program launched by Billy Collins. Shy is the author of four collections of poetry. The most recent, *What the Postcard Didn't Say,* received an Outstanding Achievement Award from the Wisconsin Library Association in 2008. Her work has been anthologized by Random House, Marion Street Press, Midmarch Arts Press, Grayson Books, and others. Shy works for the Wisconsin Humanities Council in Madison, Wisconsin, and has helped create, coordinate, and facilitate poetry programs for the annual Wisconsin Book Festival in downtown Madison each October. She is also the founder of Woodrow Hall Editions, which sponsors the *Poetry Jumps Off the Shelf* initiative, and the Woodrow Hall Jumpstart Award program.

Thesaurus Is Not a Four-Letter Word

Despite the dubious reputation that it has acquired as a literary crutch for the lazy, a *thesaurus* is the bible for many writing exercises. Poets who censure the thesaurus miss not only the enrichment of their vocabularies but also innovative ways to create images that accompany new words. These images are the backbone of this exercise, which teaches the creative process through easy and tangible steps beginning with the simplest writing tool ever invented: one word. One word, or perhaps a few words, a thesaurus, a pen, and a piece of paper are all you'll need to fuel the power that unleashes the poems within you. I call the exercise *branching*.

On Thesauruses I strongly recommend J. I. Rodale's *The Synonym Finder,* both for comprehensiveness and expediency. For traveling, I suggest the paperback *Random House Roget's Thesaurus* that has both synonyms and antonyms. I also use it regularly as a partner with *The Synonym Finder* to find antonyms, which are very helpful when incorporating contrast or conflict into a poem. I use these two thesauruses so heavily that I extend their lives by covering them with recycled leathers. Once when I was writing in a coffee shop, a woman asked if the leather-covered Rodale's was a Bible. I said, "Yes, yes it is—a bible for poets."

Procedure

I. Finding Your Topic

If you already have a topic, go to Step II. If not, think of something about which you feel strongly, that makes you think deeply, or that fascinates you. It can be anything: painful, loving, hateful, irritating, humorous. It can be something you've read, experienced or observed; it can be someone else's experience. The key is that you have a strong interest. Your position on the subject can be conflicted. Ambivalence can lead to self-growth and rewarding poems.

Step I is a solution to writer's block, as well as a tool for isolating the subject of your poem.

II. Finding the Roots

Once you've selected the topic, choose the word that most closely describes a main thought or feeling you have about it. If you can't decide between several words because they are equally important or represent polar parts of the topic (and this tends to happen when your topic is complex), then use them all: Write them side by side along the top right-hand side of a sheet of paper. Reserve the left half of the page for later.

III. Beginning to Branch

Use your word from Step II, or one of your words at a time if you made a list. Then find the word in a thesaurus. Read each synonym carefully. If you can possibly see yourself using any of them in connection with how you're thinking or feeling about your topic, list them under the root word so that you have a column of words. If you have no list by the end, then find another root word and do the same thing. Keep searching root words in your thesaurus until you have at least one list. Ideally you should work with several lists.

Now look up each of the words on your lists and do the same branching, also on the right side of the page. Circle words that you really like. This can become quite mesmerizing. Keep looking up words until images or ideas start to form. Write those images/ideas in short line form on the left side of the paper. This will lead you into your poem.

It may sound like work, but the process is playful, and it simultaneously develops your poem. About now is a good time for a break from the exercise. Overnight is best because this is when the subconscious goes to work filtering the words and images you've collected.

IV. Alternate Branching and Writing

Take frequent breaks, perhaps working on multiple poems and alternating, to give the poems time to brew. You'll be amazed that often, when you return to a poem after a break, you'll know how to start the poem and where to take it. Pursue these thoughts on the left side of the page. Soon you'll be developing actual poem lines that you want to keep.

Having branched words on one side of the paper and phrases and lines on the other creates a visual bridge that allows you to go back and forth freely between what's happening in your mind and the actual poem. Go to clean sheets of paper when necessary, but keep the stack of papers in chronological order so you can refer to them as you continue to work on the poem.

You're in the process of getting to the essence of your poem—going beneath the surface to the *why* and *how* of it. When the subconscious acts as muse in this branching way, it can take you places you have never been, and that's the beginning of exciting poetry.

V. Fine-Tuning the First Drafts

When you have something that resembles a first draft on the left side of the page, start polishing, even if the poem isn't all you want it to be yet. This polishing also works under the surface as you live with the poem.

Here's a way to polish the poem by using the thesaurus again: go through the lines word by word and see if each word is really the best one for what you want to say and for the rhythm and sound of the poem. To do this, just branch each of the words in question and read the line or stanza, alternately substituting the words in your branching list for the one you've used in the poem. You can often tell immediately if the word improves the line. Reading the poem aloud will help you decide. This extended branching will help you tighten your piece, to say more precisely what you mean, to find a title, to avoid cliché, to develop alliteration, assonance, contrast, and internal rhyme.

Detailed editing of this kind is especially important to poetry because it's the writing genre most dependent on precise, concise word usage. You want to make each word count.

An Example

Branching is my personal creative process and the crux of the workshop I teach. It has been an instinctive way of writing for me, starting with my first poem. Following is a recent one, "An American Haibun," with the branching process detailed.

The Topic and its Roots I was inspired to write this poem one day when I went out my front door for a morning walk, and the entire flock of sixty-some wild parrots that has inhabited my city for the past several decades descended into my yard and made themselves at home for a half hour. I was stunned to the extent that I knew instantly I had to write about it.

The first step was to figure out exactly what impacted me so much and why anybody else would want to know:

- The implausibility of wild parrots, indigenous to South America, living and propagating in Northern California
- The honor of receiving their company for this extended visit
- The beauty of their bright colors, cheerful sounds, and entertaining antics
- The inspiration induced during and after
- A state of mind less involved with self and more with others
- A sense of restoration

Next, I identified how I felt during and after the experience: blessed, distracted from problems, optimistic, happy, celebratory, big-hearted, repaired—as if I'd witnessed part of some kind of small miracle.

Beginning to Branch I chose a word for each feeling that might anchor my poem. The root words were: *blessing, distraction, optimism, happiness, celebration, miracle, magnanimous,* and *repair.* Next, I branched the synonyms that appealed to me in relation to what I might want to write. The chart on the facing page will help you to visualize the back-and-forth nature of this exercise.

Celebration holiday, festival, frolic, gaieties, revelry

Blessing sacred, exaltation, gift

Optimistic cheerful, bright, sunny, hope, faith, radiance, upbeat, elated

Happy euphoric, elated, joyful, positive, untroubled, lucky

Miracle marvel, wonder, extraordinary

Distraction diversion, entertainment, solace, comfort, consolation, restorative, jubilation

Repair restore, mend, improve, rebuild, renovate, remodel, remedy, renew, heal, cure

Each of the synonyms in a given list created slightly different images. I noticed that many of the images were related to the sacred. So I branched *sacred* and listed *holy, religious, spiritual.* And then I branched the word *holiday* because it felt right, and I listed *carnival, frolic, festival, celebration, Christmassy.*

Branching and Writing With this last branch, I had found my way into the poem! It was an electric moment. After that, the lines on the left practically wrote themselves. I had found not only the lifeblood of my experience, but also a metaphor that I could extend into a conceit.

I didn't, however, forget about some of the subsidiary branched words that could be developed to enrich the poem, for instance, the immigrant and the health slants. Over the following couple of weeks, I used various thesaurus exercises to perfect the poem to the version you see here.

I wrote my poem as a haibun—a combination of concise, imagistic prose paragraphs interspersed with haiku. (See "The Pie Plate: Serving Up a Slice of Time Travel Through the Haibun," page 177, and "Circling the Pine: Haibun and the Spiral Web," page 196.) The haibun originated in Japan long ago as a form of travel writing. I chose the haibun form because nature is so prevalent in the content and is fitting for the haiku sections—also because travel is an important aspect in the poem, both the parrots' journey and the narrator's.

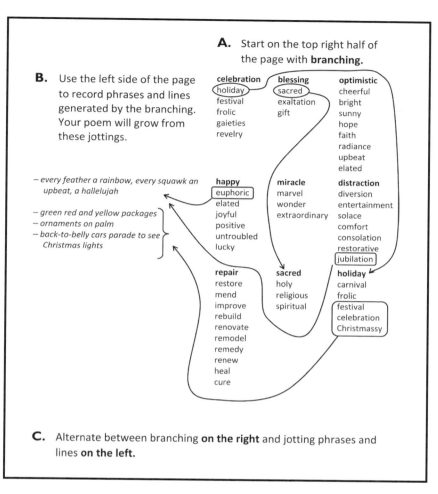

A. Start on the top right half of the page with **branching.**

B. Use the left side of the page to record phrases and lines generated by the branching. Your poem will grow from these jottings.

celebration   blessing   optimistic
holiday   sacred   cheerful
festival   exaltation bright
frolic   gift   sunny
gaieties   hope
revelry   faith
                            radiance
                            upbeat
                            elated

– every feather a rainbow, every squawk an upbeat, a hallelujah

happy   miracle   distraction
euphoric   marvel   diversion
elated   wonder   entertainment
joyful   extraordinary solace
positive   comfort
untroubled   consolation
lucky   restorative
                           jubilation

– green red and yellow packages
– ornaments on palm
– back-to-belly cars parade to see Christmas lights

repair   sacred   holiday
restore   holy   carnival
mend   religious   frolic
improve   spiritual   festival
rebuild   celebration
renovate   Christmassy
remodel
remedy
renew
heal
cure

C. Alternate between branching **on the right** and jotting phrases and lines **on the left.**

An American Haibun

Mini-flocks of eight or ten wild parrots often emblazon the trees in my yard. A stopover en route to or from the Home Depot parking lot. As though picking up supplies for ongoing nest repair.

> Green red and yellow
> packages slur the airwaves
> Jingle of chatter

Today bells ring the sky from blocks away. The entire flock arrives as I close the front door behind me for my walk. The surreal surprise of sixty-some parrots. Bodies built for South America that have branched the skies of Northern California for thirty years. Their evolution from a few slave-traded rebels and rejects. And their sheer spirit for survival stops me mid-step.

> Ornaments on palm
> filbert cherry blackberry
> Breeze of wings folding

I refuse to relinquish either the exercise or the parrots. So I walk fast circles around the driveway. Tree-to-tree talk, as affable as small town gossip over clotheslines. Drowning echoes of the morning's *Mercury* crimes-corruption-jobless-foreclosure-war *News* . . . and the crinkle of worry by fingers on fabric over a breast lump.

> Beaks fill with nectar
> from eucalyptus blossoms
> Bright pink petals fall

Dizzy now, I switch to a house-wide back and forth stride. Envision that every Silicon Valley soul in torment could line up right here. Like the way back-to-belly cars parade slowly around this cul-de-sac to see Christmas lights.

> Sprinkler shower play
> Parrots groom one another
> The sun sends glitter

Every feather a rainbow. Every squawk an upbeat, a hallelujah. An invitation to plan the next thirty years. Even the native crows acquiesce their territory to this gift. But it is I who am repaired.

Ellaraine Lockie lives in the San Francisco Bay area and writes nonfiction books, essays, children's stories, and poetry. She has published eight chapbook collections, the last of which won the 2010 San Gabriel Valley Poetry Festival Chapbook Contest, and she has received eleven Pushcart nominations. Her ninth chapbook, *Wild as in Familiar,* is forthcoming from Finishing Line Press. Lockie began writing poetry ten years ago and has accrued more than 400 awards in the genre. Her personal creative process formed the basis for the poetry workshop she teaches, and here she shares the main writing exercise from it. Lockie is also a freelance editor, professional papermaker, and poetry editor for the lifestyles magazine *Lilipoh.*

Line Dancing

This exercise is helpful in getting around blocks. It's an enjoyable way to engage with the work of writers we love—an associative muscle-builder. All it requires is the text of someone else's writing—work that elicits a visceral emotional reaction (inspiration, envy, awe). It truly doesn't matter if it's a poem or a novel, flash fiction or an essay—just that it moves you.

Procedure

Take the first line of your chosen piece, take its leash off, and follow where it runs. Approach the exercise as the language of the line inspires you, without rules or inhibition. Let the other writer's language build associative momentum; then follow it where it leads. The key to this exercise is getting out of the way.

When a line in someone's work just knocks us down, there are powerful and personal reasons: it's in the language itself, but it's also in the power of our conscious and subconscious associations with the language, the word order, the rhythm, the particular quirks of what the writer does and how it fits into our unique psyche's receptors. This exercise is designed to use that subconscious push to get us writing in a new direction.

You might use the first line exactly as it is, following it down new paths as associations lead you. You might alter it by shifting the place or person of the piece: perhaps the line reminds you of something or someone. You might repeat the line, using it as a refrain, or scramble it in repetitions, letting each new word order create new meaning, new direction for the poem. You might mirror the form or content of the piece you're using as a springboard, or you might find yourself careening off in entirely other directions.

Variations

- Use the last line of a piece instead of the first. You could use the final line to prompt a "what happened after that?" poem, or just let the language lead somewhere new.

- Use a line that stands out to you at any point in the piece. If the line that knocks you down is in the middle of the book or poem, so be it.

- Choose your line from a work you loathe—one that was forced on you. Talk back to it.

- Pull several powerful lines and use them as materials for collage, altering and combining until the language becomes your own. See where the collage takes you.

Recommended Lines to Get Started

Stuck? Some intriguing lines to chase:

"Geryon was a monster everything about him was red"
> first line from Anne Carson's *Autobiography of Red: A Novel in Verse*

"I am not going to give you any advice"
> first line from Beatrice Hawley's "Advice" from *The Collected Poems of Beatrice Hawley*

"that violence ever after would be obsolete"
> last line from Adrienne Rich's "VI" from *Twenty-One Love Poems*

"Now, when the waters are pressing mightily"
> first line from Yehuda Amichai's poem of the same name in *The New Yorker,* January 10, 2005 (translated from the Hebrew by Leon Wieseltier)

"I know. I also left a skin there."
> last line from Louise Glück's "Cottonmouth Country" from *The First Four Books of Poems*

"composed of everything lost, in which everything lost is found"
> last line from Mary Oliver's "Honey at the Table" in *American Primitive*

"That was the strange unfathomed mine of souls" or
"uncertain, gentle, and without impatience"
> first and last lines from Rainer Maria Rilke's "Orpheus, Eurydice, Hermes" from *Ahead of All Parting: The Selected Poetry and Prose of Rainer Maria Rilke*

"Now the water's low. The weeds exceed me."
> middle line from Theodore Roethke's "Praise to the End!" from *The Far Field*

Examples

Following are two short poems of my own that employ line dancing—the first taking off from the Roethke line, the latter inspired by several lines from the list above.

Cove

Now the water's low
the weeds exceed me

Roethke in my head, walking spits
through rushes and mud. Two herons:

I almost step on one. It rises
in wingbeat uprush, deafening,

but neither of us startle. We press
through August sludge, thick sky.

Weed exceeded.
Flying low.

Collage

I know. I also left a skin there
where the waters press mightily;

unfathomed mines, souls red
and composed of everything lost.

Everything lost is found, uncertain.
Without impatience even monsters

are gentle: like advice, violence
ever after shall be obsolete.

Jessamyn Johnston Smyth has had work in *American Letters and Commentary, Red Rock Review, Cezanne's Carrot, Nth Position, Abalone Moon, qarrtsiluni,* and other journals and anthologies. Hers is one of "100 Other Distinguished Stories" in *Best American Short Stories 2005*. Smyth has received a Pushcart Prize nomination, a Bread Loaf Writer's Conference grant, a Vermont Community Foundation Artist Grant, and a writing grant from Change, Incorporated. She has several books in progress: a poetry collection, a novella, a fable series, and a couple of place-focused collections that explore the boundaries between forms. She lives in Southern Vermont, where she spends as much time as possible in the forest with her dog.

Twenty Ideas for Titles
to Pique the Curiosity of Poetry Editors

I've begun to notice that magazine and journal editors (including me!) seem to be attracted to poems with interesting and unusual titles. There are more than enough poems titled "The Wedding," "Memory," "Elegy," "Daughter." Below you'll find a list of ideas for unusual titles. The next time you're looking for a subject for a poem, one of these titles may suggest a poem you will feel compelled to write.

Sometimes, it works the other way around. A title you jot down here may fit a poem you've already written. If you like the idea of this exercise, you may want to keep a list of possible titles, using the twenty suggestions here as page headings in a notebook. And, remember, you can add your own ideas and cross out any of these that don't work for you.

Twenty Ideas for Titles

1. A polysyllabic noun
2. A string of adjectives with a noun
3. A question
4. A gerund or an interesting participle
5. A strong or unusual verb
6. A familiar adage
7. An announcement or the beginning of a set of directions
8. A shocking statement
9. A newspaper headline
10. An unusual combination of nouns or verbs linked by a preposition
11. A title with a proper noun or proper nouns
12. An unusual fact
13. A song title
14. A title that uses a number
15. A quotation from Shakespeare
16. A scientific term
17. A striking word or phrase in a foreign language
18. The name of a state or city where you've never been
19. A pair of synonyms, antonyms, or homonyms separated by a slash
20. A body part or parts

An Example

Dry Heiligenschein

Halo and shadow
ring the surface of winter wheat.
Instead of blinking, I scan the day,
avoid stagnant pools. If I
told you what I know, you'd question
my solutions. The morning chimes.
Bees waver in sunlight. This is
a dream field with vapor trails pinned
against the sky. An old dog
chases his tail before he will sit.
He worries his bone.
Once as a girl I ran through
fields like these a sheep dog
at my heels or cantered bareback
through blistered furrows.
But chaos has strange attractors,
and now a low-grade fever
beats behind my eyes until I adjust
my stance, until I begin to see
dog shadows fade and a bright
spot reemerge.

Susan Terris

Dry heiligenschein is a scientific term for an optical illlusion where on a dry or dusty surface one can see a corona of light.

Susan Terris has published several poetry collections, including *Contrariwise, Natural Defenses, Fire is Favorable to the Dreamer,* and *The Homelessness of Self.* Her work has appeared in *The Iowa Review, Field, Colorado Review, Prairie Schooner, Shenandoah, The Southern Review, Ploughshares,* and elsewhere. She had a poem from *Field* published in *Pushcart Prize XXXI.* Terris published two new chapbooks in 2009 and two more in 2010. She is the editor of *Spillway* and a poetry editor for two online publications: *Pedestal Magazine* and *In Posse Review.*

Writing Play

Compose a poem in which you play the part of an employee who is antagonistic towards a supervisor. Make up all the details you like. It's okay! The point here is to tune in to the way you might use words to attack each other in the workplace. Keep in mind that you don't need to hold anything back. You're free to experiment in this break room without consequences.

Next, write a poem from the supervisor's point of view. It's always useful to role-play, to become your shadow, in this case your boss or supervisor. How does she really see the situation? What do you really look like and sound like to her? How do you hear her? This is your opportunity to mirror that. For example, here's my poem from the perspective (I imagine) of a principal in Klamath Falls who forced me out of a job.

Correcting the Big Mistake

What was I thinking, hiring that guy?
He doesn't fit. He's from over the hill
Where all those "enlightened" people live.
He's pushy. That first day, sure,
I was ignoring him because I can,
Because he needed to learn his place,
But he just kept chirping at me.
He was stirring things up, trouble,
Like with that meditation thing. Come on!
We're all Christians here—except him.
I know better than he does what these kids
Need, like job skills and ROTC.
He looked down on me. He
Didn't respect me or my authority.
Well, he hanged himself, and good riddance.
There'll be no radicals on my watch.

Now go back to the employee's role and imagine communicating in other ways. Imagine speaking with compassion, expressing the desire that the other party come to terms with whatever is tormenting her or him. Perhaps he has a wife and children who depend on him. Would you really feel overjoyed to see him fail? Suppose you celebrated the woman's promotion even if you do not understand it. Send her flowers, a card signed with personal blessings. What would you say in the card—or to others—about her promotion? Suppose you prepared a special dish for a colleague who is out sick for a period of time, a colleague you've clashed with in the past? What kind of energy would these responses send through the company? Would it be poisonous or rejuvenating?

Here is my effort to reverse what I wrote above about the principal. Here I'm writing with compassion.

How You Are

Though I may have a hard time seeing it,
I know you're doing your best. Yes,
you've irritated the heck out of me, and yes,
I've made snap judgments and blamed you.
But what do I really know about your job,
the pressure you're under as education in America
collapses like a badly built house of cards?
You've spent years working in education,
showing up every day for ten to twelve hours,
showing up nights and weekends for all kinds
of extracurricular events. When you're at school
your door is usually open to anyone, and just
recently I learned that your wife has been ill.
I know how much you love her and your kids.
This alone is a lot to shoulder, and you do
in spite of the conflicts and misunderstandings
that rise on any given day to meet you. Yes,
like the rest of us you're doing all you can.

I believe you'll discover that you're reversing negative energy by projecting positive emotions through positive speech and action.

Robert McDowell is the author of the best-selling *Poetry as Spiritual Practice: Reading, Writing, and Using Poetry in Your Daily Rituals, Aspirations, and Intentions* and eleven other books. His newest book is *The More We Get Together: The Sexual and Spiritual Language of Love,* released in 2011. Co-founder and former editor/director of Story Line Press and Development Director for Earth-Rise Retreat Center at the Institute of Noetic Sciences, McDowell is the Executive Director of Cloud Mountain Retreat Center in Washington.

Place Picture Poems

One of my favorite prompts is a simple one, but it can generate a rich variety of poems.

Procedure

Take a piece of paper and a pen and in a limited amount of time (ten minutes is more than enough), write a list of what comes to mind when you picture physical places you have been in your life that have some meaning to you. Don't stop until you've got a reasonably long list. Then pick one "place picture" to work on and save the rest of the list for another day.

My first list included *the rooftop in Crete where we stayed in 1971, walking with Dad in the woods with his dog,* and *our first apartment after divorce,* all of which became poems, although not the day they were listed. In your mind, take yourself back to the place, look around. Notice details, colors, mood, weather. If it is a difficult memory, find something peaceful or beautiful. It's all right to depart from memory and go in another direction. You can write in any style you like. Remember that a first draft is always rough, and don't be afraid to rework the poem later until you feel good about it.

Tips

Another way to write from this list is to do some research on the Internet. I remembered going to Crete in 1971, but I forgot the names of the ruins I visited. I wanted to describe them, so I looked them up. Internet search engines such as Google are great resources for detailed language.

It may also help to look at some great poetry that combines memory and a sense of place. Doing so will give you insight into the devices poets use to write about their experience. Try using some of the same devices. Here are some place poems that are readily available on the Internet: James Wright's "A Blessing," one of my favorites; Hayden Carruth's "Regarding Chainsaws"; Jack Gilbert's "Summer at Blue Creek, North Carolina"; and Meena Alexander's "Central Park, Carousel."

Examples

Here's a poem I wrote from the prompt *our first apartment after divorce.* I should explain that this was my second marriage, the result of a very bad decision, and so I am not writing about my children's father.

after leaving him

such a gentle landing:
sun-filled kitchen,
pots and pans.

my children dance,
play games,
cuddle at bedtime.

secrets spill from small throats.
we make a pact
never to see him again.

Another place poem I wrote is "Herons," thinking about a kayak trip I took with a poet friend.

Herons

we occupy a space
between wing and wet,
between soar and ripple.
green boat slips over floating logs,
through red fallen blossoms
by hemlocks and maples.
heads bow to protruding branches
we weave beside bluebirds,
redwing blackbirds, wrens.
human noises fade.
a primeval call.
above us on highest, thinnest branches,
huge rough nests, just twigs and moss,
each holds a pterodactyl,
spreading wings, long
as our two-man kayak, but nimble,
spindly legs hanging down,
twigs in beaks instead of fish.
this is their world, not ours.
when the water is high, we may enter.

turning back, regretfully.
each man-made thing
seems false,
except for our shoes,
caked with lake muck,
baptized by dinosaur droppings.

Lori Desrosiers spent her youth frolicking on the banks of the Hudson River but now calls Westfield, Massachusetts, her home. Her full-length poetry collection, *The Philosopher's Daughter,* is forthcoming from Salmon Poetry in 2012. She has a poetry chapbook, *Three Vanities,* a chronicle of three generations of women in her family (Pudding House Press, 2009). Her poem "That Pomegranate Shine" won the Greater Brockton Society for Poetry and the Arts award in 2010. Her poetry has been published in *BigCityLit, The Smoking Poet, Concise Delights, Blue Fifth Review, Ballard Street Poetry Journal, Common Ground Review,* the Gold Wake Press five-poem mini-chapbook series, and elsewhere. Desrosiers is the editor of *Naugatuck River Review,* a journal of narrative poetry, and she also publishes *Poetry News,* an online newsletter of poetry-related events in the Connecticut-Massachusetts region. She earned her M.F.A. in Poetry from New England College and teaches English at Westfield State College.

The Question of Attraction: Ekphrasis

The response of one art form to another, ekphrasis creates a unique opportunity for collaboration that traverses history, place, and perspective. Coming from the Greek verb *ekphrazein—ek,* meaning "out," and *phrazein,* meaning "speak"—ekphrasis can be traced to vivid imagery depicting a range of objects, from household utensils to weapons of war. In the *Iliad,* Homer devoted extraordinary detail to Achilles' shield—one of the earliest known examples of ekphrasis. Centuries later, W. H. Auden returned to the famed shield for his own version of an ekphrastic poem, "The Shield of Achilles." Across the years, how the wheel turns and reinvents this catalyst for writing!

Phase I: Preparation

When we introduce the concept of ekphrasis, we acquaint students with several classic ekphrastic poems, including Keats' "Ode on a Grecian Urn," Rilke's "Archaic Torso of Apollo," and John Ashbery's "Self-Portrait in a Convex Mirror." There are numerous other examples in textbooks and anthologies.

After reflection and discussion, we encourage students to visit a museum, art gallery, or other venue in order to explore a range of art. While they are considering possible choices for their writing, we ask students to observe the following guidelines:

I. Select a work of art of any medium that evokes a response, either positive or negative.

II. Make note of the artist's name, title of the work, place of creation, and other identifying information that might be needed later to properly identify the artwork and to enhance a poem for potential publication.

III. Free-write your first impressions, concentrating on sensory responses. Also, pinpoint how this work affects you emotionally.

IV. Decide if you are attracted to the entire work or a fragment.

V. Maintain detailed notes on such aspects of the work as subject matter, time period, materials, colors, shapes, textures, and even curiosities.

VI. Take a photo of the piece, if permitted; make a sketch; or locate a postcard or book on the work, should it be available.

VII. Determine how you might approach the piece by answering the following questions:

1. Are you the viewer? Are you a character in the scene? Are you the commentator?
2. Are you going to consider your selection as a starting point for a metaphorical journey? Or are you more interested in being faithful to reproducing the piece, based on your understanding of the artist's intentions and your own perspective?
3. Are there questions you have for the artist? How do you think s/he might respond?
4. Are there specific language techniques you think might best represent the artwork while staying true to your style and chosen poetic form?

Phase II: Expansion

When students are comfortable with engaging in ekphrastic pursuits, we require them to explore art through an additional prompt: why they select a particular piece. The new challenge invites students to engage more fully to discover the source of resonance—even empathy—the work engenders in them. This is the nexus of where the artist's vision and the poet's words join to create a new work.

To accomplish this goal, we ask students to rapid-respond to a series of questions in five words or less. Depending on skill, knowledge, and resource availability, examples might include:

1. Why do you find yourself drawn to portraiture as opposed to landscape?
2. Why do the textures of clay or fabric invite a poem versus sculpture or metal fabrication?
3. Why does a specific culture seem more stimulating than another?
4. Why select art that challenges? (Think Picasso's *Guernica*. Think Mapplethorpe. Think Serrano.)
5. Why does one quality of work engage or fascinate more than another? (For example, the robust sculptures of Fernando Botero versus Alberto Giacometti's elongated torsos.)

Examples

Taking both processes into account, here are two examples demonstrating our own approaches to ekphrasis that include the above considerations—careful examination, research, meditation, exploration of form and structure, and choice of poetic techniques.

Madelyn discovered the fabric scarf *The Milky Way,* by Taos weaver Gorus, during the fall she was immersed in Brian Greene's book, *The Fabric of the Cosmos: Space, Time, and the Texture of Reality.* Head spinning with tantalizing words and speculative theories—string theory, Planck mass, protons, neutrons, quarks, and braneworld, to name a few—she responded to the scarf's texture, size, and colors in philosophical and emotional ways. At the crossroads of quantum physics and art, she needed the reassurance of what she could see and touch. The *why?* Driven to explain what seemed unfathomable in ordinary terms, she saw in the fiber art, science made manifest. This collector of black-and-white fine-art photography, who had never purchased a weaving, knew for that moment in time that the scarf answered her speculative search for meaning.

The Quantum Loom

The Milky Way, fiber art by Gorus

Ancient weavers knew the weft
of molecular threads
long before Galileo set the earth off-center.

Time: piled undressed wool,
now carded, now spun
into three dimensions of

      space

divided by simple sticks fixed
parallel to flat line horizons,
ridged hinged sky,

weighted by gravity's invisible hand.

Infinity: the notion of edge:
   selvage, border, fringe
the point at which the universe vanishes
in black dissolve.

   ∞

The night sky still patterns
into golden Aries:

waves of suns filling the cosmos
even as the woven motions of dyed fibers—
   sunflower, madder, and indigo
flicker into form.

∞

The theory of everything
embedded here in the shivering strings
of unfolding fabric—
a scarf.

Madelyn Garner

While Madelyn's poem explores the tension between experiential reality and theory, Andrea's poem approaches the sacred in everyday life. Spending hours viewing the extraordinary collection of *bultos* and *retablos* at the Harwood Museum in Taos, New Mexico, she perceived that although the carved figures depicted suffering, there was a curious silence about them. It led her to ponder what it would be like to live in the world of the *santero*, or saint-maker, and how she would deal with such silence in her own life. What are the implications of silence?

This is the *why* that prompted the process of writing her response to the entwined figures carved by *santero* Carlos Barela. This process included Andrea visiting several museums over a period of time, researching the lives of female saints, and reading extensively on the technical aspects of carving. She wished to begin and end the poem with questions. Also, her choices of poetic techniques were specific and deliberate—especially imagery and diction—to heighten the tone of the poem. Finally, she engaged the audience through the use of the second person.

Sleeping in the House of Saints

   Don't you want to ask—

*Why must the wife of the santero wear
earrings made of earth and wood?*

By day, his women balance silence.

In the nicho, la Guadalupana wants
the sun, stands above the moon.
Hers is the cloak of cold heaven,
crown of December pearls. How beautiful
su mandoria, body halo tipped almagre
through topaz heart of flame. Mira:

Our Lady of the Rosary: He has carved *her*
out of cottonwood, entwined the child
with its roots. The sadness of her face.
The robe spinning ribbons and veins.
She cradles the kneeling world
between candles and rainbow of God.

By night, in the chapel of their bedroom,

the wife of the saint-maker is unveiled,
a ruby at her center. His fingers sculpt
her hair to juniper, skin gessoes
to his touch. Paradise. This, and then, this:
She is the perfumed altar of midnight.
He is the deepest moment of dark.

Don't you want to ask—

What must our lady suffer to wear
earrings made of blood and stars?

Andrea Watson

In the exploration of the attraction of ekphrasis, students discover new depths
in art through the act of writing. Simply stated, they may not always know for
certain the theme or significance an artist intends, but they can use art to focus
and shape a poetic response about their lives or the world about them. Ekph-
rasis confirms the truth about this collaboration of art and poetry: within
each artist is a folio of images; within each poet, a museum of words.

Permutations on a Single Theme

- In the tradition of the original use of ekphrasis, expand the field of choice
  to include the unexpected: wallpaper, tattoos, folk art, fetishes, video

games, graffiti, anime, taxidermy, soup cans, medical imaging, or plastination. The list is as infinite as the imagination of a writer or an artist.

- In one of our sponsored shows, we asked artists to create an art piece based on a poem of their choosing. The artists had little trouble selecting a poem, and many said later they felt they were encouraged to move outside of their comfort zone. Participants involved with this show thought it produced works of art neither expected nor in their usual styles.

- Another variation: the *why* changed from the reason a certain work was chosen to the question "What was there about one selected work that attracted a deeper response?" Poets then were challenged to look within the artwork at fragments or details that echoed for them. Not one response was the same.

- In the most adventuresome permutation, artist David Hinske suggested a show based on the old Gossip Game. The concept was to alternate an artwork with a poem in a cycle in which each participant responded only to a preceding work. Beginning with *Aegean Sea Scroll*, by Bill Rane of New Mexico, the name of the artist or poet was not to appear on any piece, nor could the title be evident. On the night of the resulting show, *Interwoven Illuminations,* each response was uncovered to the delight of the audience. It was the first time in over a year that anyone had seen the full scope of the project.

Madelyn Garner has led the educational community as a creative writing teacher, administrator, and editor. Her work has been recognized with numerous honors, including the Colorado Governor's Award for Excellence in the Arts and Humanities. She is the recipient of an Aspen Writers' Conference fellowship, the D.H. Lawrence Award from the University of New Mexico, and the Jackson Hole Writers Conference Poetry Scholarship for 2010. Her writing has appeared in *Margie, Harpur Palate, Calyx, Saranac Review, Water-Stone Review, American Journal of Nursing,* and elsewhere.

Andrea L. Watson has had poetry in *Runes, Ekphrasis, Cream City Review, The Dublin Quarterly, International Poetry Review, Nimrod,* and other publications. Her show, *Braided Lives: A Collaboration Between Artists and Poets,* was inaugurated by the Taos Institute of Arts in 2003 and has traveled to San Francisco, Denver, and Berkeley. She is co-editor of *Collecting Life: Poets on Objects Known and Imagined.*

Chapter II:
Exploring the Senses

If you follow trustfully, it's surprising
how far an image can lead.

James Merrill

Cyra S. Dumitru

The Mind's Eye: Listening as Seeing

Our culture is excessively oriented toward the outwardly visual. This focus on how people and things look *out there* can hinder the ability to see inwardly—to imagine and to recall sensory details stored in memory. Because imagery and metaphor are essential elements of poetry, writers often need practice connecting with inward sight. We need exercises that orient us toward the mind's eye as opposed to the social eye. Listening to poetry, receiving the images and narrative of a poem repeatedly through the ear, can stimulate the mind's eye. It can shift our attention from seeing externally to seeing internally.

Phase I: Listening and Drawing as Preludes to Writing Poetry or to Deep Analysis of a Poem

The purpose of this phase is to help enter the sensory world of poems. It can be transformational for writers who feel distant from poetry. However, it is relevant to writers of any age and with varying levels of experience reading and writing poetry. It is designed not only to help writers comprehend imagery but also to help us grasp the moment or situation that lies at the heart of a poem, thereby grasping the root of the poem's meaning.

At the heart of nearly every poem there is a central moment or situation that the poem's speaker focuses upon, with the desire to recreate or reflect or respond. If writers can *name* this moment or situation, we can see the center of the poem. Once we recognize the center of the poem, we can more readily understand how the elements of the poem—imagery, narrative arc, line length, stanza shapes, pauses and white space, rhythm, and emotional tones conveyed by sound—interconnect to form the multi-dimensional life of the poem. This recognition helps writers see analytically into poems as readers and as writers revising our own work.

Procedure

I. Materials You will need an audio recording of a poet reading a particularly imagistic poem. You can hear numerous poems spoken by their authors online at the Academy of American Poets, The Writer's Almanac, and YouTube (which includes recordings of poets and others reading poems, as well as numerous videopoem versions). You might want to sample poems by Elizabeth

Bishop, Robert Bly, Naomi Shihab Nye, Mary Oliver, William Stafford, or William Carlos Williams. Currently, for example, the website of the Academy of American Poets has audio files of Elizabeth Bishop reading "The Armadillo," Robert Bly reading "The Greek Ships," and Naomi Shihab Nye reading "Making a Fist" and "Streets."

You will also need white or cream paper, 8.5 by 11 inches, as well as large index cards (the larger, the better) and several colors of markers, pencils, or crayons. More colors should be within easy reach. Keep these supplies on hand for Phase II of this exercise.

II. Listening If you are working alone, close your eyes as you play the recording of the poem. Listen to the poem all the way through at least once without drawing. Just focus on what your inner eye sees as you listen. Listen to the poem a second and even a third time—as many times as you like as you begin to draw.

III. Drawing The purpose of the drawing is not to create a museum piece, but to represent what you see inwardly as you listen. Making stick figures to represent people is just fine. If you are working with a group, you can consider reading the poem aloud. If you are the voice for the poem, be sure to read in a relaxed, vibrant voice and to pause significantly at the end of the poem so that listeners understand that the poem is over, before you begin to read it aloud a second time.

IV. Writing Once drawing time is finished, write several sentences that describe what you have depicted on the index cards. These sentences become a kind of summary of what the poem is about, often voicing or coming very close to the poem's central moment or situation. (Note: if you are working with a group, allow time for all to share their drawings and read their statements.) Consider that what you have drawn reflects the imagery of the poem—the concrete, sensory language. You are getting a handle on the poem and its emotional meaning.

This exercise can open resistant writers to poetry. For experienced poets who haven't drawn in years, it can liberate the hand, and broaden the symbol-making part of the mind.

Phase II: Expansion First, Then Compression

The purpose of this phase is to give writers the opportunity to write freely and then select images and arrange them into a poem. It uses prose freewriting as a way to keep inexperienced poets from falling into sing-song rhyme and as a way for experienced poets to step outside of what might be well-established habits of shaping poetic line. It heightens awareness of white space or pauses and emphasizes compression. Using large index cards as a canvas for arranging poetic lines is surprising as well as playful, and it facilitates thinking in small units of imagistic thought.

Procedure

Take a quick walk outside and pick up several objects that catch your eye, e.g., shells, stones, leaves. If weather keeps you inside, take a quick walk through your home and select several ordinary objects that appeal to you, e.g., pottery, wooden boxes, spoons. Don't overthink your choices.

Allow about fifteen minutes for the first three steps.

I. The Senses Choose one of your objects. Freewrite a brief paragraph focusing on the object's sensory details—how it looks, feels, smells, tastes, and sounds. Describe its weight and texture in the hand.

II. Comparisons In a second quick paragraph, compare the object to something else and then something else and then something else.

III. A Memory Freewrite a memory triggered by the object, any association with your own experience. You can also invent a memory.

IV. Selection, Compression, Arrangement Review what you have written. Using a pen, colored pencil, marker, or highlighter, underline the words and phrases that are the most vivid, musical, satisfying, and necessary. On one index card, copy the underlined words and phrases, one under another, like lines of a poem. Read through. Are transitional or connective words needed here and there to create greater unity among the diverse images? Would rearranging the order of images make more sense?

Begin the process of playing with sequence, line lengths, and stanza lengths. Examine verb choices throughout, and see if any passive-voice verb constructions could shift into active. Would couplets, tercets, or quatrains serve the content well? Do any lines want to repeat? Does the content want to become mostly a memory poem, or does the memory-related material seem burdensome for a poem spare and lyrical in nature? In other words, decide if the memory part should be amplified, trimmed, cut, or moved elsewhere.

If you do this exercise as part of a group, you can read various versions to one another for reader-response feedback. You can also exchange first index cards with one another and try writing a poem from someone else's gathering of phrases, images, and possibilities.

An Example

Black Rock

It is utterly black, like a chunk of night,
a chunk of moonless and starless night
that fell from the sky and solidified.

When I hold this black rock,
my hand fills with smooth weight.
My palm can feel which side settled
upon the river bottom,
flattened slowly
beneath the press of waves.

My fingers curl over
the round side of the rock,
and imagine a river otter ready to dive
below the flowing surface.
As I listen to this fallen chunk of night,
it tells me that for hundreds of years

it lived at the bottom of the Chama River
and dreamed about the moon.
It tells me about the everlasting waves
that stream through rivers after heavy rain,
how no two waves are exactly alike
and each one necessary.

Cyra S. Dumitru

Cyra S. Dumitru has had poetry in national journals such as *Nimrod, Southern Poetry Review, WLA: War, Literature and the Arts,* and *Windhover,* as well as regional publications such as *The Texas Poetry Calendar* and the anthology *Big Land, Big Sky, Big Hair.* She has published three books of poetry: *What the Body Knows, Listening to Light,* and *remains.* She teaches poetry writing and composition courses at St. Mary's University in San Antonio and is a freelance writing consultant for Methodist Healthcare Ministries and other clients.

Metaphor: Popcorn, Popcorn, Leaping Loud

Over many years of doing poetry workshops for groups from kindergarten children to graduate students to nursing home patients, I have focused on the skills employed by poets. Otherwise, it seems to me, we often teach the simple spilling out onto paper of words, memories, and emotions shaped somehow to look like a poem. This exercise, which I originally borrowed from a poet I heard on the radio back in 1968, is intended to introduce the use of metaphor in poetry. I first tried the exercise with a group of at-risk neighborhood children in a special program in Warren, Ohio. I have continued to use the activity successfully with students of almost every age and economic level. The name of the one who originated the idea of the popcorn poem I have forgotten, but I hereby tip my metaphorical hat to him.

Materials

Popcorn You'll need an electric skillet or popcorn popper and appropriate extension cords, as well as oil, salt, and small disposable cups for sharing popcorn at the close of the exercise.

Poetry Have printed copies of poems—or excerpts—in which metaphor plays a central role. These might include the following:

- Ezra Pound's famous two-line poem "In a Station at the Metro"
- Richard Lederer's *The Miracle of Language,* which includes several student poems mirroring Pound's poem
- Walt Whitman's "A Noiseless Patient Spider"
- Simon and Garfunkel's lyrics to "The Dangling Conversation"
- X. J. Kennedy's "Summer Children" from *Dark Horses*
- John Donne's "The Flea" or "The Compass"

Preparation

I usually begin the exercise by explaining some of the skills used by poets to turn emotions, ideas, and experiences into poetry. One of those tools is metaphor, the making of an image more interesting, vivid, and memorable by comparing one thing to another. I use examples, including the lines from Pound: "The apparition of these faces in the crowd; / Petals on a wet, black bough." I almost always use a poem from Richard Lederer's *The Miracle of Language* (Pocket Books, 1991). Written by a student, this poem mirrors Pound's: "A child in the slums, / A withered flower in a dirty bath." I also include a line by Donna Blackwell, one of my second graders on Tinker Air Force Base, Oklahoma, in the 1970s: "The sun is a big dandelion in the sky."

More discussion and examples usually follow the exercise itself, when the discussion can be expanded to encourage the practice of finding comparisons to express things for which we have no words. One example I often share is the struggle I have had for years to find a way to express the color of winter grass.

Procedure

The exercise begins with students closing their eyes and listening to popcorn popping, trying to think of everything possible to compare to the various sounds they hear, from the first sizzle, the first snapping sound, to the full jamming together of puffy explosions, and at last to the trailing muffled pops. When all is silent (and aromatic!), students are asked to begin jotting down their ideas, trying to form poems or lists or whatever comes. Meanwhile, I salt the popcorn and pass out small cups for everyone to munch while working.

Outcomes

I never limit anyone to an exact assignment. I encourage free-ranging adaptations. Here are sample metaphors for popcorn popping that came from one group of students:

- hail hitting a street sign
- the Boston Tea Party
- a snare drum's rat-a-tat-tat
- a grandfather clock tocking
- sand blowing around

When I taught on the integrated staff of a not-yet-integrated at-risk school in Indianapolis, Indiana, one among my thirty-four second graders gave me my all-time favorite line from this exercise. He said, "It sounds like an army of ants marching over the roof." I wrote the children's ideas on the chalkboard for them, as neither their reading nor writing skills were yet developed enough to write down their own. It can be useful to collect answers on the board for other groups of students. I have found it necessary for younger children and also for seniors with dementia. I made their lines into a class poem that they could take home in a "newspaper" of their writings.

In the 1980s, among fifth graders in the Academic Center for Enrichment for Mid-Del Schools in Oklahoma, a few of the boys decided to parody William Blake's "Tyger! Tyger! burning bright." They began their poems with "Popcorn! Popcorn!"

This exercise always ends in munching and sharing, followed by my suggestions for other activities students can do on their own. Sometimes, instead of popcorn popping, I use one of the variations listed on the following page.

Examples

These were written by fourth-grade students at Will Rogers Elementary, Edmond, Oklahoma, 2002.

> The sizzle sounds like a snake hiss
>   rain coming down by the pipe
>   someone small tapping at the door
>   Slow.
> It sounds like water boiling
>   someone hammering a nail
>   a balloon popping
> or a tiny little dog barking
> or birdseed being dropped
>   into the container.
>
> *Kathryn Hook*

> Tons of balloons popping
> Someone playing the drums
> Like a horse race
>   . . .
> A grandfather clock
> or knocking.
>   . . .
>   dolphins jumping in the water
>   guns shooting off during a war
>   . . .

a movie theater sound
   . . .
an "ahhhh" from a student
   . . .
Popcorn sounds like a march squad's feet
    firecrackers
       thunder
          knocking on the door
             a snare drum's rat-a-tat-tat
            hail on the roof

Josh Keller

It sounds like punching a punching bag
    like a puppy's paws as it walks down the hall
        like a parade
    tennis balls shooting out of the electric pitcher
the sizzle sounds like a snake slithering
   . . .

Brandon S. Dale

Variations

Sloshing Water If the group is too large to share popcorn, or if I'm not sure a popper can be used, I sometimes shake a half-filled jar of water to slosh the sound into each student's ear. "What does it sound like?"

Lemon Drops Give each student a lemon drop to suck on. "What does it taste like?"

Spice Rack Pass around little containers of spices to be sniffed. "What do they smell like?" A favorite from this exercise was written of oregano: "It smells like the old sweaty gym clothes inside when I open my locker."

Variations: An Example

With teenagers, who, surely, everywhere, love to write broken-hearted pieces that say "You broke my heart, I am so sad, I'll never get over it," I sometimes share a poem, one of the first I ever wrote, way back in the late 1960s, when everything in my life was terrible. It was influenced by my tendency to understand life by comparing one thing or person with another, also by the only poet I had yet learned to like, John Donne, and surely by my love at that time of the music of Simon and Garfunkel and their rendition of "Are You Going to Scarborough Fair?" Here is my poem:

Myself

I am dried up
    Thyme
        Oregano
            and Basil
I exhale desiccation
    Tarragon
        Turmeric
            and Sage
I am bottled and colorless
    Marjoram
        Bay
            and Curry

I have come from far places
Been hung in the corner
And now I sit on the shelf
And am sprinkled out
Once in a while.

Carol Hamilton, Poet Laureate of Oklahoma 1995–97, received the Oklahoma Book Award for a chapbook of poetry, *Once the Dust,* in 1992. She has two new chapbooks—*Umberto Eco Lost His Gun* and *Master of Theater: Peter the Great.* Her work has recently appeared in *South Carolina Review, Cold Mountain Review, Tulane Review, Wisconsin Review, Southwestern American Literature,* and numerous other publications. Winner of the Byline Literary Award for both short story and poetry, as well as a five-time nominee for the Pushcart Prize, Hamilton received the David Ray Poetry Award in 2000 and the 2002 Warren Keith Wright Prize for Poetry. She has been a featured poet in *Voices International, Piecework, Chiron Review, Potpourri, Westview, Drury's Gazette, Newsletter Inago,* and *Prisa.* A former elementary school teacher, she has had a distinguished teaching career at the college level. Hamilton received a Distinguished Alumni Award from the University of Central Oklahoma in 2007.

Birds in the Classroom

Calling the people who come to a workshop students makes me squirm. This could be because I started teaching poetry when I was eighteen; I still had milk-breath and anarchistic ideas. Poetry is a process of creation in which teacher is student to the craft, and student is teacher to others, and those combinations are endlessly parabolic.

The most important teaching I hope to engender in writers is trust in their own impulses—internal affirmation sufficient to let them commit to a poem entirely. So I refer to all in the room as writers and require that they identify as such, even if just for the length of their stay. I also call them birds, just to myself.

The birds of chance and spirits of spontaneity show up in my curricula more reliably than any other pedagogical creatures. I draw direction from experiments with the raw materials—psychic and physical—that each writer brings to workshop. From these materials, a live, energetic process emerges that teaches writers to trust their process and find inspiration anywhere.

I depend on the concept that each person already has the creative material he or she needs—both within and at hand in the environment nearby. Like birds who come down to ground level to pluck up materials for their nests, writers find material by probing the ground beneath their feet, changing position, changing perspective, looking at the same old things differently.

Here is an exercise I use. It's modeled on an exercise delivered once by my mentor, Elizabeth Alexander.

Procedure

Ask each writer to search his or her pockets and bags and bodies for one interesting object to add to the center of the table. This exercise has yielded pecans in shells, plastic reptiles, foreign money, wisdom teeth, and the ever-present sunglasses, keys, cell phones, tampons . . .

Make a pile of all these objects and mix them up.

Ask each writer to select an object that is not his or her own and write for thirty minutes. Prompt options include:

- Investigate the material history of the object.
- Allow the object to speak in first person.

- Follow your own associations emotionally and visually.
- Explore a persona which has lost this object or is obsessed with it.
- Write an ode to the object.
- Use the object as a metaphor or symbol.

After each writer has written, invite participants to show the object they chose, describe the prompt or route they took in their process, and read their new draft aloud. Then, return the object to its original owner. If the owner of the object wishes to reflect aloud about what was revealed during this sharing, make time for that. Often, the original owner of the object will be moved by the creative work it sparked and want a copy, which builds relationships in the workshop community.

Variations

A variation on this exercise can be done as a follow-up or as a stand-alone exercise. It uses the same method of looking at a familiar thing from an entirely different vantage point, working to turn the tables of the imagination. The instructions are the same as above, but instead of using an object, writers bring in a childhood photograph. They are paired up and trade photos, without telling each other anything about the childhood or the moment snapped long ago. Prompt options include:

- Describe exactly what you see in the photo.
- Speak in the voice of the child pictured.
- Invent—or intuit—backstory to the scene pictured.
- Imagine what—or who—is not in this picture and why.

Follow-Up

Bringing in published poems can deepen the conversation. Some poems that build interestingly upon either of these two exercises include "The Fishing Tackle" by Bertolt Brecht; "I Go Back to May 1937" by Sharon Olds; "Emancipation" by Elizabeth Alexander; "From a Photograph" by George Oppen; "The Want Bone" by Robert Pinsky; and "Persimmons" by Li-Young Lee.

Pass these poems out after the writers in the room have composed their own, so as not to unduly influence their language. Consider asking writers to read a published poem aloud in choral voice, or read it aloud going around the room, a line or stanza per person. That way, every bird gets to add some sound to the song.

An Example

The assortment of objects offered when the poem below was composed included several Slim Jim-type beef jerky sticks, which propelled the writer into a vision of gas-station food as the epitome of Americana and a fantasy of living on the road as a trucker, consuming America's processed foods with gusto.

Ode to Meat Sticks

All our food should come in a stick shape—
then, we could be truck drivers!
We could toot our horns as we pass each other hauling 90 down
        I-10 at 4 a.m.
We wouldn't have to stop for food; we could pee
in an empty soda cup with George Michael's *Faith* album cranking
        on the stereo,
crack the window for an icy blast of air to keep us awake,
park for twenty minutes to grab a nap in the sleeper,
with two tons of lettuce wilting in the back.
An old trucker on dope will have a stroke in the shower at the Flying J.
I'll put a pack of meat sticks in my back pocket and leave without
        paying—
sustenance for another thousand miles!
When the sun rises, you'll tell me to stop because you saw a bill-
        board for the World's Largest Cow Skull,
and you'll cry because you left your shower flip-flops in Tucumcari.
We'll eat chicken fried steak and corn for breakfast
and I'll steal more meat sticks for you, because you like them so much.
In the cab, we laugh: you pocketed an air freshener shaped like a tree
and a CD by Los Tigres del Norte!
Oompa oompa doo-dee-doo-dee-doo!
Phoenix in the distance, LA by nightfall.
You are enchanted with this country and its intestinal highways;
I am enamored with sleep, the road's elusive mistress.
She taps my eyelids then falls under the wheels and you whisper
in my ear, "Maybe we should get some books on tape?"

Monique Daviau

Abe Louise Young was born in New Orleans, Louisiana. She is an award-winning poet and journalist, who has long worked to nurture writers in unconventional settings. Her projects range from interviewing Holocaust rescuers and Hurricane Katrina survivors to leading writing-for-social-change workshops with gang-affiliated youth. A former Beinecke Scholar and Michener Fellow in Poetry, she holds degrees from Smith College, Northwestern University, and the University of Texas at Austin. Young has recently published in *The Nation, New Letters,* and *Witness,* and is the author of one chapbook of poetry, *Ammonite.* Her anthology, *Hip Deep: Opinion, Essays, and Vision from American Teenagers,* was published by Next Generation Press.

A Crack in the Cup

I don't give many exercises, though perhaps I should. In semester-long workshops at the senior and graduate level, I tend to require students to read a collection by one (assigned) contemporary poet a week, and I'll give a flexible assignment based on the poet's book, asking them to write a poem for the following week based on a characteristic method, style, form, or theme they find in that poet's work.

But here is one particular exercise I have given in undergraduate classes and in other workshops. Between each of the following instructions, I pause for a minute or so to give everyone time to write.

Procedure

1. Picture yourself in a kitchen that is familiar to you. It could be one in a place where you live now or one you remember from the past.
2. Imagine that you find a cup or bowl in one of the cupboards, on a shelf, or on a countertop.
3. Pick up the cup or the bowl. Hold it with both hands. What does it feel like? Describe its texture, its shape, its weight. If you set it down on the counter, what sound does it make?
4. Do you know if it belongs to anyone, or if anyone in particular uses— or has used—this cup?
5. Hold it again, in your hand. Look down into it. At the very bottom is a crack.
6. What happens next?

I give the students time to write freely for about ten minutes and then ask them—between now and our next meeting—to "play" this piece of writing into a poem that we'll discuss in the workshop. They are to decide what form the poem will take (free verse? a sonnet? couplets? another form entirely?) and tell us why they chose that particular form.

An Example

Poet Liz Garton Scanlon tried her hand at this exercise. "Everywhere there are cracks," she begins, and then goes on to explore a cracked bowl as a metaphor for one kind of marriage. Scanlon expands beyond the details of a particular dish, but the image of a cracked bowl anchors her poem in the specifics of a single consciousness.

The Bowl

Everywhere there are cracks, even hidden in the cupboards of your
      own home
This bowl like a marriage, so familiar and capable, but my god—all
      that holding

Something's got to give, and it does, there is no mistaking two
      pieces for one
Oh, gaping fault line, folks on either side, looking down into the
      crevasse

Saying, "Who's to blame for this? Who's to blame?" because some-
      one must be
The alternative is just too damn bad, that some things can't help but
      crack wide open

The alternative is just

Too damn bad

Liz Garton Scanlon

Notice that the writer does not include every part of the exercise. For example, she doesn't describe her bowl's texture, shape, or weight. When you try this exercise, don't let it confine you. Let your imagination shape the poem that comes of any exercise.

Wendy Barker has a novel in prose poems, *Nothing Between Us: The Berkeley Years,* runner-up for the Del Sol Prize and a finalist for the 2010 Texas Institute of Letters' Helen C. Smith Memorial Award for Best Book of Poetry. Earlier full-length collections of poetry include *Poems from Paradise* (WordTech, 2005) and *Way of Whiteness* (Wings Press, 2000). Barker has published three chapbooks, most recently *Things of the Weather* (Pudding House, 2009). Recipient of an NEA fellowship, a Rockefeller residency fellowship at Bellagio, the Writers' League of Texas Book Award, and the Mary Elinore Smith Poetry Prize, Barker has also been a Fulbright senior lecturer in Bulgaria. She is Poet-in-Residence and a professor of English at the University of Texas at San Antonio.

Thirteen (Give or Take) Ways (of Seeing): A Study in Scrutiny

My father was, as they used to say, handy. He could build things and fix things and did not need (or have) Home Depot's vast resources at his disposal. When he died, most of his tools were rusted over, except for one— which would never rust—his spirit level. It looks like a two by four, painted red, with two windows in it, and within each window a small tube (one horizontal, one vertical) containing water (or alcohol, a "spirit"), in order to determine if a surface was truly flat.

We are not a family of possessions. Don't get me wrong—we were not averse to possessions, but neither side of my family inherited anything of any monetary value, and my parents were not sentimental about what they would have called "junk," items that reminded them of harder times. (My father, who worked as a draftsman for the Big Three car companies his whole life, had no nostalgia for the stick-shift once automatic transmission became popular.) Of course, I am a little more sentimental, and one of the few items that would remind me of my father was his spirit level. (Of course, this term was made famous to readers of poetry by Seamus Heaney.)

There are few poets who *don't* write about the dead. I am no exception. I have attempted many poems about my father: many elegies, many narratives. Some are better than others. I thought that approaching grief through a closer study of this object, so identified with my father, might help (at a time, really, before I knew him—I was a late baby). I looked to Wallace Stevens' essential "Thirteen Ways of Looking at a Blackbird" for help. (Always go to the best.)

Of course, Stevens' poem does not describe the blackbird; in each section he mentions the blackbird; the bird is a reminder, a through-line. Some vignettes are reminiscent of a brief Asian figure. The blackbird is a constant, creating shapes and rhymes, asserting presence even when physically absent. I wanted the red spirit level to be a presence, a source, a jumping-off point into various sorts of reverie. I used Stevens' poem to remind me that the level need not always be literal, nor actively symbolic. I used his poem to remind me to trust the object I had chosen and to trust the subconscious to choose an object that "mattered," that would lead me into and through the poem.

Procedure

I. Choose an object. Do not choose something that smacks of obvious sentiment—no photographs and, ideally, nothing "artistic." Choose something that seems artless, that could even be described as "useful." If not useful—if it is ornamental—don't let it in the slightest be cute.

II. Describe the object. Start with size, color, shape, texture, any special features. Do not content yourself with surface detail. What is inside the object? What is seen from far away and from close-up? Stare at the object. Scrutinize, scrutinize. Find metaphors or similes. What is the object like and not like? Stare not only at the object, but at its name: how does the name relate to the object? What would exist in the absence of the object? You are trying to look at this object from every possible angle and perspective, to conceive of the various ways it could be used or perceived. All that staring should provide you with enough information, at least of the physical sort.

III. Invent a history. Tell a few stories—in draft form—of the object, its owner, your relationship to both object and owner. Stay away from mush.

IV. Combine your stories and your observations. What you are really doing is telling the story of the object *and* the story of its owner *and* the story of the narrator's relationship with the owner and object, interspersed with detail, both literal and imaginative. For the poem on page 64, I chose to craft two parallel (or intersecting, depending on your geometric tastes) stories: one of people and one of the object, and I divided the people story into small pieces—clauses, short sentences. Each brief piece of story owned its own section of description; I began with physical, literal description of the spirit level, then moved into more metaphorical reaches: riffing on the word *level*, on the color red, on T. S. Eliot's objective correlative—a brief examination of an object standing in for an emotion, of memory's functions and inadequacies—and ultimately on the admission of loss.

This exercise helps students write a poem with emotional intensity that is not directly written from a personal memory or anecdote (which they are often unwilling to amend). Using an object requires them to demonstrate their descriptive and metaphoric powers, which will ultimately connect with and comment on a narrative or will subsume what a student thinks he or she knows about his or her relationship with the object or its owner. The object, which has some vague talismanic value, comes into its own in the course of the poem and allows the poet to access a more complicated amalgam of emotions.

Variations for a Large Group

- Bring in an object for the class to study. Have each person provide one "way" of approaching the object. You may need to assign them individual tasks: one student (or several) can be assigned physical attributes, another small group assigned metaphor, another assigned history (which they will invent), another assigned its name, another assigned its absence.

- Bring in a group of objects, and ask individual students to write poems that describe or use several of your objects. This ends up being a collage poem, and I have found that it brings out the best in students. Something there is about an object or two....

An Example

It takes a patience I do not often have to sit and stare, but in the course of doing so, I came to understand the potency and value of this object, for me, and allowed myself to express in a non-clichéd fashion my great grief for my father, now twenty-three years gone.

I did not reach thirteen ways; I reached eleven. That will have to do. It's not the number that's important.

Red Level

I. *I found it leaning in the basement.*
> Device for establishing a horizontal
> line or plane. Like the wheelbarrow
> in color, a working man's prop.

II. *His draftsman's tools gone, no straight edge or compass remains*
> Two by four, two windows bound,
> slightly bowed tubes, water within,
> air bubble in each (the chicken in
> every pot) that falls between thin,
> black lines to mark the center,
> if the surface is as named.

III. *and the photograph of a young man in RCAF uniform*
> Two small canoes scooped out on each
> wide flat. One hole from which to hang it
> in the shop. Red paint shot with gray.
> You can lay it on its side or stand it up.

IV.   *with his cargo plane went to the future*
                     Apt palindrome, each side
                     meeting in the "v"—two arms
                     that join at the crotch as of a tree

V.   *patriarch who loves it as he can.*
                     cleaved by lightning where
                     trunk and branch unite or part,
                     depending on the heart's conjugations.

VI.   *My brothers find me sentimental and don't mind*
                     In a gloss of stratum, red's the sunken
                     shelf that shrines the gem's bathing
                     gangue, vein of the unrefined pulse.

VII.   *say take whatever junk you want.*
                     Even Eliot might like it if correctly
                     correlated: humble properties,
                     lone purpose—to ensure an even
                     surface in the face not of the odd
                     but the imbalanced. Air and liquid
                     kindred, wood and window wed,
                     you and I, you and I level-headed,
                     even-keeled, nonplussed.

VIII.   *My mother, who remembers to forget*
                     Obligations to object hinge on history.

IX.   *and visits the cemetery often when she's lonely*
                     Objectivity lives in the level's
                     wide-eyed evaluation.

X.   *wonders how she raised a child*
                     If I close my eyes, I see the world
                     divided, not into matter and ether,
                     darkness and light—into those who
                     take object as subject and those
                     who refuse to subject their objects
                     to the mutinies of memory.

XI. *with such capacity for sadness.*

What can be done but make do
with the token left behind—
unsold, unlauded, earns its scars

—is that the person you are?
The one you blame, you miss, you
fear, you yearn to be? Be near?

Patty Seyburn won the Green Rose Prize with her third book of poems, *Hilarity* (Western Michigan University, 2009). Her two previous poetry collections are *Mechanical Cluster* (Ohio State University Press, 2002) and *Diasporadic* (Helicon Nine Editions, 1998), which won the 1997 Marianne Moore Poetry Prize and an American Library Association's Notable Book Award for 2000. Her poems have appeared in numerous journals, including *The Paris Review, Poetry, New England Review, Field, Slate, Crazyhorse, Cutbank, Quarterly West, Bellingham Review, Boston Review, Cimarron Review, Third Coast* and *Western Humanities Review*. Seyburn grew up in Detroit. She earned a B.S. and an M.S. in Journalism from Northwestern University, an M.F.A. in poetry from the University of California at Irvine, and a Ph.D. in poetry and literature from the University of Houston. She is an assistant professor at California State University, Long Beach, and co-editor of *POOL: A Journal of Poetry.*

Kurt Heinzelman

The Window Poem

What is a window? It is an aperture through which we see—both in and out. Our English word comes from the Old Norse *vindauga*—literally "wind-eye." That great painter of windows, René Magritte, did not paint, to the best of my knowledge, a window with an eye in it, or an eye in the shape of a window, but these would have been surrealistically logical and Magritte-worthy inventions. Magritte did paint, however, a picture—*The Palace of Curtains, III*—that contains an irregularly shaped, seven-sided window with a beclouded sky painted in it and mounted on what looks to be a solid wall. Hung next to this is another "window," identical in every way except that it is blank and the word *ciel* ("sky") is inscribed within it. What Magritte's entire oeuvre reveals, with great abundance, variety, and inventiveness, is that a window is also a means by which something is framed—framed as a painting is. One of Magritte's most famous paintings—*The Human Condition*— shows a painting on an easel in front of a window in which the scene represented within the frame of the easel is exactly what is outside, framed by the window.

But windows frame the world in all sorts of ways, and the frame can have many different shapes (oval, round, square, oriel, bay). As I write this, I am seated in front of two double-hung sash windows with eight panes above and eight panes below, each window making a sixteen-part square but the two windows side by side making a horizontally-oriented rectangle. These panes are clear glass, but windows may utilize many different kinds of material (horn, mica, canvas) and may be convex, concave, tinted, even frosted or waffled so that they are translucent, the windows admitting light but in a way that one can't see beyond that light.

What you see through a window depends in part upon what you are looking to see. It also depends on how far away from the window the looker is. In his memoir, *Speak, Memory,* Vladimir Nabokov writes of getting so close to the glass that all he can see is his own reflection, his own eyeball looking at itself trying to look through the glass to what is outside. But even if your eyelash is not touching the pane, you may see aspects of or deformities in the glass before you see through the glass. William Virgil Davis' poem "October: With Rain" begins, "The way the light lasts longest on a single spot / of window-pane, some small distortion in the glass / that keeps its final clasp of wind and rain as well, / has caught my eye again." Windows may catch our eyes in many ways, sometimes making us able, with a kind of purposeful bifocal vision, to look both into the glass and through it at the same time. And sometimes our sight is arrested by the window frame itself. The artist James Turrell, himself a Quaker, designed the Friends' Meeting House in Houston with windows that had no mullions—those rectilinear pieces of wood or leading that separate individual lights or panes—because he didn't want parishioners to see crosses when they looked at the windows.

Now, for instance, I'm seeing a bank of nandina atop a cinder-block wall—flora and wall about a meter in height each. I notice how cracked and irregular the cinder blocks are compared to the relatively monochromatic plants. But then I see that I am seeing that coruscated wall through window panes that are smudged around the edges, some old paint still adhering. And the screen beyond the window (yes, of course, windows can have another cover over them, blocking their transparency between us and the world) has small holes in it; cobwebs have accumulated between it and the glass; and then I notice, lining up my sight-line with a crack in the wall outdoors, that the window itself has a small hairline fissure. I use one to sight down the other. And then I see that the wall, which was a moment ago in sun, is now in shadow, but a light from inside the room where I am sitting is striking a copper plate on the wall beside me, and that plate is reflected now in the window and superimposed on the shadowy wall outside like a kind of dimpled and amber sun.

Windows, in short, comprise a way of looking. Or they engage multiple ways of looking all at once. Or, perhaps more accurately, they are a way of being positioned, a way of being put in place and a way of putting things in place, as Robert Creeley suggests in his very suggestive poem "The Window": "Position is where you / put it, where it is . . . ." And the poem ends, "It / all drops into / place. My // face is heavy / with the sight. I can / feel my eye breaking." Creeley himself was blind in one eye, but it really can break your eye, that attempt to see out of a window and also to see all that is in the window—understanding *in* in all its senses (framed by, reflected across, etched upon).

The point of the following exercises is perception, using the window as a guide or matrix or device to think about how and what one sees, how seeing is a kind of positioning. Each exercise is a way of teaching ourselves how what is perceived is a function of where the perceiver is positioned and how difference or change in what is perceived is a function of that positioning. "A window is a verb," as the young British poet Katharine Kilalea puts it.

Procedure

Exercise I. Compose a poem in which someone, a person of a different gender and age than yours, is looking out a window.

Exercise II. Compose a poem in which someone is outside a window looking in. This person could be the same person as in Exercise I, or not; looking into the same window the person in Exercise I is looking from, or not.

Exercise III. This one should be done in stages. First, write a description of what you see from a window. Be as detailed as possible. Notice changing things—a passing shadow, say, or a butterfly, or a shadow of a butterfly—as well as things that don't change. Second, start looking at yourself looking. In other words, notice the window itself and how it is framing what you see and pay attention to what you see in the glass, not just what you see on the other side of it. Pay attentions to flaws, reflections. Third, start to shape a narrative of how the person looking out the window got to this position and why this person is noticing certain things in particular. Now add a second person looking out the same window or looking at the window from outside. Or maybe looking at the window from another window—one across the street, for instance. By adding this invention to your perceptions, you will need to concoct a story.

The first two exercises can be done as practice in the art of description, remembering what Ralph Waldo Emerson said in his essay "Nature"—"Every object rightly seen unlocks a new faculty of the soul." What will emerge, in addition to any sea-change in your soul, is a kind of landscape painting. You may place your perceivers in any position that suits you—near the window, in a room at some distance from a window, in a room behind an open door into another room that has a window, wherever. All of these motifs are ones that the American painter Edward Hopper likes to use, and, although Hopper's paintings often imply a story, they just as often don't.

Examples

The use of the window as a device is as old as windows themselves and is nearly universal in all national poetries. In our own language Thomas Hardy perhaps uses this device as often as anyone, and with great effectiveness, with window poems such as "Nature's Questioning," "Overlooking the River Stour," "Shut Out that Moon," "We Sat at the Window," "Faintheart in a Railway Train," "The Curtains Now Are Drawn," "The Face at the Casement," "Love Watches a Window," "Outside the Casement," "Heiress and Architect," "The Background and the Figure," and "Domicilium." Here is one of my favorites:

The Fallow Deer at the Lonely House

One without looks in to-night
Through the curtain-chink
From the sheet of glistening white;
One without looks in to-night
As we sit and think
By the fender-brink.

We do not discern those eyes
Watching in the snow;
Lit by lamps of rosy dyes
We do not discern those eyes
Wondering, aglow,
Fourfooted, tiptoe.

Thomas Hardy

What you will begin to see, as you start reading poetry for windows, is that sometimes poems are, in effect, window-poems even if there is no window mentioned in the poem. One of my favorite examples of this is Francis Ponge's prose poem "Rain," whose detailed explication of how the rain looks, how it sounds, and how it changes what it dampens could only have been constructed from indoors, from behind a window (though the window has passed invisibly away). Susan Stewart also has what I would call a concealed window poem—we don't discover that her blurred perception is caused in part by her looking out a window until the very end of "The Owl."

The wonderfully idiosyncratic anthology called *A Book of Luminous Things*, edited by Czeslaw Milosz, contains a number of window poems, such as the following: "Dusk in my Backyard" by Keith Wilson, "Vacation" by William Stafford, "Zen of Housework" by Al Zolynas, "The Window" by Raymond Carver, and "Woman at Lit Window" by Eamon Grennan.

Finally, I offer my own poem "Bifocals," about a person who may need to start wearing new eyeglasses—and about the problem of seeing bifocally what is both near and far. The poem concludes with a picture of a window that the setting sun has painted into an opacity of its own.

Bifocals

April. So it's April
again, is it, its
flag on the breeze
unfurled? And just as you
were wondering how

you'd know if you needed them,
another mild afternoon,
the third in a row, settles
hard against your house,
the side that is peeling.

Between the shoots
of forsythia, the first
tawny spears of spirea,
what *Peterson's* calls
"confusing spring warblers"

have shaken their shakers,
dusting snowdrop and crocus
with New World spices—
splashes of Tabasco,
whole spoonfuls of saffron!

And oh
if only your own
palms could rise out of their
Oaxacan bowl
in which they've been tossing

the diced and the seeded
with lozenges of
just-ripe Brie
and wing their way
over to them, the wings

on the other side of the pane
from this rinsing of
linguini, arugula,
and hold them OUT THERE—
a *koan*—

in focus now because
turned from, seen into
because seen through.
But you can't, see?
You can't see

any more
how to turn even
the tap off, now the whoosh
of water's spooked them.
Once more, then, silence,

the evening's greens
draining and the sunset
in the windows showing
winter's fingerprints
all over them.

Kurt Heinzelman co-founded and for ten years edited the award-winning journal *The Poetry Miscellany;* he also co-founded and is now Editor-at-Large of *Bat City Review.* His latest book of poetry is *The Names They Found There* (Pecan Grove, 2011). A book of translations (of Jean Follain's *Territoires,* published originally in 1953) is forthcoming in 2011. Heinzelman has been a multiple nominee for the Pushcart Prize, and his two previous books of poetry, *The Halfway Tree* (2000) and *Black Butterflies* (2004), were finalists for best poetry volume of the year from the Texas Institute of Letters. He has published or edited three other books in the fields of British Romanticism, Modernism, and 20th-Century Art, as well as numerous articles on literary, economic, and cultural history, and he is on the Board of Directors of the Dylan Thomas Prize in Wales.

Katherine Durham Oldmixon

Lyrical Bees:
Writing Poems Inspired by Biology

One spring day, a colleague came to me waving a poem one of our students had shared with her because it included the word *feral*—a word the student had learned in my colleague's Environmental Biology course. The student, then a first-year English major, had recognized the word for its suggestive beauty and quasi-scientific tone and set it in another context, applying it to human behavior—which brought a smile to both her biology and poetry professors. My colleague still reminds me of science's muse-moment, and we've noted others since then.

It's a cool word, *feral*, although you don't have to take Environmental Biology to discover it. In fact, you might come across it in any number of poems, perhaps May Swenson's "Little Lion Face" ("strange feral flower asleep"), Judy Jordan's "Prologue" ("the tunnels turn feral"), or Jack Gilbert's "I imagine the Gods" ("That the nights / will be full enough and my heart feral"). Still, my student learned the word in its biology context. What else might she have learned from reading in science, especially environmental sciences? She might have learned about sericulture, the way silk is traditionally produced in a small village in China, or about life in clouds—real clouds, not the kind in poets' heads. And what would she do with that information? What fresh associations might she make, or metaphors spin?

Let me clarify that what I am calling biology poems are not simply poems that include words gleaned from biology, and I'm not including all nature poems, although one could argue that any poem about life is a biology poem. What I mean by biology poems are poems that are informed by an investigation of scientific literature, dissection or experiment, and/or by direct observation deep into the processes or behaviors of living organisms. These are poems that happen when poets approach the world as biologists but remain poets.

What do biologists and poets, especially poets who write about nature or the environment, have in common? A need for keen observation, a love of precise language, a desire to experience life through the senses and contemplate it deeply. . . . We recognize the continuity and interconnectedness of living beings. We want to see into things, and we *look*, at the beautiful, yes, but also at the grotesque, the disturbing, the small and seemingly inconsequential. We share a love for collecting information about whatever fascinates us, and a joy in live observation and experience.

What poets do is see the connections and exploit them, which is to say, articulate them to raise them in our awareness and bring them to new contexts. That is, poets show us the deeper meaning in the realization that squid fly or help us to see unapparent connections. A fish bladder looks an awful lot like a peony, as Elizabeth Bishop shows us in her widely anthologized poem, "The Fish." We long for the beauty of the "Conjugation of the Paramecium," after Muriel Rukeyser leads us to contemplate it.

Procedure

I can't speak to the process by which a brilliant and accomplished poet like Elizabeth Bishop or Muriel Rukeyser approaches biology with poetry, but I think my process is worth experimenting with as a poetic exercise. The steps are simple: pay close attention to non-human life; look deeply and long; read, study, and ask experts about what you see and experience. Sleep on it. Dream, if you will. Write what you see and don't be afraid to write again what you only hazily see, what you only partly understand. Don't try to explain. Describe, feel, express.

I. Observation

What is most critical is personal observation and experience. It may be that you live in a city and never leave your apartment. There you will want to watch the spiders that spin cobwebs in the legs of a chair or the rails of a stairwell or balcony, or the moth dancing about a reading lamp. Or perhaps you venture into the pocket gardens, peer through the fences at giant dahlias or wander through city parks and gardens with an eye open for dragonflies and emerald beetles. You might return to the same park bench day after day, contemplating the small changes that occur in your immediate environment. If you have a garden of your own, you might want to institute a meditative practice so that you spend time being still and observing. Even if you have a great expanse of outdoors surrounding you, you will want to focus on the miniature sometimes and revisit the same place in different light again and again. Repetition is the poet's and the scientist's strategy.

II. Expert Knowledge

Solitude intensifies our experience of the natural world, but we are also social animals. We want to test our hypotheses and share our observations. We might want to consider what those who study what has caught our attention know and think. We might want to talk to the experts.

"But I don't know any experts," you say. Of course, you do. There is the neighborhood master gardener or the local nursery worker who can name a plant by looking at a leaf; the amateur bird watcher who knows the seasons of nesting and distinguishes the sparrows from the wrens; and the county extension agent who knows which wasps eat tent-worms and how to deter fruit flies with apple cider vinegar. Writing a biology poem is an excellent time to seek out a conversation with people whose hobbies have fostered considerable expertise in areas they might not have studied formally. It might be an opportunity to reach out to older people in your family or community who have accumulated not only scientific knowledge about the natural world but also folk wisdom.

You also should not be afraid to contact the biologist, physicist, chemist, or natural historian at your local college or university. People who have spent years studying science are often delighted to talk about their specializations to anyone who will listen. So you are interested in the mating practices of dragonflies? Someone has spent years writing about just that behavior.

III. Libraries

There is also the old-fashioned and wholly satisfying visit to books in the library. Perhaps the only books in the grown-up library more colorful than the giant art tomes are the science volumes, full of plates and often beautiful, precise photographs and illustrations. You don't even have to read, if you are not so inclined, but look; consider the diversity of life forms and the peculiarities that distinguish members of the same species. And how delightful to touch the covers and smell the paper! Who knows what you will discover in the creases between the pages?

IV. Electronic Research

The Internet, of course, facilitates informal information gathering. While an Internet search has the potential to deliver quick information, for someone contemplating a facet of nature for a poem, the Internet presents an opportunity to explore leisurely, moving from site to site at random, collecting information as if gathering shells on a beach walk. If the abundance of information on the Internet is overwhelming, then certain sources might be privileged, perhaps those posted by faculty for their students (.edu sites), those in online science magazines (such as *Scientific American*), or—my personal favorite—

the science articles posted on *The New York Times* online. In this practice we would be in good company; the poems in Kimiko Hahn's most recent book, *Toxic Flora* (Norton, 2010), are all responses to scientific articles in the *Times*.

Examples

Often I seek my mother's or biologist friends' help identifying a bird, flower, or bug that has caught my eye or ear, but field guides, books, and the Internet are my quick references. When I one day began to ponder a nest of paper wasps on my patio, I turned to the Internet to glean everything I could about wasps; for weeks I kept reading and looking back to the garden. All that information stirred my dreams and waking thoughts. When I wrote a poem about wasps, then, what emerged was a poem about the ways of wasps, fully open to other interpretations, beyond the biology and beyond my consciousness.

Poesis in Plato's Garden

Look how they cluster on paper
nests built of their spit and feed
their brood on stunned bodies
of butterfly young before sucking
nectar from shallow cup figworts,
stealing honey stuff from the golden
feet of lyrical bees.

See these who craft elaborate mud
knots so dense they seem fact
sing themselves shrill anxious songs.
Their discharge warp-binds weavers;
their secretions quick-seal winged kin
in pulpy tombs. Some lay histories

in their sisters' urns, eat the eggs
to replace with their own drone
warriors, who devour one another.
Listen: the blood-red hum
of mandibles, translating truth.

Similarly, after one night in the garden when I was mesmerized by a cloud of insects, mostly moths, circling a lit floodlight, I hit the books, curious about the common names of insects and musing the relationship of appellation and behavior. The poem that emerged has as much to do with the eerie feeling I had as when—after observing for as long as I could stay awake—I went through the nightly ritual of turning out the lights and entering the house.

March Rites

Dancing about the floodlights
an ecstasy of moths convenes—
the old army type, black witches,
gypsies and sphinxes; in their midst
two or three glistening green lacewings flitter,
and a trinity cloaked as dust or bark
trembles in the shadows.
A rapt virgin tiger clasps
the long white filaments
of a Maya hammock
suspended from the necks
of those beguiling lamps,
as purple wisteria censes
the night air.
Down below, dervish beetles
whirl about their heads
on sand-yellow tile.

After-hours in my garden—
the cult, eclectic as Americans,
worships an electric god
I could turn off with one flick.

Another poetic experience I had that found me deeply musing a life smaller than my own was swimming in a bioluminescent bay of Puerto Rico. In these lagoon waters are tiny dinoflagellates that phosphoresce when they are stirred. The result is a silvery wet wing attached to a treading human arm, a stream of tiny stars glistening behind a trolling finger. I struggled to describe this in multiple drafts of a poem on the first experience of this phenomenon:

Bahía las Cabezas de San Juan

A moonless night—we drop into the dark waters
of a bioluminescent bay, imagine
ourselves fallen angels. Above us brilliant hordes
pervade black heaven; with a flashlight, our boatman
spots stars that lead sailors to unseen continents.
Alongside us droves of tourists astride kayaks
emerge like giant thrashing dragonflies from dense
mangrove thickets, where hidden iguana sentries
keep watch as humans invade their marvelous red
lagoon, five-hundred times saltier than the sea.

We seraphim distress millions of small creatures—
dinoflagellates whose presence we only sense
bathe us when we stir their fires to see ourselves glow.
So we wave our bare arms as if we were leaving
impressions in snow and a cloud of light follows.
So beautiful we seem, so aware our power—
and yet so much depends on the invisible,
like veiled glints on the breath of conquistadores.

Clearly a poem is not a scientific treatise, even when it borrows the language
of science. What happens is something of a chemical, rather than a physical
change, as the poet processes the matter of science and that of his or her own
subjective experience, of context. The poet's free-associating thoughts and
feelings, the tendency to metaphor and connection in aesthetic ways of un-
derstanding act upon the scientific information and create the poem. The ad-
vantage of being a poet, rather than a scientist, is that the experience doesn't
have to yield the same results every time to be true.

Katherine Durham Oldmixon is the daughter of a research chemist who
changed his major from music, and an English teacher who first studied nurs-
ing. She is the author of *Water Signs,* a chapbook of three sonnet crowns, each
loosely set in one of the zodiac's water seasons. She has recent poems in *Bor-
derlands, Poemeleon, The Normal School, qarrtsiluni, Bellvue Literary Review,
The Texas Poetry Calendar,* and *Big Land, Big Sky, Big Hair: Best of the Texas Po-
etry Calendar.* Oldmixon teaches creative writing and literature and directs the
writing program at historic Huston-Tillotson University in east Austin, Texas.

Chapter III:
Echoing the Familiar

Originality is nothing but judicious
imitation. The most original writers
borrowed one from another.

Voltaire

Ways of Looking

The poem that I feature in this exercise is Raymond Patterson's "Twenty-six Ways of Looking at a Blackman," inspired by the famous Wallace Stevens poem "Thirteen Ways of Looking at a Blackbird." Patterson's poem was originally published in 1969 in his collection of the same title, and it appears in *The Vintage Book of African American Poetry* (Vintage, 2000), whose editors, Michael S. Harper and Anthony Walton, claim that "the infinitely various, seamless shifts between philosophical contemplation and dark humor mark the poem as one of the more significant and subtle poetic evocations of the interior lives of blacks ever written."

Procedure

I. Reading After reading Stevens' "Thirteen Ways of Looking at a Blackbird," we read "Twenty-six Ways of Looking at a Blackman." We discuss how Stevens' poem renames the blackbird—and examines it from different angles. Sometimes, I talk about Wallace Stevens apparent disdain for people of color.

I contrast the Stevens poem with the Patterson poem. Some students have been surprised that Patterson does not address stereotypes. Instead, he creates metaphors and phrases that evoke what it may feel like to struggle for dignity ("the seeds / Of rainbows are not unlike / A blackman's tear") or just to execute simple tasks ("The blackman dipped water / From a well. / And when the well dried, / He dipped cool blackness"). I ask students to find the images that stand out to them and have them explain why those images resonate.

II. Point of View We discuss how the subject of the poem is examined from a different point of view in each section, switching from first person ("I would think of blackmen / Handling the sun") to second person ("You thought it was like the troubled heart / Of a blackman") to third person ("The fingerprints of a blackman / Were on her pillow"), as well as from singular to plural.

Changing points of view allows the poet to assume different perspectives on the subject of the poem. The brevity of each section isn't rooted in a fixed form. Each short section is rooted in an observation made by the subject or by someone or something else. For example, a spider sees itself differently than a human, an insect caught in its web, or the web itself sees the spider. The exercise that follows forces the writer, and readers, to examine the subject in different contexts outside those that are easily seen.

III. A Subject After reading and discussing the poem, I ask students to pick a subject that is close to their experience and that takes on different facets in their life. Students may explore a person or a type that's relevant to them—for example, Ways of Looking at a College Student, Ways of Looking at (A Member of a Particular Cultural Group), or Ways of Looking at a Mother (Father, Sister, Brother . . .).

IV. A Poem in Short Sections After students have made their choice, I ask them each to look at the subject in at least thirteen sections of several short lines or less. This kind of poem can also be written in groups, but I would expect it to be longer than thirteen sections.

An Example

Ways of Looking at a Blackwoman

I. On the corner, we saw black curvature,
     nothing else.

II. Work shapes history. Who has not
      been bombarded with housekeepers
      removing plates and smiling?

III. In morning rain,
       a blackwoman gathers umbrella
       and scarf, fragile promises she clings to.

IV. Always I hope to see
      the blackwoman I know
      loved as much as any man.

V. The silhouette thickens
     a soft power.
     Call her a vulnerable fist.

VI. The options of gender
      were excised at birth.
      Pruned beings,
      roles of attitude
      for a blackwoman
      are circumscribed.

VII.   When the beach filled,
grains of sand calculated
how many hoped to be her.

VIII.   Honey, cocoa butter,
shea, incense, pink lotion,
sweat, baby's milk, tears—
a blackwoman, canister of scents.

IX.   Blackbird, every woman,
dear mama, Shakeela,
gangsta bitch, ill na-na,
a blackwoman always rides
in a lyric's seat, but never drives.

X.   Her eyes match the talons
in her whispers. Who she
think she is anyway?

XI.   Every woman every woman
an anthem soaring, flipping
her facets in the light.

XII.   Brooks palmed the Pulitzer
first, but Stevens saw
coon claws nimbly turning
the clubhouse key, dreading
her den of cubs to come.

XIII.   She carries her heart singly
unlike dull, bruised apples
in a crumpled brown bag.

XIV.   Rumors said she kept
testicles in jars, cruel experiment
in a lab to which she never had keys.

XV.   Steatopygia, cellulose,
hamhocks' aftermath blessing us
or anorexia's brown opposing cousin

depends which way her hips sway
when you say her name.

XVI.   When she is called she hears
cradle, bridge, scale, pillow,
bed, kitchen, doormat, cape,
weight, burden. Her name
is voice too far away.

XVII.   When dusk arrives,
a blackwoman's hands
twist cotton candy pink,
orange and plum above heads.

XVIII.   The gloss shimmers
across her full lips
almost moonglow
across her shoulder.

XIX.   Her story is everyone's pedestal
except her own. The relationship
between staircase and vertebrae
is no coincidence.

Tara Betts

Tara Betts is the author of *Arc and Hue,* her debut collection on Aquarius Press/Willow Books. Betts is a lecturer in creative writing at Rutgers University in New Brunswick, New Jersey. She is also a Cave Canem fellow. Betts' poetry and prose have appeared in *Callaloo, Crab Orchard Review, Bellevue Literary Review, Columbia Poetry Review, Hanging Loose, Drunken Boat,* and numerous other journals, as well as anthologies such as *Gathering Ground* (University of Michigan Press), *Bum Rush the Page* (Three Rivers Press), *Power Lines* (Tia Chucha Press), *Poetry Slam* (Manic D Press), and *Black Writing from Chicago* (Southern Illinois University Press).

Let's Take It Outside

This exercise comes from our work with Split P Soup, a poetry and creative writing outreach program sponsored by the University of South Carolina and the South Carolina Poetry Initiative. The program places M.F.A. students and community writers in schools (from elementary to high school) and various community organizations (we've had workshops at libraries, women's shelters, churches, and the local gay and lesbian community center).

The Split P model focuses on invention and process. We use time limits in conjunction with exercises to get students in the habit of *writing* rather than *thinking* about what they want to write, or worse, waiting for inspiration to hit before they can write. The following exercise is one we developed primarily for students who claim that they can't find anything to write about.

The exercise helps them to write a poem in sections or a series of small poems, but it also depends on direct observation. Rather than ask students to imagine an object, we take them outside to find an object. While the exercise extends into a series of prompts based in associations, we find this appeal to direct experience is great for student writers. In the Split P program, we've offered workshops at the local zoo and botanical gardens, but a local park, your school playground, or your own backyard can be just as productive. Locate and observe—then let the exercise take over.

Many of the exercises we use are designed to get students to recognize or call attention to the value of the everyday object and to focus on the concrete object as the means by which to explore the abstract. Bringing objects into the classroom or pointing out objects in the classroom helps start their thinking. For instance, what can the light switch teach us about love? What does the door knob know about abandonment? The conch shell is the end result of what emotion or mistake? Helping students think through these imaginative possibilities provides some startling discoveries, but they are often quick to end it there or—worse—to limit the object to clichéd associations.

Too often students also worry about making sense; they are not willing to take risks that endanger the meaning of the poem. We suspect that a good bit of this trouble comes from a lack of experience with poetry, but it could also be a result of space itself. The students are already working through entire sets of predetermined factors that classroom spaces present in terms of authority and correctness.

Procedure

I. Getting Outside Taking students out of the classroom opens channels for them to engage with objects using their own senses. We like to use Wallace Stevens' "Thirteen Ways of Looking at a Blackbird" as a model. It provides students with a good example of the way a poem can play with ambiguities by focusing on the image of an object and the associations it provokes rather than defining an object by its properties. In order to help students work through this kind of process, we came up with an exercise that borrows from Stevens' structure but allows flexibility. We call it "Let's Take It Outside."

II. Finding an Object Taking students outside allows for greater possibilities with the poem. Trying to picture an object and imagine all of its possibilities is a tall order. Give your students a moment to find an object such as a bird bath or (as one following example shows) a park bench, and you give them something tangible to explore. Also, taking them outside allows them to discover unexpected objects. Sometimes it helps to go to an area with the entire class and demonstrate the exercise (or at least various parts of it). It may help students to see specific natural objects in relation to their surroundings (a pine cone on the sidewalk, a leaning maple fighting for sunlight). Point out objects that may not be obvious choices for students.

III. Writing Students generate material for their poems by writing to each of the following prompts.

1. Use at least four senses to describe what you are looking at.
2. What secret does the object hold?
3. What is its mood?
4. Relate what you are looking at to a familial figure.
5. List what the object is like (association and comparison). List at least three things. For example: *The pine needle is a sword for idiots. It is a frustrating toothpick. It, like us, breaks too easily.*
6. Tell what it is not like (disassociation). Write only one. It should follow the list of what the object is like. For example: *The pine needle is a sword for idiots. It is a frustrating toothpick. It, like us, breaks too easily.* **It is not an instrument of hope.**
7. Give directions for how one could invent/build the object.
8. Create an ancient myth about it.
9. Let the object speak. What would it say, and to whom?
10. What is its relationship to its current location?

Variations

The exercise can work in a variety of ways. It could lead to one poem in ten sections—or ten separate poems that work as an organically linked series. Of course, the exercise might yield only a few strong sections. If so, the writer may choose to omit the weaker sections in the final version.

Examples

Eight Ways of Looking at a Fallen Tree Trunk

after Wallace Stevens

I. The fallen tree trunk is rough,
   sturdy, mottled where insects
   have chewed away its bark.

II. The fallen tree trunk is an uncle
    who passes out on the couch
    after Thanksgiving supper.

III. The fallen tree trunk sleeps on
     a bed of dirt and leaves, covered
     by a quilt of woven twigs and moss.

IV. The fallen tree trunk is a pit
    stop for weary hikers. It is
    a termite tenement. It is
    a poster child for Earth Day.

V. The fallen tree trunk is not
   a renewable energy source.

VI. The fallen tree trunk
    was a stilt for the gods.

VII. "Help!" cries the fallen tree trunk.
     "I've fallen and I can't get up!"

VIII. The fallen tree trunk keeps its secret:
      it didn't make a sound when it fell
      because no one was around to hear it.

William Dye

Ten Ways of Looking at a Cedar Bench

I. A pitted cedar bench
    turned grey with age
    soaking up the rainwater
    creaks with the weight
    of a man.

II. The bench could teach you
     to continue living
     after death.

III. An orange cat licks his paw
      and washes his face
      on a grey bench.
      A noise frightens him
      and he runs away.

IV. A son never married,
     struck down in his prime,
     weeps upon
     a grey park bench.

V. A red fire
    dies out
    when nothing is left to consume.
    All that results
    is the ash grey bench.

VI. A cedar bench
     does not even dream
     of trying to be
     an upholstered couch,
     but remembers when
     it was a stool.

VII. Kill the soul
      of a tree
      and bend it to your whim.
      Breathe clumsy life
      back into it
      and you have a bench.

VIII. The grey mountain
is the bench
of the clouds.

IX. Any bench
would tell any other bench
tales of the only world
they know.

X. The grey bench
is in the garden.
The boulder
is in the wood.

Vic Mirmow

Ray McManus is an Assistant Professor of English in the Division of Arts and Letters at the University of South Carolina, Sumter, where he teaches creative writing, Irish literature, and rhetoric and composition. He is the author of three collections of poetry: *Driving through the country before you are born* (winner of the South Carolina Book Prize, USC Press, 2007), *Left Behind* (winner of the South Carolina Poetry Initiative Chapbook Competition, Stepping Stones Press, 2008), and *Red Dirt Jesus* (winner of the 2010 Marick Press Poetry Prize, Marick Press, 2011). His poetry has appeared in many journals throughout the United States and Canada, most recently in *The Asheville Poetry Review, Borderlands,* and *The Arkansas Review.* McManus is the founder of Split P Soup, a poetry writing program housed under the South Carolina Poetry Initiative, which has worked with thousands of South Carolinians since 2001.

Born and raised in rural Arkansas, **Ed Madden** is an Associate Professor of English and gender studies at the University of South Carolina and writer-in-residence for the Palmetto Center for the Arts, a magnet high school. His poems have appeared in *Borderlands, Los Angeles Review, Poetry Ireland, Southern Humanities Review,* and other journals, as well as in *Best New Poets 2007* and the Notre Dame anthology *The Book of Irish American Poetry from the Eighteenth Century to the Present.* His first book of poetry, *Signals* (USC Press, 2008), won the South Carolina Book Prize. Madden has a second collection, *Prodigal: Variations* (Lethe Press, 2011). A third book, *Nest,* will be published by Salmon Press in 2012.

My Summer Vacation:
"I wish I didn't know now what I didn't know then"

In the Split P workshops (see page 85), we focus on invention and process, and we encourage student writers to use their own experiences, to trust that their experiences are worth writing about. That often also means getting them to focus on the concrete rather than the abstract (love, hate, dream, reality). We also like to use models—not for form, exactly, but for ways of thinking through and structuring the work. In particular, we like to find a contemporary poem that has an interesting syntactical or rhetorical structure—a tic, a repetition, a shift, a leap, a turn, a movement—that students can replicate as a structure for writing about their own experiences. Sometimes we begin with the model and read it with the student writers, teasing out the structure or the shift that makes the poem interesting; sometimes, instead, we base a series of prompts on the poem, then read the poem with the students after they've begun their own writing.

This exercise grew from using a model—in this case, Paul Allen's "A Tangle of Angels"—and from our inclination to use works by local or visiting writers whenever possible. We had been working with a group of high school students at the Palmetto Center for the Arts, a magnet school. To encourage our students to attend the South Carolina Book Festival and to hear and to meet writers there, we held our regular Sunday afternoon workshop at the convention center during the festival. We knew Paul Allen would be reading from his latest work (*Ground Forces*, Salmon Poetry, 2008) in a poetry session scheduled just before our workshop (a session students might have been likely to attend), so we decided to use one of his poems as a model for student writing.

In the poem, there is a series of reflections about a place the narrator used to visit during summers as a child. Allen begins:

> You can't grow up spending summers
> in your aunt's trailer
> across the river from lights
> of the country club
> without learning something—
> *good, bad, hard, easy, Mom, Dad,*
> *river bed in time of drought*

but fairways green as green—
about something, even if you don't know what.

It's quite an opening, suggesting that we learn things even if we don't know, really, what we've learned. That is the idea at the heart of this exercise: taking the traditional school assignment—what I did last summer—and transforming it into something mysterious—what I learned (but didn't know I was learning) last summer. It's a different kind of learning, a learning based in experience, not textbooks.

It is also a poem grounded in the specificity of place. Our experience has been that place-based poems work well with student writers, encouraging them to write with concrete and specific details as they think through personal memories or experience. At the heart of this poem is an engagement, a vacillation between the abstract and the concrete—the ways we associate certain ideas with particular places.

This is a poem about a memory of a place. The primary objective of the exercise is to write about—and through—our personal memories of place. In doing so, a secondary objective is to learn how to move between the concrete and the abstract as we move (as Allen does) between the past experience and the present reflection on that experience. We approach the mysteries of *how* and *what* we learn—inevitably abstract—through the specific and concrete details of place, of *where* we learn.

The poem is built in three sections—one focusing on a place, another focusing on something that happened there, a third bringing us back home, literally and figuratively. The only required material is a copy of Allen's poem. For the purposes of this exercise, we focus on four sections of the poem.

Phase I: Preparation

I. Think about a place where you spend time in the summer—either a place you have visited regularly or maybe a place that remains important to you. Or if not the summer, maybe someplace you go regularly at holidays. Maybe it's a relative's house you visit or a particular place your parents or grandparents like. Maybe it's a family reunion. Think of some of the things that regularly happen there, as well as maybe some unusual things that have happened there. Write about that place, using as many specific details as possible. Write at least one page. This will be the raw material for the poem.

II. Read Allen's poem. With our students, we focus on four moments, four short sections in the poem:

1. the opening stanza
2. a section about seeing something you didn't expect to see
3. a section about driving home (and noticing particular things on the drive)
4. the end of the poem

We spend some time on the first stanza. Notice the list of oppositions in the first stanza—suggesting the kinds of things the narrator learned as a child at his aunt's trailer. If you're working with a class, you might ask your students what those oppositions suggest and which other details in the stanza and in the poem (e.g., the trailer across from the country club, or the green fairways and the dry riverbed) suggest things he's learning.

Phase II. A Poem in Four Steps

Starting from the page of writing already drafted, work on a poem, using the following four steps adapted from Allen's poem.

I. Using as a model Allen's first stanza, which is about learning something you didn't know you were learning, write an opening section for your poem. Write in second person, using *you*.

> You can't grow up spending summers
> in your aunt's trailer
> across the river from lights
> of the country club
> without learning something—
> *good, bad, hard, easy, Mom, Dad,*
> *river bed in time of drought*
> *but fairways green as green—*
> about something, even if you don't know what.

With beginning writers, we encourage them to use Allen's rhetorical and syntactic structure: "You can't grow up spending _____ [summers, Christmas, vacation, etc.] at _____ without learning something about _____." Use a list of phrases, perhaps some oppositions like his, to describe what you learned there (even if you didn't know, at the time, what you were learning).

II. For the second section, describe the place again, but describe yourself looking for something but seeing something else—something you didn't expect to see—or listening for something but being surprised to hear something else. Allen writes:

From your aunt's porch,
you watched the fireflies between you
and the club, their green lights.
You lost every bet with yourself
where the next blink would be.
Then where you were guessing next,
or very close, some other kind of lights
came out—from the club itself.
Three. Gold. No *on* and *off* to those.
They fanned out like a fleur-de-lis,
three brilliant flakes of gold,
floating down the black back nine.
This was no doctor's magic trick.
So beautiful and new and sudden,
like a meteor, you wondered for a moment
whether you truly saw it—everything
so utterly going back to how it was.

We learn later in the poem that what the narrator saw at a distance—those three gold lights—was three people on fire. Three women dressed as angels in an amateur theatrical production caught on fire because of an electrical accident, and they ran out of the building and onto the green before being put out by cast members. As he writes, "You learned that what you saw, / was what you saw, but what you saw was something / else as well."

III. For the third section of the poem, bring us home. Describe the drive. Describe something you always remember seeing or someplace you always stop. Allen writes:

Take different routes home
(to pick up or drop off this or that on your way),
but they all come out here
at the one stoplight at the warehouse.
In time you've come to know the bricks
(the brick by brick) of the building's base.
And on the slight ledge
where the dry-rot clapboard begins,
the crumbling mortar and a beer bottle.
And up where one of the graying boards bows,
the makings of a sparrow's nest.

What are some of the things that you recognize as you get closer to home? Is there a particular building you always see? Use specific details.

IV. For the fourth and final step in the process, close the poem and bring us back to its beginning.

Allen ends his poem:

> You don't know what you know—
> or where, why, when.
> Just that you're stopping at the light now,
> and on your way home again.

You may want to close your poem similarly—echoing your opening, bringing us back to where we started. (You might even rhyme, as he does, to give the poem a sense of closure.)

Variations

With groups, start by asking people to describe places they've visited, or summer vacations, family trips. Conversations help to generate a range of ideas and possibilities.

With older writers, we may talk about the risky use of second person, but how the use of *you* lets you write to yourself in a different way from the first-person *I*. You can address yourself in the past, explain to yourself what you were learning even if you didn't know it then. With younger writers, we may not read the section of the poem about the women on fire—or the full poem—until *after* they have written their own poem, since the macabre element of this can sometimes make them think they have to do something equally dramatic. After reading Allen's poem, we might also talk about how quiet surprises are equally powerful.

An Example

We offer this poem, "Summers in Charleston," written by Ashley Cohen-Burnell when she was a high school senior at the Palmetto Center for the Arts at Richland Northeast High School.

Summers in Charleston

inspired by Paul Allen

You can't grow up spending summers
in Charleston with family without learning

something about cooking, a movie you haven't seen,
style, *The Young and the Restless*,
about something, even if you don't know what.

I'm pushed as I try to head in line for
Granny's soul food.
Granny always told us
not to push.
Black-eyed peas, macaroni and cheese, fried chicken,
and upside-down cake.
The smell makes me smile.
I look forward to cutting into Auntie's
homemade pound cake,
right on the left hand corner of the dessert table, its usual spot.
Only to find a store-bought coconut cake
of yesterday.

We ride through the narrow Charleston streets
as we head home.
The open field stays occupied where kids chase
each other in circles and slide down the rusty red slide,
the only piece of the playground set left and
though the basketball hoops and court are worn and torn,
the guys still love their regular five on five.

Ashley Cohen-Burnell

Ed Madden and **Ray McManus** collaborated on two exercises for *Wingbeats*.
See page 89 for their biographies.

The Element of Surprise

Successful poetry operates on conscious and unconscious levels, blending material from both realms in a single poem. Indeed, one of the definitions of *poetry,* as opposed to *verse,* is that in poetry an image ferries the reader from the conscious world to the unconscious world.

Typically, unconscious material is a surprise to the poet. So let us focus on two of the ways that we may use surprising elements when we write. First, we may surprise by the choice of an unconventional or unlikely subject. Second, we may couch a message in surprising imagery within the poem.

Examine "For the Sleepwalkers" by Edward Hirsch—reprinted below. Read this poem aloud at least twice. Then examine the poem, using the discussion that follows as a prompt to your thinking. If you are in a class, use the discussion topics and questions to prompt the conversation.

For the Sleepwalkers

Tonight I want to say something wonderful
for the sleepwalkers who have so much faith
in their legs, so much faith in the invisible

arrow carved into the carpet, the worn path
that leads to the stairs instead of the window,
the gaping doorway instead of the seamless mirror.

I love the way that sleepwalkers are willing
to step out of their bodies into the night,
to raise their arms and welcome the darkness,

palming the blank spaces, touching everything.
Always they return home safely, like blind men
who know it is morning by feeling shadows.

And always they wake up as themselves again.
That's why I want to say something astonishing
like: *Our hearts are leaving our bodies.*

Our hearts are thirsty black handkerchiefs
flying through the trees at night, soaking up
the darkest beams of moonlight, the music

of owls, the motion of wind-torn branches.
And now our hearts are thick black fists
flying back to the glove of our chests.

We have to learn to trust our hearts like that.
We have to learn the desperate faith of sleep-
walkers who rise out of their calm beds

and walk through the skin of another life.
We have to drink the stupefying cup of darkness
and wake up to ourselves, nourished and surprised.

Edward Hirsch

Discussion

I. Title As poets, we continually strive to embody our unique vision in unpredictable and resonant language. To accomplish this goal, it is crucial for us to remember that the body of the poem begins on the first line of the poem, which is the title.

In this poem, Hirsch begins the surprising revelations of his poetic vision by composing a poem about a group most of us have never considered. Additionally, the poem's axis of orientation is aligned by the *For* in the title. This is a crucial grounding that enables the poem to function at times as a tribute or a gift rather than a study or journalistic rendering.

II. Tercets How many successful contemporary poems have you seen written in tercets? If you feel they are successful, what makes them so? Compare them to Hirsch's poem. Why do you think Hirsch chose tercets for this poem?

How does Hirsch keep the energy of the poem flowing through the tercets? Notice that in Hirsch's poem the first two stanzas keep their momentum because they are one sentence with only the last two lines becoming endstopped. Would he have been able to obtain this same effect by use of couplets or quatrains?

III. The Shift Before we can discuss the italicized section, we must acknowledge the importance of the material that precedes the colon. Hirsch alerts the reader by both syntax and diction that he/she must enter the italicized section with a different set of expectations than are employed in the previous stanzas: "That's why I want to say something astonishing." This is only the second time within the initial five stanzas that a sentence begins within a tercet rather than with a tercet's opening word. In addition, *astonishing* must multi-task to create the mood for what follows and provide a glimpse into the persona of the poet.

IV. The Realm of the Unconscious After the colon, the reader enters into the realm of the unconscious. It is at this point that the poem truly soars. By unabashedly sharing imagery from deep within the unconscious, Hirsch furnishes the most hauntingly beautiful and disturbing section of the poem. In doing so, he continues to ground the reader ("our hearts" recurs three times) while revealing images that cluster around themes of darkness and searching.

One way to think of this italicized section is that it is a message from the unconscious, much like a nighttime dream. Thus, this section can handle wild, bizarre, and potent images. Indeed, the figurative images here have a mesmerizing quality that seems rooted in the dream world.

V. Return After the startling images of the italicized message, the poem returns to the almost commemorative energy of the first five stanzas—but with an important shift. Hirsch grounds readers by the repetition of "our hearts" and pulls them further into the poem by switching from the first-person singular to the first-person plural. It's almost as if the shock of the imagery from the unconscious in the italicized section has emboldened the poet to connect more intimately with his reader. Hirsch's *we* functions to embrace the reader. Then the poet furnishes a dark encouragement.

VI. Sound Notice how Hirsch weaves the letter *s* throughout the poem. He also weaves *w* into the first four stanzas.

Procedure

Write a poem in tercets about an unlikely group. Mimic Hirsch's sentences and end-stops. Make sure that your punctuation and syntax follow Hirsch's. About midway through the poem insert a colon and after it, tell us something wildly and overtly beautiful or poetic, funny or bizarre. Then, after this italicized portion, return to the structure of the poem and tell us what we learn from this group. Weave one letter throughout the poem, but do so subtly.

In class, I encourage students to write as closely as possible to the prompt poem's structure when encountering an assignment for the first time. We will then use a different prompt poem for a number of weeks, with each student poem following the model's punctuation (or lack thereof), line length, mood, tone, function of stanzas, and overall structure. Then, later in the semester we will work at making these first attempts *our own*—we will see if we might vary any of the structural, syntactical, or grammatical components to help the poem become what it wants to become.

An Example

For the Ballerinas

Now I want to say something ethereal
for the ballerinas who dedicate themselves
to illusion, the illusion that legs

are made with springs
that vault slim torsos through space,
that arms unfold seamlessly and float on air.

I admire that ballerinas are committed
early on, willing to forsake birthday
parties and dates to spend hour upon hour

in stark, windowless studios.
They stretch and bend, farther and deeper,
polish pliés, jetés, and pirouettes until

one day their limbs are lithe
as reeds, sturdy as I-beams.
I want to say: *When you take the stage,*

in yards of ribbon and tiers of tulle,
hair pulled in small, tight buns,
our hearts become pastel

soaring in the wake of violins,
hovering in the strains of cellos,
sliding down harp strings.

We have to strive for illusion,
learn the discipline of ballerinas
who dismiss pain, bleeding into pink satin

for an encounter with perfection.
We have to embrace sacrifice
and emerge inspired, one step closer.

Ann Reisfeld Boutté

Notice that Boutté has chosen to vary (at times) the punctuation and whether the lines are end-stopped or enjambed in a way that differs from Hirsch. For instance, in the third stanza, she forgoes the end-stopped commas after both the second and third lines in order to quicken the pace. In the fourth stanza, she keeps the beautiful moment of complete pause with the end-stopped first line but increases the pace in the rest of the tercet so as to come to a satisfying resting point at the end of the line: "as reeds, sturdy as I-beams."

In the seventh stanza, when the unconscious message has the reader in its sway, Boutté accentuates the phrasing in a manner different from Hirsch's since her message from the depths is different both in tone and mood from Hirsch's message. We see these differences, also, in her decision to use parallel structure rather than repetition in the penultimate stanza.

Boutté has woven the letter *s* throughout her poem. Its emphasis carries beautifully from stanza one, line one—*say something*—to the important elements of dance in stanza two, with *springs* and *space*. Many of the poem's important words begin with *s*: *studios, stretch, sturdy, stage, satin, sacrifice, step.* However, the art of the poem keeps the reader from recognizing this dynamic upon an initial reading.

Sarah Cortez is the author of the poetry collection *How to Undress A Cop.* Winner of the 1999 PEN Texas literary award in poetry, she has edited *Urban Speak: Poetry of the City* and *Windows into My World: Latino Youth Write Their Lives,* winner of the 2008 Skipping Stones Honor Award. She has also edited *Hit List: The Best of Latino Mystery* and *Indian Country Noir.* Her latest editing project is the anthology *You Don't Have a Clue: Latino Mystery Stories for Teens* (Arte Publico Press, 2011). A co-editor for the journal *Lineup: Poems on Crime,* Cortez has been a police officer since 1993. She lives and works in Houston as a freelance editor and writer. She serves as the national treasurer for the Wordcraft Circle of Native Writers and Storytellers.

Emulating Walt Whitman

from Song of Myself

A child said What is the grass? fetching it to me with full hands;
How could I answer the child? I do not know what it is any more
    than he.

I guess it must be the flag of my disposition, out of hopeful green
    stuff woven.

Or I guess it is the handkerchief of the Lord,
A scented gift and remembrancer designedly dropt,
Bearing the owner's name someway in the corners, that we may see
    and remark, and say Whose?

Or I guess the grass is itself a child, the produced babe of the
    vegetation.

Or I guess it is a uniform hieroglyphic,
And it means, Sprouting alike in broad zones and narrow zones,
Growing among black folks as among white,
Kanuck, Tuckahoe, Congressman, Cuff, I give them the same, I
    receive them the same.

And now it seems to me the beautiful uncut hair of graves.

Tenderly will I use you curling grass,
It may be you transpire from the breasts of young men,
It may be if I had known them I would have loved them,
It may be you are from old people, or from offspring taken soon out
    of their mothers' laps,
And here you are the mothers' laps.

This grass is very dark to be from the white heads of old mothers,
Darker than the colorless beards of old men,
Dark to come from under the faint red roofs of mouths.

O I perceive after all so many uttering tongues,
And I perceive they do not come from the roofs of mouths for
     nothing.

I wish I could translate the hints about the dead young men and
     women,
And the hints about old men and mothers, and the offspring taken
     soon out of their laps.

What do you think has become of the young and old men?
And what do you think has become of the women and children?

They are alive and well somewhere,
The smallest sprout shows there is really no death,
And if ever there was it led forward life, and does not wait at the
     end to arrest it,
And ceas'd the moment life appear'd.

All goes onward and outward, nothing collapses,
And to die is different from what any one supposed, and luckier.

Walt Whitman

Procedure

I. Speculative Questions Write ten different questions that you imagine
a smart and sensitive child, or a time traveler from the distant past or distant
future, or a visiting extraterrestrial, might ask about the world as you know it.
Choose one of your ten questions that you would like to explore further.

II. Speculative Answers Write a series of ten imaginative guesses, specula-
tions, thoughts, wishes, or hopes that address or attempt to answer the ques-
tion you chose. Try to use words and images that connect with the senses as
well as the emotions.

Note: If you prefer, you may use all ten of your questions and write a different
response for each question.

III. Using Whitman as a Model You may use the selection above from
Walt Whitman's "Song of Myself" as a model for your own poem. Notice that
Whitman's poem is not metrical; nor does it rhyme. Instead it is built upon
an accumulation of poetic comparisons, or metaphors, through the use of

anaphora, a practice of rhetorical repetition common to oral and written poetry and prose. This poetry writing exercise is inspired not only by Whitman's marvelous work, but also by Mark Doty's insightful discussion "On 'A child said, What is the grass?'" on the website of the Academy of American Poets. I recommend it for further reading.

A scientist might have tried to answer the child's question with accurate botanical information. However, this poet admits right away that he cannot provide that kind of answer. Instead, he uses the question to pursue a different method of inquiry, demonstrating a poet's process of thinking through figurative language and sensory imagery.

Whitman thinks about grass in a metaphorical way. Rather than giving definitive answers, he offers a series of poetic comparisons. He turns the poem from fact to metaphor, thus shifting our attention from the referential *What is the grass?* to the poetic: *What is like grass?* or *What is grass like?* or *What does grass remind me of?* He thinks about the grass in a poetic, figurative, or metaphorical way. *What does the grass resemble? To what might it be compared?* In successive lines and strophes, the poet imagines what the grass might be, generating possibilities and accumulating layers of meaning by comparing the grass to several other things, such as a waving green flag that matches the speaker's hopeful mood, or a perfumed handkerchief deliberately dropped to attract the speaker's attention, or a message written in an ancient script.

An Example

Moon, Why Are You Following Me?

Because I am hungry
and you are plump.

Because I am cold
and you are tender.

Because I am tired
and you, you—

> Do you ever stop
> to think of me?

My arc, a slow tremolo solo.
My light, blind flight.

Draw me down to you.
Sigh into my nautilus ear

and the air crackles honeysuckle.
Bite me: salt.

Can you hear me hum, shining
you in my mirror?

Lean from my silvered bow to fill
my tin cup with the night's cool seas.

Pull in my battled anchor.
Let me feed you from our ocean's bowl.

I fall, you rise
brighter and brighter—

Judy Jensen

Note: Poet Judy Jensen started by collecting ten questions children have asked. Her poem grew out of question eight from her list, reprinted below:

1. Were you around when the dinosaurs were still here?
2. Why don't spiders stick to their webs?
3. If you're 34 when I'm 4, how old will you be when I'm 68?
4. Were Froot Loops black and white when you were little?
5. What does God look like?
6. If I break my head open, would all my ideas spill out?
7. Why didn't you write your list in your brain so you can remember it later?
8. Why is the moon following me?
9. What happens to your tattoos when you go to heaven?
10. What kind of blood do bugs have?

Harryette Mullen is a professor of English at the University of California, Los Angeles, where she teaches creative writing, African-American literature, and American poetry. The author of *Recyclopedia: Trimmings, S*PeRM**K*T, Muse & Drudge* (Graywolf Press, 2006), and *Sleeping with the Dictionary* (Univ. of CA Press, 2002), Mullen is the recipient of the 2009 Academy of American Poets Fellowship, awarded to a poet for distinguished poetic achievement.

Karla Huston

Aping the Masters: Poems in Imitation

Writing imitations—in homage, of course—of others' poems is one way not only to mimic another's style, but also to practice craft in the same manner that someone imitating Van Gogh's style might learn his skill with a palette knife or someone practicing Clapton's guitar riffs might learn his chords. And if your writing is blocked, imitating someone else's poem is a good way to get out from behind that impediment.

One poem that lends itself to successful imitation is Peruvian poet César Vallejo's "Piedra negra sobre una piedra blanca," known in English as "Black Stone Lying on a White Stone," a sonnet in which the writer pictures his death—the actual day, the setting, the weather, and who might be in attendance. When writers get past their squeamishness about imagining their own deaths, most actually enjoy the serious play involved in this act of creation.

Black Stone Lying on a White Stone

I will die in Paris, on a rainy day,
on some day I can already remember.
I will die in Paris—and I don't step aside—
perhaps on a Thursday, as today is Thursday, in autumn.

It will be a Thursday, because today, Thursday, setting down
these lines, I have put my upper arm bones on
wrong, and never so much as today have I found myself
with all the road ahead of me, alone.

César Vallejo is dead. Everyone beat him,
although he never does anything to them;
they beat him hard with a stick and hard also

with a rope. These are the witnesses:
the Thursdays, and the bones of my arms,
the solitude, and the rain, and the roads.

César Vallejo, tr. Robert Bly and John Knoepfle

In the first stanza, Vallejo announces he will die in Paris on a rainy day. He adds details about which day and the season of the year. In stanza two, Vallejo decides definitely he will die on a Thursday because he has put his "arm bones on wrong," a surprising figurative leap. He also concludes that for all the roads ahead of him, he is alone. In stanza three, Vallejo is absolute: he is dead. He lists the abuses he has suffered at the hands of others. Finally, in stanza four the poet reasserts his premises: he is dead, his witnesses are the day, the solitude, the rain, and the road.

Procedure

I. The Model Read and carefully examine the Vallejo poem. Make notes about how you might imagine your own death.

1. When will you die?
2. Where will you die?
3. What will the weather be like?
4. What kind of day will it be?
5. Which other details will you include? Note the elements that Vallejo repeats: the day, the weather, his death.
6. What figurative leap will you make? Maybe it will be the personification of inanimate objects as I have done in my variation on the opposite page.

II. Your Poem Begin the process of writing and revising.

1. You may want to begin writing with Vallejo's line, "I will die. . . ." Or you may want to begin with, "These are the witnesses . . ." and work from the other direction.
2. Announce your own or someone's death—as Vallejo has announced his. Do this anywhere in the poem.
3. Play with form. Many variations on Vallejo's text are not sonnets—or at least not strictly metered and rhymed sonnets. Yours could be a sonnet—or not.

III. Other Models An Internet search will find numerous other imitations of Vallejo's poem, including Donald Justice's "Variations on a Text by Vallejo," which begins, "I will die in Miami in the sun." Read some of the other variations available online, as well as my own poem opposite. How have these been constructed? What of Vallejo's poem/structure have these authors chosen to keep or reject? How have the imitators made the poems their own? How have they varied the text?

IV. Making it Your Own Allow Vallejo to lead you to poetic discovery. Then make this poem your own. Change it, play with it. Perhaps you may want to give the original poet/poem "thanks" or "apologies" under the title.

An Example

Variations on a Text

I will die at my kitchen table on a fidgety day.
I will finger a cigarette, stare down
the dregs in a glass of red wine.
Between puffs, the sky coughs a lung
full of rain and god's hand pokes through,
wags a smoky finger at my transgressions.
It will be a day someone might remember.

This will be a Tuesday, the sun trying
to come out, wind sighing anxiously in the trees.
Mourning releases a new page, a rattling song,
thin as the light behind my eyes, sad
as the skin over my knuckles.
A dog shivers, violets clench their roots.

All the poets are dead, their words used up
like coins flipped in a gritty gutter.
Once the sun shone on the sea, on lilac eyes,
waves moving in the street like soot.
Cars bleep their exhaustive voices.
Fire comes as witness,
fingers writing with ash.

Karla Huston

Winner of the 2003 *Main Street Rag* chapbook contest, **Karla Huston** earned an M.A. in English/Creative Writing from the University of Wisconsin–Oshkosh. She is the author of six poetry chapbooks, most recently *An Inventory of Lost Things* (Centennial Press, 2009). She has published poetry, reviews, and interviews in many national journals, including *Cimarron Review, Eclectica Magazine 5 A.M., North American Review, One Trick Pony, Pearl, Poet Lore, Rattle,* and *Smartish Pace*. Her broadside *What to Wish On* is forthcoming from Page 5.

The Notebook Poem

Pima Road Notebook

My mother's voice echoed me nearer toward home.
Sad quail in the brush, searching for her children.
Her stained glass hobbies, her knotted macramé.
Bougainvillea papering the window, blood light.
Jackrabbit in summer, beating white heart.
A pheasant blown off-course into plate glass.
The vulture hopped as it ate, puppet-like.
No one she could talk to like she wanted to talk.
Down street, the boy who stuttered but could sing.
I should've been her lovely girl.
My father said he made something from nothing, like sons.
The temperature of silence was always rising.
I could hear the needle of the palo verde drop.
Javelina bristled for water outside my sleep.
Brothers were other animals.
Coyotes gathered and chattered in guttural moans.
All night she thought the howls were only dogs.

Keith Ekiss

Pima Road Notebook

In desert light, in thirsty light, out past the houses.
Out past the idea of roads toward the dry wash.
Always the abandoned mattress springs in the arroyo.
And sunlight dusting tattered afternoon curtains.
Her medicine cabinet a cave of tints and scents.
I twisted her lipstick, a spiral root.
Smelled the sweet clay of Sunset Red emollient.
Who broke the necklace of the river?
Blue relief, our chlorinated swimming pool.
I straightened my dive through infertile water.
My body's better use, casting a shadow for a dove.

I watched the tame hawk return to its hooded wrist.
She dropped me off at school, Cherokee Elementary.
Heat pulsing in my temple and sweat.
I found a nest of rabbits hidden in the cholla.
The young are born helpless, naked, and blind.

Keith Ekiss

Procedure

Write a poem modeled after Keith Ekiss' "Pima Road Notebook" series from his book of the same name (New Issues Press, 2010). Begin by making a list of observations, claims, memories, and descriptions of the street (or a street) on which you grew up. (You can also use the street where you currently live.) Don't be afraid to use fragments, and feel free to widen your descriptions to include family, neighbors, animals, anyone or thing you'd find on the street. Keep the language as concrete as possible, making one statement or claim per line. Consider how each moment expresses a tension or series of tensions. Once you've generated a page full of lines, choose the best ones, rearrange them to maximize tension, and see what happens. Title the poem "[Your Street Name] Notebook."

What I love about Ekiss' "Notebook" series is the way he uses disconnected end-stopped lines to create an often mysterious but evocative experience of place and personal history. I always introduce this exercise by reading aloud a couple of the Ekiss poems, inviting the class to discuss what they reveal about place and the speaker's past. What specific moments are the most resonant and why? What does the poem gain from its fragmented structure? And how does the particular arrangement of the lines affect our reading of them, strengthening tensions, setting up figurative possibilities, etc.?

Of course, this is essentially a list poem, a great exercise for students who have a tendency to over-articulate the tensions and themes of their poems. As Ekiss demonstrates, simply placing one description or claim in proximity to another invites the reader to make meaningful connections between them. The trick for the poet is to choose vivid, suggestive moments and to arrange them to create the most surprise, tension, and meaning possible. My students always love this exercise and, from it, many produce their best poems of the semester.

An Example

Willow Creek Road Notebook

We lived in the last house on a road at the edge.
Came to a point like the prow of a boat which seemed pointless.
Topping a ridge, it was all downhill from there to the ocean.
Mushrooms grew in cow dung in a pasture across the way.
I never found out if they were psychedelic.
The trail led through a fern forest filled with sylphs and fairies.
My son had a tiny friend named Pong with blue hair.
Deer avoided the redwoods claiming they poisoned the stream.
The house was haunted by the spirit of an old sea captain.
Even the idea of people set him off on rifle shooting sprees.
He lay dead in the house for weeks before someone found him.
Smelled still of demon rum and bourbon with a hint of salt.
Sunsets tasted of pastel jelly beans and swept us into night.
A silver manx came by at full moon, decided to stay.
Taught us to love the unexpected.

Carol Alena Aronoff

Bruce Snider is the author of *The Year We Studied Women,* winner of the Felix Pollak Prize in poetry from the University of Wisconsin Press. A former writer-in-residence at both the James Merrill House and the Amy Clampitt house, he has been a James A. Michener fellow at the University of Texas Michener Center for Writers as well as a Wallace Stegner fellow and Jones Lecturer in poetry at Stanford University. He currently lives in San Francisco.

David Meischen

Lost—and Found—in Translation

As Act II of *Three Penny Opera* draws to a close, the libretto offers up a delicious little piece of cynicism when Macheath, flinging challenges in the face of conventional morality, sings out, "Erst kommt das Fressen. Dann kommt die Moral." Translators have been tripping over *Fressen* ever since—because for this German word, English has no equivalent. If we stick to the syntax of the original, Macheath is saying, "First comes eating (or food or grub). Then comes morality." But German has two words for the consuming of food. *Essen* connotes what human beings do when they sit down to the table: we bring civilization with us when we eat. *Fressen* is for the animals, the brutes. It evokes images of eating without pause or manners or silverware—eating stripped of everything but appetite. We are beasts, Macheath is saying. Satisfy our animal hunger and then perhaps we'll climb the evolutionary ladder and come to morals.

As writers we have much to learn from moments such as these. They draw our attention to language, to the shortcomings of the words we use. They issue a challenge to the creative spirit: No way of saying *fressen?* What are you going to do about it?

But that's what we do when we sit down to write, isn't it? We search for words, with all their shortcomings, to say what can't be said. Last fall, in a piece for the *New York Times,* Michael Cunningham had this to say: "Writing itself is an act of translation—putting a vision into words. Trying to match the vision with words."

It seems to me, then, that translation as an exercise—translation from one language to another—can heighten our sensitivity to words, so that we return, strengthened, to our own language. And more adept with the tools at hand.

Procedure

1. Choose a short poem from another language, preferably one that is widely available in English translations. You needn't be proficient in the language. When I completed the exercise that follows, my German had rusted almost beyond repair. But I had in front of me a German poem that I had loved in college. If you love Neruda in English and you have something of an acquaintance with Spanish, consider putting your hands on a favorite in Neruda's native tongue. If you love Shakespeare's sonnets and your college French comes back to you watching films by Truffaut, you might want to reverse the process. Find a French translation of one of your favorite sonnets. Put the original aside and take the French version back into English.

Note: It's okay to choose a poem for which you are aware of one or more translations. However, do not consult a translation before or during the exercise itself.

II. Read the poem aloud. If possible, listen to an audio version read by the author and/or a native speaker. Absorb the poem's cadences, its music.

III. Line by line, write out a literal translation of the poem. Consult dictionaries. Consult the Internet. I have used the short bi-lingual dictionaries in the back of my *Random House Unabridged*, as well as Internet translation tools. I have consulted friends and former students who know another language well.

IV. Next, you will turn your work into a poem. Consider the original's most prominent features. If it's a highly imagistic poem in iambic pentameter, end-rhymed, will you try for all of those in your own? A confession here: I'll do everything I can to capture the images, the feel, of poetry in another language, but I almost always give up on rhyme. That said, searching for English words that will do justice to images has vastly enhanced my admiration for Rilke, among others.

Let go of the literal. Arrange and rearrange. Consult your thesaurus. Go back and forth between the original and your own attempt. Try to capture the voice, the spirit, the image, the music of the original.

V. When you have arrived at a final draft of your translation, actively search for published translations. I recommend the online catalog of the university nearest you. I recommend a trip to the library itself. Study the translations you can find. Notice how they differ from one another, how they differ from yours. Which parts of which translations, your own included, do you most admire and why?

An Example

During the summer of 2000, I came across a photograph of my younger son Jack, at about three, on the carousel at Golden Gate Park in San Francisco. I thought briefly about writing a poem to go with the photo, but then I remembered Rilke's "Das Karussell." I pulled *Neue Gedichte* from my shelves and read the poem to myself—lip-reading at first and then aloud—over and over again. At the University of Texas library here in Austin, I found two translations.

They differed so radically it was hard to believe the translators had started with the same German words. The first was doggerel, a sing-song rhyming mess. Rilke's poem rhymes—and beautifully. Still I was relieved when I saw that the second translator had decided against rhyme. But his version was dull and flat—drained of Rilke's lovely meditative wonder.

I went to work on my own translation, which later that summer accompanied the carousel photo of my son, in a little book of poems and photos I had put together in the aftermath of his high school graduation.

For the sake of brevity, I'll focus on my work with Rilke's opening stanza:

> Mit einem Dach und seinem Schatten dreht
> sich eine kleine Weile der Bestand
> von bunten Pferden, alle aus dem Land,
> das lange zögert, eh es untergeht.
> Zwar manche sind an Wagen angespannt,
> doch alle haben Mut in ihren Mienen;
> ein böse roter Löwe geht mit ihnen
> und dann und wann ein weißer Elefant.

First, I did a literal translation, staying with the German syntax, despite its awkwardness in English.

> With a roof and its shadow turns
> itself for a short while the stand
> of colored horses, all from the country
> that long hesitates before it perishes.
> To be sure many are harnessed on the carriage,
> though all have courage in their demeanor;
> an angry red lion goes with them
> and now and then a white elephant.

As you can readily see, this stage of the work turned out to be a lesson in loss. Frost was right. Poetry *is* what gets lost in translation. Take the last line. In Rilke, it's iambic perfection. *Dann* und *wann* have a natural emphasis that *now* and *then* just can't muster. Notice the natural rhyme, too, with *dann, wann, Elefant*. Say it in English and only the information survives—dull, flat, voiceless information. This is perhaps the most disappointing lesson of translation—that a literal rendering takes the life out of the words.

Next, then, I tried to transform the poem beyond the literal, to move it in the direction of Rilke's poetry. I failed, of course, except that in the end I admired Rilke's poem—his mastery of words—even more. Here's what I sent my son at summer's end:

> In the shadow falling from the roof
> the herded horses circle, many-colored,
> a little while at least, all of a world
> that lingers, as if to stay, before it vanishes.
> Several as well are harnessed to a carriage
> though courage strains against their bridles;
> a lion red with anger runs with the horses.
> And now and then an elephant, pale and white.

It doesn't rhyme, though I like to think it has a trace of what before I called Rilke's meditative wonder. The most important benefit of the exercise was this: I came back to my own poems with greater skill (I hope)—and certainly with greater care—because I'd spent this kind of time in Rilke's company.

Follow-Up

I have long since misplaced the translations I consulted a decade ago, but early this year, I went back to the library for another look. I pulled three translations from the shelf—two by Edward Snow (*New Poems,* North Point Press, 1984 and 2001) and one by Stephen Cohn (*New Poems,* Carcanet, 1992). I found much to remark on, not least that Snow revised himself considerably in the 2001 edition. His 1984 translation follows Rilke's text closely, perhaps too much so. Snow's opening line is an exact translation: "With a roof and its shadow it turns." This rendering is virutally identical to my literal translation. By 2001, Snow had eased his grip on the literal. His new opening line: "With a canopy and its shade it circles." These might seem small differences, but over the course of the poem, the effect accrues. The 2001 translation, while not my favorite, is deft and confident. It reads like Basho doing Rilke.

Stephen Cohn's translation is breathtakingly good—because, from the outset, he lets go of a fussy need to follow Rilke from phrase to phrase, as if such deference will produce the best translation. Cohn's opening line runs thus: "The team of painted ponies spins around." He saves "the shadow of the canopy" for the second line. He uses rhyme, uses it subtly and effectively—but not Rilke's rhyme scheme.

I read to the end of these three translations wondering what the poets would do with my favorite of Rilke's images—a smile from one of the carousel riders that becomes the poet's focus in the closing lines.

Rilke closes thus:

> Und manchesmal ein Lächeln, hergewendet,
> ein seliges, das blendet und verschwendet
> an dieses atemlose, blinde Spiel . . .

Here's what I did with these lines:

> And sometimes a smile tossed out:
> blissful, blessed smile, it dazzles, then disappears
> upon this blind and breathless whirl.

Snow's translations are not all that different from mine. Both versions have "a smile, turned this way." The version of 1984 closes with "this blind, breathless game. . . ." This line is closer to the original than my own. *Spiel* translates as *game*. I chose *whirl* because it felt right. In 2001, Snow revised himself, closing with "this blind, breathless play . . ."

Here again, as with the poem's opening, Cohn frees himself from slavish devotion to the original. His closing lines have no smile at all, but rather this: "And sometimes children's voices unrestrained / sound out in brilliant laughter." There is no *laugh* in Rilke's words, but oh, can I feel the joy, the laughter in his poem. Cohn must have heard it too. I like his translation almost as much—in its own right—as Rilke's carousel.

Doing a translation exercise and then studying your work against one or more published translations will reveal much to you about the challenges of language and about your own tics as a writer. A minute ago, I noticed, for example, that Rilke and all three of the published translations referred to above close with ellipses while mine closes with a period. Over the years, you see, I've read so many banal and/or sloppy and/or pretentious sentences that wander into the mist of spaced periods that I simply will not let myself use them, except, in academic papers, to indicate omitted material in a quotation.

All writing is translation. All writing is reaching—and reaching again—for the one word that makes me hear a *yes* inside myself—*yes,* this is true to the spirit of my experience, or *yes,* this is true to the spirit of the poem I'm recasting in my own tongue. Finding the right words is the work that makes writing worth the bother.

David Meischen has been writing poetry and teaching the writing of poetry for twenty-five years. He was the Master Teacher in English for UTeach–Liberal Arts, the teacher preparation program in the College of Liberal Arts, University of Texas, Austin, 2002–2006. He has had poems in *The Southern Review, Southern Poetry Review, Borderlands, Cider Press Review,* and other journals, as well as *Two Southwests* (Virtual Artists Collective, 2008), which features poets from the southwest of China and the United States. Meischen has participated in two collaborative poetry and art shows—*The Art in Fiber 2011* at the Copper Shade Tree in Round Top, Texas, and *Threaded Lives: Poems from the Fiber World* (Taos, New Mexico, Rane Gallery, 2009). He is a co-founder and Managing Editor of Dos Gatos Press. With a recent M.F.A. in fiction writing, Meischen has short stories in or forthcoming from *Bellingham Review, Superstition Review, Prime Number,* and *Talking Writing.*

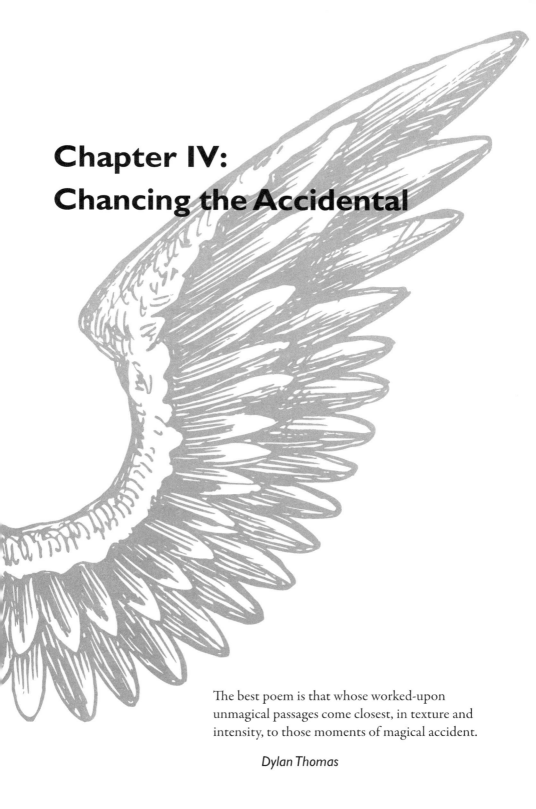

Chapter IV:
Chancing the Accidental

The best poem is that whose worked-upon
unmagical passages come closest, in texture and
intensity, to those moments of magical accident.

Dylan Thomas

Author byline

Naomi Shihab Nye

New Combinations:
Nouns and Verbs

I was tired. I was dragging.

After working as a visiting poet exclusively in middle schools for inner city San Antonio Independent School District for a few years, after ten years working at all levels around Texas—I needed a spa. (None of the other artists-in-residence for the district at that time would agree to visit middle schools, so I had blithely said I'd visit them all.) Driving to work in the rain one day, I heard an NPR announcer say, *Today is the anniversary of the discovery of gold,* and I thought, *Is anything shining?*

What could a visiting poet do to spark energy when the atmosphere sagged, seemed humdrum or hopeless—that day or any other? I hadn't yet found my devotion to lugging large wicker baskets of fruits and vegetables around—encouraging students to smell, touch, identify, connect. That would come the following year and give me, and a herd of young writers stunned by their own insights, renewed enthusiasm for many seasons. But at that moment the spirit at Ralph Waldo Emerson Middle School was not quite living up to the self-reliant gusto of its namesake.

In class, when the students read their poems, I was struck by how easily we fall into simple noun/verb ruts—birds *soar*, streams *trickle*, waves *roll,* blah blah blah. After our luminous toddler-metaphor years, we learn the dull patterns and they take us over.

Could breaking basic noun/verb patterns alone be one key to rejuvenated images and language?

Certainly poetry has always tried to transfuse language with possibility—but how to do this on the most elemental level?—with sweet sad kids whose heads were lolling on their arms—*oh no, Miss, I never write anything good, I can't do it, really, not me.*

Procedure

I. Clipping Nouns and Verbs That night I found two old-fashioned brown paper lunch sacks. I wrote NOUNS in large letters on the front of one, VERBS on the other. Then I sat down with scissors and a heap of glossy magazines, wildly snipping and clipping every intriguing noun or verb I could find—no proper nouns, only common—but verbs with all sorts of endings were admissible—gerunds, past tense, present, etc. Before placing them into their bags I made a patchwork of clipped words on the table and enjoyed simply seeing them in their dazzling many-fonted line-ups—strange combos already sparking possibilities in my weary brain.

II. Finding Unexpected Combinations The next day in class, I focused on reading poems that sprang language and imagery alive simply by making new combinations of nouns and verbs. I had everyone list five nouns they liked and five verbs, and draw lines between some of them to make unexpected combos (I talked about strange sandwiches being more interesting than traditional sandwiches, and we discussed *STRETCHING* with language so that unexpected metaphors might pop up). Everyone wrote wacky sentences in which clouds talked, pillows dreamed, hearts wrote, peanuts danced....

III. Sharing Model Poems Then I read them a nice bouquet of poems using new combinations in many lines—Langston Hughes, Gwendolyn Brooks, Octavio Paz, Carl Sandburg, Denise Levertov, Robert Bly, and the poet who would become my favorite for this exercise's examples, the late Bert Meyers, who had lived in California. I loved his two books *The Wild Olive Tree* (West Coast Poetry Review, 1979) and *Sunlight on the Wall* (Kayak, 1976), which provided these lines:

> the rusty nail shrieked
>
> pulled from the place where it lived . . .
>
> Flowers burst from the walls.
>
> The boat, a huge altar, dissolves in the fog.
>
> Sunlight plays its flute in the treetops.
>
> Night's swept away like a broken glass.
>
> the fallen man curls around a wall like smoke . . .
>
> At noon an airplane, a hard drop of sweat, rolls down the sky's big forehead.
>
> The light drips like oil from an old machine.

I had them pick out the unusual noun-verb combinations in each line. We talked about how images and whole stanzas were able to unfurl simply from those glittering little rubs of strangeness. Did I only imagine it or were they sitting up straighter? Looking more alert?

You don't even have to have a *thought,* I said. (They liked this.) No ideas necessary. Just let new combinations, new intersections of words, lead you.

IV. Pairing Clipped Nouns and Verbs Then I wandered the room with my sacks. Everyone had to pick three nouns and three verbs. They could couple them in any ways they liked, rearrange them, then write images and lines and see if a poem would grow out of it. They could even trade with someone near them if they liked. They could add endings to words or change the tenses or make a singular plural. Okay, go!

I remember feeling, that first day we did this, as if I'd had a blood transfusion—strength came roaring back into me. Or trickling, maybe. Anyway, poetry and surprise seemed more palpable in that room, despite the various murmurs and disclaimers (*Miss, there's no WAY these words could go together! Stretch! I said. Stretch!*)

I have probably tried the New Combinations exercise 999 times since then. Sometimes my writers wanted to tape or paste their actual nouns and verbs from the bags onto their pages. Sometimes I could get them to give the words back. Sometimes I had the chatterboxes who finished fast thumb through magazines and snip out more nouns and verbs for other people to use.

New Combinations is not a bad thing for any of us to do when we need a poke, a language revival. It gets things going on the page.

Examples

I have actually been able to dig back and find a few of the *first* poems written by students the *first* day we ever tried this. I included them in my anthology *Salting the Ocean* (Greenwillow, 2000) with beautiful illustrations by Ashley Bryan, which has just gone out of print. (Please buy a used copy if you can find one; you won't be sorry.)

> As I walk in the moonlight
> I sing of darkness,
> I sing of clouds,
> big black clouds,
> how they change like people,
> they meet and they flee.
>
> I sing of people, rainbow's light,
> empty roads and wooded nights.
> My voice is deep.
> It sparkles to your ears
> and swirls dust away.
> My voice flaps and moves

like a river.
It whispers to the world,
sometimes it shouts,
but yet it has a heart.
My voice can be a swan
and speak with its wings
but behind it is a shadow
that looks like the world.

Vangie Castillo

Vangie, I think, drew *voice, river, swan, speak, flap*, and *sparkle* from the lunch sacks. She was full of disclaimers when she handed this to me—*This isn't a poem! No way! It couldn't be!* But I found it so breathtaking, I could only say, *Fine then, Vangie, don't write poems, just write things like this.* Years later I would run into her working in a department store and she would say, *Do you by any chance have a copy of that first poem of mine that wasn't a poem? As a matter of fact....*

I sing deep songs.
I fly like a river on the wind.
I dance like dreamer corner.
I remember the star like loose white jagged bones.
I open darkness like snow on a chicken.
I shout like an empty sail in the air.
I bounce like a broken ribbon on a window chime.
I sparkle like the golden road.

Dillard Yates

Now, Dillard had his own way of doing it, which was fine with me. For years to come I would remember this boy *who opened darkness like snow on a chicken* and feel everything was going to be okay.

Naomi Shihab Nye was born in St. Louis, lived in Jerusalem, and moved to San Antonio, Texas, at age sixteen. She has worked as a visiting writer all over the country and world. Her thirty books include *Habibi, Going Going, Sitti's Secrets, Fuel, Honeybee, Red Suitcase, You & Yours, Come with Me: Poems for a Journey, A Maze Me,* and *Never in a Hurry,* as well as eight anthologies of poetry for teens, including *Is This Forever or What? Poems & Paintings from Texas.*

Scissors & Gluesticks: Re-Visioning the Poem

How to keep the managerial self from over-managing the poem? How to keep inviting our associative, intuitive intelligence into the poem, especially during revision, when the managerial can override the magical? That's the intention and focus of this revision exercise.

I'm always interested in finding fresh points of entry, for my students as well as for myself, when a poem is in a generative stage and still taking shape. When we begin with the blank page, it is easy not to over-think, or think at all. There are no words staring or sounding back at us from the paper or computer screen. Starting the poem can be an edgy kind of silence or blankness, but it can also hold all the promise and play of "crossing unmarked snow"— the image William Stafford brought to the early generative writing time, and also the title of his book on the creative process.

Crossing the unmarked snow, spilling some words and images onto the page, the generative energy in the life of a poem has so much promise, but we sometimes fail to keep that energy and promise going for the duration of the poem's making. Once we sense a real poem taking shape inside the generative spill of words, we enter a delicate place. At times we demand too much from the poem; other times we don't challenge the poem or ourselves enough. Sometimes, we privilege our self-conscious, pedestrian minds in the poem's narratives and images. We allow the same logic we would use to balance our checking account in directing our poem's shape, texture, and language. As we start thinking about the poem, attempting to revise and make it stronger, the poem can seize up under such scrutiny; it can stop feeling and being because we are now working with it too much in our heads and not enough in our intuitive body. It's ironic how as we become more conscious of the poem through our successive revisions, we can sometimes subvert its associative, luminous energy. The poem can start to feel more rigid, more static. Less playful, less kinetic. Yet as long as the poem still feels unfinished, it needs us to keep wondering it into being.

I want revision time to be as promising and playful as the generative origins of the poem. I am always looking for ways—in the words of Pablo Neruda—to keep the "pure nonsense, pure wisdom of someone who knows nothing" alive in the poem throughout the whole arc of its making. To use Stafford's and Neruda's metaphors, revision time is how we re-cross the marked snow and keep both nonsense sense and wisdom evident in our tracks. I favor revision strategies that disrupt and unsettle the ground my imagination has laid for the poem, and I offer here a strategy that can shake the stalled poem loose, and upend its preliminary structure and intentions.

This exercise is a simple "cut and paste" approach to revision, yet it has startling possibilities in how it privileges the wild and intuitive mind over the managerial mind. When I use this exercise with students, I have them work in pairs, but it can also work very well for an individual writer. I have used this strategy myself when I sense that my poem might grow from a revision technique that subverts my focused, logical control, and summons instead my intuitive presence, and perhaps also the latent energies of the poem. I will describe the exercise for both group and individual contexts. Both approaches can have evocative and productive results.

Materials

- Two typed copies of a problematic poem.
- Two envelopes.
- A few sheets of colored paper, scissors, and tape or glue.

Procedure

Select a poem that is in a draft stage and that has been more frustrating than satisfying to revise. Choose a poem you still care about but aren't yet satisfied with. Maybe it's a poem where you are experiencing an impasse, and nothing you try seems to bring it to fruition or completion but you are not ready to give it up altogether. If you try this exercise with a writing partner, it is best to use poems that you have not yet shared with each other.

Make two copies of your problematic poem, preferably with 1.5- or double-spacing between the lines. Place one copy in an envelope, seal it up, and address it to yourself. Then set it aside. This is an intact draft of your poem, and it will serve as a point of reference later, after the more radical revisions of this exercise have occurred.

Scissors

Take the other copy, and with scissors in hand, cut the poem up, line by line. Beware! Just doing this simple preparatory step can profoundly liberate your managerial self from your current draft of the poem. Place the cut-up strips of poem in the other envelope, and address it to the person you are paired with for this exercise. If you are doing this exercise by yourself, just label this envelope so that you can distinguish it from the uncut draft copy.

Now exchange envelopes containing the cut-up version of your poem with your writing partner. If you are doing this activity by yourself and not exchanging poems, I would recommend a time lapse of several hours or days between when you cut the poem up and when you return to this envelope. Time away from the poem should give you more distance and objectivity when you return to it. You want to try to simulate the fresh and unknowing perspective of the writing partner who opens this envelope to "revise" your sliced up lines, not having heard or seen your original poem.

Gluesticks

Now you have someone else's poem (even if it is your own!), all cut up in an envelope. Invite the poem to discover itself anew. Use the colored paper and begin to revise—to re-see, re-hear, and re-write the poem. The colored paper gives visual contrast from the text; it seems to implicitly help create a sense of play, and invites the visual energy of collage for the revision. Don't do any gluing or taping until you feel the poem has had a chance to find its newly revised shape and sound. It is both playful and productive to be able to move lines around so physically and freely. Be sure to read the poem aloud to yourself, letting the poem's sonic energy direct you as much as its visual or imagistic energy. Be experimental: the cut-up lines at your fingertips are a more immediate and tactile prompt for constructive re-vision than the cut and paste commands on the computer screen, so you want to take full advantage of the tactile aspect of this activity.

Although you want to try to honor the integrity of the lines as given to you, you may also give yourself permission to cut some lines up if doing so seems to enhance or strengthen them. Also, you don't need to use every line, or every word or phrase that was in the envelope. You might also decide to repeat certain lines or phrases for emphasis, repetition, incantatory energy. (I had one student make a palindrome out of the poem he received in the envelope.) You can also add a few words or phrases to help with syntactical cohesion, but you want to be respectful and not over-impose your voice on the revision. If you are working by yourself and with your own poem, go ahead and give yourself full permission to free-write and free-associate whole new lines, phrases, images for the poem. It could be that by cutting the poem up in the first place, you have already given yourself permission to dispense with the least engaging lines of the poem, and some entirely new images and insights might usher in.

Your task is to trust your own intuitive impulses about making the most kinetic and sonic poem you can out of the scraps of loose lines. Let go of any compulsion to guess at, or restore, the poem in its original draft; this is not a puzzle but a poem in the works. If you think you've found the poem's original emphatic lines—the first or last lines, or the title—you should feel no compunction to place such emphasis on these lines unless they seem to call for it. Listen to the lines themselves. Is there a line that calls out to be the first or last line in the poem? Which lines propel the poem forward, and which lines lack interest, energy, and pulse? When you learn to listen this closely to a poem, even when it is not your poem to begin with, you are engaging in something that goes far beyond revision; you are assisting the poem in a metamorphic process. Your scissors and glue revision may or may not ultimately help the writer when she returns to her poem, but 1) it certainly helps you learn a new technique with far-reaching impact for your own creative process, and 2) it helps to shake and unearth the poem from the managerial mind that might have controlled the drafting process up to this point.

Once the poem begins to find its shape for you on the colored paper, go ahead and tape or glue it down, and give the poem a title. Then read it back to your partner. Let him know why you made the choices you did with his lines. Which were most evocative and engaging for you? How did you decide upon a structure, shape, form, and name for this poem? Ask the writer to articulate what she hears and/or learns from her poem in this new version. What might the writer want to keep or dismiss from this exercise when he returns to the self-addressed envelope that contains the intact previous copy of his poem?

If you are working in groups, you probably want to allow plenty of time—at least an hour—for this exercise. When I've offered this exercise to students, I can feel an intense level of creative focus as each writer opens the envelope of cut-up lines and begins to make a new poem from someone else's cut-up draft. Further, by working in pairs, writers have an opportunity to experience both freedom and constraints while working with someone else's poem, and likewise to usher those juxtapositions back into their own creative process.

Discovering a New Poem

For the writer, the next step of this exercise is to compare the new version of the poem with your intact copy. Your partner may have discovered some associative leaps in language, image, and narrative that can now strengthen your original poem. You may now see some lines or passages that you can delete because you realize that they aren't compelling enough for your partner to include, and—more important—nor did you miss them when you heard the revised version of the poem your partner constructed from your lines.

Maybe there are some lines or images you are still attached to even as you acknowledge that your poem is better without them. You can take these lines and file them for another time. For the writer working by herself, a variation of this activity is to keep a file of lines (I keep them in a small wooden box near my desk, but you could also create this file in your computer). Sometimes when I get stuck working on a poem or I'm starting out with the blank page in the generative time, I open the box and pull out a random, long-forgotten image or line. Not always, but sometimes it becomes the little permission slip that gets me crossing snow again.

Before, During, After: An Example

Student Allison Barrett chose the poem below for this exercise. Student Garret Lee Milton created the gluestick version on the following page.

Gretel

Acid tears melt a perfect china face
Desperate wails prevail through the placid night
Little hummingbird heartbeat quickens
No light to illuminate this ugly world
Only the menacing moon.

She weeps and blubbers in search of mother
Distraught fingers tear at wretched pink lace
Miniature shiny shoes scuff desolate dirt
No one hears howls in the hush of shadow
Only the menacing moon.

Surrounded by looming, scraggly trees
Never has the forest felt so Grimm
Without white pebbled path
Nor companion or friend
Only the menacing moon.

Allison Barrett

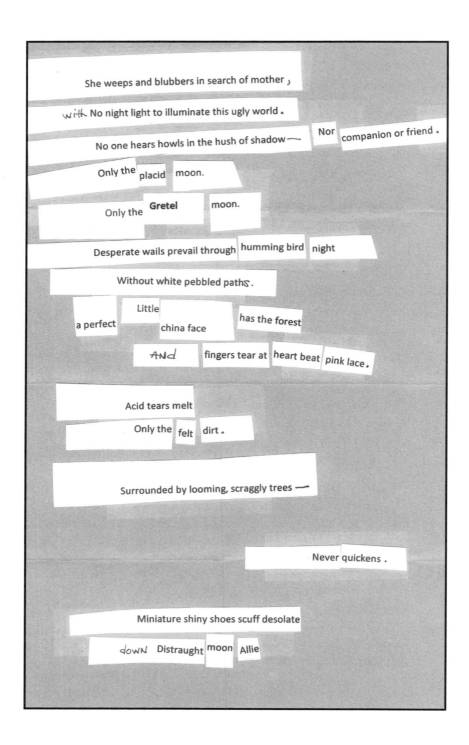

She weeps and blubbers in search of mother ,

with No night light to illuminate this ugly world .

No one hears howls in the hush of shadow — Nor companion or friend .

Only the placid moon.

Only the **Gretel** moon.

Desperate wails prevail through humming bird night

Without white pebbled paths .

a perfect Little china face has the forest

AND fingers tear at heart beat pink lace.

Acid tears melt

Only the felt dirt .

Surrounded by looming, scraggly trees —

Never quickens .

Miniature shiny shoes scuff desolate

down Distraught moon Allie

Using Milton's gluestick work, Barrett revised her poem. See below for the final version.

Distraught Moon

Little, perfect china face has the forest.
She weeps and blubbers in search of mother,
without night light to illuminate this ugly world,
only the placid moon.

Fingers tear at heartbeat pink lace.
Miniature shiny shoes scuff desolate,
surrounded by looming, scraggly trees—
                    Never quickens.

Acid tears melt,
only the felt dirt.
Grimm leaves cackle—
                    Awaken wickedness.

Desperate wails prevail through hummingbird night.
Without the pebbled path,
no one hears howls in the hush of shadow,
Only the Gretel moon.

Allison Barrett

Laurie Kutchins is the author of three collections of poetry—*Slope of the Child Everlasting* (BOA Editions, 2007); *The Night Path* (BOA Editions, 1997), recipient of the inaugural Isabella Gardner Poetry Award and a Pulitzer Prize nomination; and *Between Towns,* recipient of the Texas Tech University Press First Book Award. Her poems and nonfiction prose have appeared widely in journals, including *The New Yorker, The Georgia Review, The Kenyon Review, Ploughshares, Poetry,* and *The Southern Review.* Kutchins has been anthologized in numerous publications, including *A Place on Earth: an Anthology of Nature Writing from Australia and North America; Sweeping Beauty: Contemporary Women Poets on Housework;* and *Woven on the Wind: Women Write about Friendship in the Sagebrush West.* She co-directs the interdisciplinary Creative Writing Program at James Madison University (JMU). A co-founder of the faculty creative arts series, Works in Progress, at JMU, she is also a faculty member at the Taos Summer Writers Conference, sponsored by the University of New Mexico.

Scott Wiggerman

Two Wrongs Make a Right: Revision through Recycling

Think of the dozens of poems you've abandoned midway in journals or notebooks. Or the file folders of poems that you've rewritten so many times it seems all their life is sucked out of them, the ones that no amount of revision seems to save. Or the poems you've "finished" but seem too run-of-the-mill to send out into the world. I know I'm not the only person with such failures. Right?

We've all heard the saying that two wrongs make a right. I decided to apply the adage to such poems as a way of resuscitating the good lines, phrases, and images in them; and while this technique is not a sure-fire route to success (a student from one of my workshops dubbed the exercise, "Two Wrongs Make a Third Wrong"), it's at least a way of bringing some new life into the many poems you've deserted, dismissed, or relegated to the foot-high "needs revision" stack piling up on your desktop.

Procedure

To start the process, find two poems of similar length that you've given up on—whether incomplete or "finished." It doesn't matter whether they're on similar topics. It doesn't matter if one is in form and the other is free verse, if one rhymes and the other doesn't. What matters is that neither of the two poems is one you feel confident enough to submit to an editor. Once you've chosen the poems (or selections), prepare to alter them—radically. If these are poems that truly seem to be languishing in limbo anyway, you've got nothing to lose. Ready?

I. Dividing One poem at a time, take each line and divide it into two parts, perhaps breaking where grammatical units fall or pauses logically occur—but not necessarily. I sometimes break a line so that the first words of a prepositional phrase are separated from their objects by the break (i.e., if "from their objects by the break" is a line, I might divide it as "from their objects by" and "the break"—not "from their objects" and "by the break"). Notice in "Mortal Wounds," the example on the following page, I've broken the third line so that the preposition *of* sits by itself; *up* and *by* get similar treatment later in the poem. In "Afterward" (also on the following page), I broke the second line so

130   Wingbeats

that one half ends with an article, "perhaps a." I have literally taken a pen and marked a line between the two halves of each line to accomplish this since I usually work with a printed copy, though on a computer it's also easy to tab a space somewhere in each line.

Mortal Wounds

I lament to watch	→	I lament	| to watch
the dead rise up	→	the dead	| rise up
with my great flood	→	with my great	| flood
of tears. I ponder	→	of	| tears I ponder
these thousand deaths,	→	these	| thousand deaths
my one life, the soul	→	my one life	| the soul
divided. Blow by blow,	→	divided	| blow by blow
sorrows add up,	→	sorrows add	| up
my worn-out heart	→	my worn-out	| heart
struck by another	→	struck	| by another
offense of love,	→	offense	| of love
rendered another scar,	→	rendered another	| scar
surprised by its next breath.	→	surprised	| by its next breath
One who in love	→	one who	| in love
dreamed a fortunate destiny,	→	dreamed	| a fortunate destiny
now hobbled by	→	now hobbled	| by
the pain of mortality,	→	the pain	| of mortality
a prodigious memory of red.	→	a prodigious	| memory of red

Afterward

They want to hear no words,	→	they want	| to hear no words
perhaps a shot of warmth,	→	perhaps a	| shot of warmth
the kind that stings going down	→	the kind that stings	| going down
but lingers afterward	→	but lingers	| afterward
like the stain of childhood guilt.	→	like the stain	| of childhood guilt
An undertow of desire	→	an undertow	| of desire
followed by a pool of silence—	→	followed by	| a pool of silence

is this what sex comes to,	→	is this	| what sex comes to
insular as a sleeping bag?	→	insular	| as a sleeping bag
Blind currents rush	→	blind	| currents rush
in a river of coupling, but fork	→	in a river of coupling |	but fork
as quickly into separate branches,	→	as quickly	| into separate branches
the narrow banks of need,	→	the narrow banks	| of need
where *you* is but a shimmer	→	where you	| is but a shimmer
on a distant moonlit wake—	→	on a distant moonlit |	wake
like *love*, another word	→	like love	| another word
they do not want to hear.	→	they do not	| want to hear

II. Combining Now that both poems are broken up, you come to the interesting part of the process. You start working with the broken up units, and combine bits from one poem with bits of the other. In some ways, it's no different than reusing a phrase or line that gets cut from a poem—only this recycling is on a much grander scale. In fact, almost every word in the new poem, "Coming Clean," stems from "Mortal Wounds" and "Afterward." (Those words that don't are indicated in parentheses below.)

Jump around both poems looking for phrases that go together or that combine in fresh or unusual ways. For example, I used syntax—the infinitives from the original first lines—to add a parallel structure to the new first line. "A shot of warmth" becomes an "*up*shot of warmth." *Hobbled* becomes a descriptor of *word,* as *distant* and *moonlit* become for *scar.* Several lines of "Coming Clean," you will notice, do *not* combine within the line with any other words or phrases, but are essentially used as they appear in the original poems; yet they are new in the context of what comes before or after them. The idea of "Two Wrongs Make a Right" is not simply to combine two poems, but to merge them in a way that creates a stronger, more interesting poem, so use whatever combinations work in doing so.

Coming Clean

to hear no words	+	to watch	→	To hear no words, to watch
one who	+	is but a shimmer	→	one who is but a shimmer
going down	+	(with a) flood	→	going down with a flood.

			a pool of silence	→	A pool of silence
divides	+ my worn-out heart	→	divides my worn-out heart,
blind	+ struck by another	→	blind, struck by another

in a river of coupling		→	in a river of coupling,
(an) up	+ shot of warmth	→	an upshot of warmth.
tears I ponder	+ afterward	→	Tears I ponder afterward,

like love, another word		→	like *love*, another word
now hobbled	+ (the) undertow	→	now hobbled, the undertow
of	+ my one life	→	of my one life.

a distant moonlit	+ scar	→	A distant moonlit scar
(on) narrow banks of need		→	on narrow banks of need,
the stain (of a)	+ thousand deaths	→	the stain of a thousand deaths:

| prodigious memory of red | | → | prodigious memory of red. |

An Example

Here (see the following page), I combined two wildly different poems—one on a relationship ("Burnt Toast") and one on the anniversary of 9-11 ("September 11")—using this same approach. Since they are longer, quite a bit of both poems did not make it into the revised poem, "Introduction to Want." However, while the new poem retained some of the narrative of "Burnt Toast," it became less prosaic with the addition of the political images from "September 11." I think "Introduction to Want" is much more fascinating—at times almost surreal—than either of the two poems it stemmed from. Combining the two wrongs into a new right added a life that was missing from both of the original poems. "Beer swilling / as the national verb" is a line I never would have composed. Same for "big ol' Rams black as burnt toast." Or "nude in my own garage." These are all lines I now love. Admittedly, I made some additional changes as I continued drafting the poem, bringing in entirely new material that wasn't in either of the original poems, but, again, it's your poem, and you are allowed to do whatever it takes to make the best poem that you can. When this exercise works—and it often does—it's well worth the effort. Go green!

Burnt Toast

He liked to make me breakfast,
omelettes with bacon and Swiss,

while I sat nude in the dining room,
staring at the old-time toasters

that lined the papered walls
on shelves just out of reach

What I remember of the bedroom
was the box under the bed

with condoms, lube, and cum rags.
My grandmother adored him,

took photos of us riding
the bronze longhorns at the Arboretum,

our tight jeans button-fly to butt.
He introduced me to *antiquing*

as a verb, dragged me
to rusty towns across Central Texas.

I made him sit through poetry.
It's how we compromised.

On Sundays we used to cruise
in circles around the Veloway.

The last time I saw him,
he was picking up the bicycle

he stored in my garage,
lifting it into the bed

of his big ol' Ram, his hair
as black as burnt toast.

I don't remember why I broke it off.
There wasn't anyone else,

but I was always testing lovers,
and now I've lost his name,

which says more about me, I think,
than him.

+

September 11

It started as one.
Then one became two,
became ten, became a hundred
before the week was through.

Like an endless loop
of incontinence-tampon-Viagra spots
or relentless commercials for
explosive-driven blockbusters,

we tired of seeing
planes proliferating,
multiplication as commonplace
as Internet pornography or American arms.

Eight years later
some want to make
9-11 a national holiday
"so we'll never forget,"

as if another beer-swilling,
fire-up-the-fat-on-the-grill
day-off from work
would make us remember

any more than we do
the sacrifices that led to
Memorial Day,
much less Labor Day.
The crisis that brought us
together lasted as long
as our collective attention span
or the latest mascaraed popstar,

and we, mired in excess,
are as divided now
as we were then,
when it all started as one.

=

Introduction to Want

What I remember of the bedroom:
planes proliferating in explosive
blockbusters, but mostly the loop
of relentless commercials. We tired
of condoms, Viagra on shelves
just out of reach, fat on the grill,
incontinence, beer-swilling
as the national verb, the latest
popstar bronze as American arms,
big ol' Rams black as burnt toast.

How we compromised, picking
our sacrifices, always testing—
takeout or delivery? paper or
plastic? extra cheese?—
staring at papered walls before
the weekends were through,
my words in orbit around
his giant screen and tiny speakers.
He introduced me to want—
of something . . . I don't remember.

And now, breakfast at two,
nude in my own garage,
I'm lost on Memorial Day.
I see him or someone like him
in fusty towns across Texas.
I seem to remember in circles.

Scott Wiggerman is the author of two books of poetry, *Vegetables and Other Relationships* (Plain View Press, 2000) and *Presence* (Pecan Grove Press, 2011). Recent publications with poems by Wiggerman include *Switched-on Gutenberg, BorderSenses, Poemeleon, Broad River Review, Boxcar Poetry Review,* and *Southwestern American Literature.* Wiggerman has also edited several anthologies and books, including *Big Land, Big Sky, Big Hair* and this one, *Wingbeats.* A frequent workshop instructor, he is lead editor of Dos Gatos Press, publisher of the annual *Texas Poetry Calendar,* now in its fourteenth year.

Over My Dead Body: Exquisite Corpse

True collaboration melds the voices of two writers into a new, distinctive one, but choose the wrong partner or stage the process poorly and it can feel as if you've been overtaken by the enemy. If you are writing for publication, it is critical that you have a collaborative partner you trust, one who works well with you. I have had mixed success with writing collaborations. One partner refused to follow the agreed-upon rules and kept changing my lines (but never his own), so that I felt defensive about every word I wrote. Another, in an e-mail partnership, took so many weeks to return his lines that the creative flow was sluggish—more frustration than motivation. With a compatible partner, though, collaboration can produce wonderful results.

Collaborative writing dates back to *The Talmud*, the King James Bible, Imperial Chinese literature. Exquisite Corpse is one of the simplest—and most practiced—forms of collaborative writing. It began as a Surrealist parlor game, played by André Breton and the French visual artists in the early twentieth century.

Exquisite Corpse for Groups (Traditional)

You are likely familiar with this exercise in its original form. If not, I offer a quick overview:

Preparation

1. Write or choose an opening line. This game works best if you have a prepared starting line: one of your own, one pulled from the cosmos, or one borrowed from a favorite poet—something you wish you'd written. Leave this line unfinished so as to lead easily to a new line.
2. Separate participants into groups of four to six, each with a sheet of paper and a pen.
3. These sheets of paper will pass from member to member. To avoid chaos, decide ahead how papers will pass and explain the route to participants.

Instructions for Collaborators

1. Write the line provided at the top of your sheet of paper. Complete the line and write a new line beneath it.
2. Fold the paper so that *only the second line* shows and pass your paper to the next person.
3. Take the folded sheet you have received. Read the visible line and add two lines of your own. Fold the sheet again—so that *only the last line* shows. Pass the sheet again.
4. Continue this process until each sheet of paper returns to the participant who started it.
5. When you receive the sheet you started, read the one visible line and add a closing line.
6. Unfold the poem you hold. Ooh and ah over your Exquisite Corpse.

Exquisite Corpse for Two Live Bodies

I have been writing collaboratively with Karla Huston since 2001. We would hardly label ourselves as *surrealists,* nor does either of us own or work in any room vaguely resembling a parlor (unless a sun room counts). All that aside, we have found the Exquisite Corpse collaborative writing exercise to be fun, inspiring, rewarding.

Procedure

This procedure mimics the process Karla Huston and I have successfully used numerous times, but, like a recipe, it can be easily modified.

1. Agree upon what you'll begin with: an unfinished first line, a stolen line, a theme? Agree upon how many lines you'll write so you know when to stop; if in doubt, the bottom of the page is as good a place as any.
2. Start with only one sheet of paper and a pen. Decide who will go first.
3. One participant finishes the first line and writes one new line below it, then folds the paper so that *only the second line* shows, and hands the paper to the other partner.
4. The second partner reads the visible line, adds two new lines, folds the page so that *only the last line* shows, and hands it back to the partner who went first.
5. The exchange repeats until you've written the agreed-upon number of lines or hit the end of the page.
6. Unfold the poem and read it. Think of it as an exquisite first draft.

An Example

Karla Huston and I started writing collaboratively through a persona named Thigh. While not all the poems we wrote over the years were about her, she was often who we turned to as a start point—both for fun and for help in jumping outside our individual writing voices. With Thigh, we created a list of possible titles and often began with one of us choosing a title from the list, in this case "Thigh Worries about Friction."

She's been fighting her twin for weeks,

it started somewhere between ~~crossed out~~
a pair of tights and Beloit
and a deep need to rub something the wrong
way for a change   one

to make a ~~spark~~

to prove she's a live wire, or just plain alive.
like rubbing hard things together creates heat
and flares when she least expects it.

But she didn't expect this evil,

being estranged from her identical twin.
Makes her lonesome for that closeness.
She came close with a guy named

Lyggin, but that was too close for comfort,

too feminine, like the wrong kind of itch
~~one~~ that doesn't need scratching,
only a soothing ointment,
tincture, tincture.

~~crossed out~~ Lubricant? Or amputate.

You can see that we have very distinctive handwriting, so it was always easy to remember whose lines were whose. If this is not the case with your partner, be sure that one of you writes in a different color.

After we unfolded and read, a few things immediately occurred:

- We agreed the poem was worth pursuing further.
- We each made some immediate edits, based on the sum of the parts.
- We decided who would take the draft home, type it up, and e-mail it to the other.
- We agreed that on our own we would edit only our own lines, that when we were together we could edit collaboratively.

If you refer to the original draft, you'll notice three choices for the poem's closing word—*tincture* (Karla's original choice), as well as *lubricant* and *amputate* (my suggggestions). Neither of us cared for the other's choice of words, but in the end—because we have a good collaborative relationship—we were able to agree on *unguent,* a word that worked for both of us and works for the poem.

Thigh Worries about Friction

She's been fighting her twin for weeks,
bickering about smoothness.
They started somewhere
between a pair of pink tights
and Beloit, a deep need
to rub something the wrong way,
to make any spark, to prove
she's a live wire, alive. But rubbing
hard creates heat, flares
familiar where she least
expects it. She didn't count on
the chafe. Being estranged from herself
makes her lonesome for that closeness.
She came close with a guy named Lynn
but that was too feminine, the wrong
kind of itch, one that doesn't need scratching—
unguent, unguent.

Cathryn Cofell and Karla Huston

Tips

Often, with Exquisite Corpse the poem is done—or almost done—when the exercise is done. This exercise encourages wildly creative flow. Don't over-think and don't over-edit. If revision works, great. If not or if you're struggling to find a middle ground, abandon the poem and move on. However, if you have a strong collaborative partner and find you're good at this game, you may want to send your work off for publication. A number of good journals are open to collaborative work. If you decide to go beyond the first draft, take an editorial look at the poem *together*. First, agree to a set of rules about the revision process. Some general questions for any collaborative writing process:

1. How do you decide if it's good enough to be called a poem? (For us, if one thought it didn't measure up, we killed it, no questions asked and no begging for mercy.)
2. Will you allow revision? To what degree? Will you revise as you write or at the end?
3. Will you allow the other writer to revise your lines?
4. Will you "fix" inconsistent structural elements such as point of view?
5. Will you revise the final draft together?
6. Will one or both of you decide when the editing process is complete?

Distance offers a balanced perspective; revising too close to the first draft can be more difficult if you are still in love with your own lines. Put it aside for a couple of weeks or even months; with time, we often couldn't remember whose lines were whose, so we were less apt to nitpick. Ultimately, the poem should not sound like two dueling voices, but one fabulous new voice.

Variations on a Corpse

You don't have to be in the same room or even the same state to do Exquisite Corpse. E-mail, text, or voice messaging is very efficient and allows you to write on your own time. Be sure to have a system in place to keep track of the order of the work:

Guidelines for an E-Mail Exchange

1. We use e-mail a lot—including a color-coded system, with my lines in blue and Karla's in red.
2. You can't fold an e-mail so that only one line shows. The first partner writes two lines and sends them to the second. The second partner copies the two lines into a master document and adds two lines. Then the second partner copies the last line into an e-mail and sends it back to the first partner, who repeats the process.

3. In each e-mail, we use a line of *X*'s in place of the invisible previous line (the one you'd fold over on paper).
4. We each keep track of what is sent to us and copy it into a master document, including the colors, the visible lines and the *X*'s.
5. When we reach the agreed-upon finish point, we e-mail each other our version of the poem, with lines of *X*'s for the partner lines we haven't seen yet.
6. One last time, each partner copies previously unseen lines from the other's document and pastes them over lines of *X*'s to produce a complete draft of the poem.

You could agree that just one person keeps the master document, but we found that sometimes one of us would slip and miss a line or two. With both keeping a master, we were sure we wouldn't lose anything.

This sounds more confusing than it is—trust us! It's easy once you get the hang of it, and it allows you to write on your own time.

An Example

We offer a closing example as evidence that collaborative writing can lead to publication. This poem appeared in *Margie.*

Thigh Considers Her Heritage

It's the sound of thunder
she dreads most.
That and boots
tramping through her veins,
boots with stiletto heels,
stuffed with snakeskin
too tight
for an average girl.
She's inside the boa,
she's inside out,
shed and
pushed like a petulant
tongue or a banana
peeled too soon.

Some days she'd like
to dance,

hang out with a man
with tattoos and wavy
black hair.
Most days it's all
she can think about,
the driving beat of his tarantella,
the dripping heat, the musk,
her body ripe
as a storm cloud, her body
a scarecrow,
her arms full
of black birds and dreams.

Cathryn Cofell and Karla Huston

Cathryn Cofell is the author of five chapbooks, including *Sweet Curdle* (Marsh River Editions) and *Kamikaze Commotion* (Parallel Press). In 2010 she produced a CD called *Lip,* putting new and selected poems to the music of Obvious Dog. She has had poetry in numerous publications, including *New York Quarterly, Oranges & Sardines, Slipstream,* and *Wisconsin People & Ideas,* in which she was selected for the 2008 John Lehman Poetry Award. Cofell is the recipient of more than forty awards for poetry and essay; she is a frequent keynote speaker, radio guest, and workshop facilitator. She currently chairs the advisory board for *Verse Wisconsin* and helps coordinate several writing festivals and readings throughout Wisconsin. Cathryn Cofell and **Karla Huston** have collaborative poems published in *Margie, Rhino, Indiana Review,* and online at *qarrtsiluni.*

See page 107 for a biography of **Karla Huston.**

Thrift Shop:
Giving and Getting, a Collaboration

Ever have a poem (or three?) where nothing seems to work? The poem isn't worthless; it's just stuck. One way to solve the problem is to donate it—give it away—preferably to another writer. A good friend is ideal. Cathryn Cofell and I have written successful collaborative poems from each other's stalled attempts. A few years ago, I had a poem that didn't work, no matter what I did. In frustration, I handed it to Cathryn, telling her to do what she wanted to it. A few days later, a new poem appeared in my e-mail inbox. Part of me was pleased and couldn't wait to see what she'd added, but another part was jealous that she'd taken something I'd struggled with and so easily made new of it. She hadn't revised my lines. Instead, she'd written between and around them. Once I overcame my bruised ego, I realized that what we had created together was better than what I'd tried to make on my own.

Materials

You'll need a pen and paper, a stuck or frustrated poem or two, and a trusted writing friend, ideally one with whom you've written before (see page 136 for comments on writing partnerships). Before proceeding, set some ground rules both partners can live by. Finally, you'll need patience. Remember that what comes back to you is often stronger than what you'd created on your own. The most difficult part is ego. Give that away, too—at least temporarily. Allow that new voice to appear as two writers merge as one.

Procedure

I. Exchange and Write Hand a frustrating or stalled poem over to a writing partner and allow it to be reinvented. Take your partner's stalled poem in a new direction. Write between and around the poem's existing lines. Don't edit the original lines; follow them in a new direction. Then return the poem to your partner.

II. Edit and Exchange At this point the writing partners can repeat the exchange. The first partner will edit her lines with the whole in mind and forward the poem to the second partner again, who will edit her lines, again with the whole in mind. At any point in the process, the two partners can meet and work together on the developing poem.

An Example

The poem "Miracle Fish" was a stalled piece I wrote in 2001. My vision of the poem and what showed up on the page were two different things. I had given up. So I offered the poem to Cathryn. The original poem looked something like the one below. (We kept few drafts of our collaborative poems. This version is only approximate, and the original lines were not as polished as the lines below.)

Miracle Fish

Place the cellophane fish in your palm
and wait. His actions will tell your fortune.
A moving head means jealousy,
a finicky tail means indifference.
See how he bucks and twists in my hand,
nearly falling over himself to get me right.
But every time I open either palm
to this red minnow, he turns a different story.

Today, I am tail over mouth: fickle.
Yesterday I was false.
I want to know how seven seconds
and a sliver of head-shop plastic
know me so well. So tell me, Miracle Fish,
which scarlet fortune do I believe,
how much of me is approximately true?

Karla Huston

Cathryn wrote between and around my lines, adding her own. Afterwards, we both agreed about the revision, still following our self-imposed guideline of revising only our own lines. The finished product contains words from both of us. It has been published and nominated for a Pushcart Prize.

Miracle Fish

Place the cellophane fish in your palm
and wait. Let him warm to you,
find your cradle, the curve of your inner
nature. His actions will tell your fortune.

A moving head means jealousy,
a finicky tail means indifference.
And so you unfold through all his stirrings.

He bucks and twists in my hand,
nearly falling over himself to get me right.
But every time I open either palm
to this red minnow, he turns a different story.
Today, I am tail over mouth: fickle.
Yesterday, his fin-flick called me passion.
Sometimes late at night, he flips
all the way and claims that I am false.

I want to know how seven seconds
and a sliver of head-shop plastic
know me so well when my own
husband holds me all night, his whole body
cloaked over mine, his whole body absolutely
still. According to the key, his silence says
I am the dead one.
So tell me, Miracle Fish,
how much of me is approximately true—
which scarlet fortune do I believe?

Karla Huston and Cathryn Cofell

A Variation

In another collaborative exercise, Cathryn and I worked across from each other at my kitchen table on stalled poems. She e-mailed the following lines to me, wondering what could be done with them.

I cling to a man who will not cling to me

I imagine he
imagines me
a sock
stuck
inside his pant leg
to be rid of me

he has to strip down
pull the electric eel
of me free
only to catch to his
sleeve his
hand as if in greeting
a first meeting
shocking as the last

Cathryn Cofell

While she worked on another piece, I added my own lines to hers. Instead of writing between and around, I worked across the page, trying to mirror what she had done. We e-mailed various versions back and forth, offering suggestions. Lastly, we wanted the poem to read not only vertically but horizontally as well, so I continued to play. The ultimate version looks like this:

I cling to

a man	a woman
who will not cling to me	stuck like static
I imagine he	wants me
imagines me	close to her
a sock	one that's lost
stuck	and wandering
inside his pant leg	the quick strokes
to be rid of me	to her sticky bidding
he has to strip down	O, I want to explode
pull the electric eel	the alarm and crawl free
of me loose	but captive still
only to catch to his	fingers sinking,
sleeve and clasp as if	unbutton(ed), fly, my
greeting	fist uncoiling,
that first meeting	this, tryst over text
shocking as the last	grip, thumbs on fire

Cathryn Cofell and Karla Huston

Finally, whatever method collaborative writers choose to use, the key element is a sense of fun and, more important, trust—in each other and the process.

Note from Cathryn Cofell: You don't have to exchange a whole poem to do this exercise. Sometimes you might have a great stanza, a great couple of lines, several stanzas, but no good ending. We've done a combination of these and most all have been great experiences both to smack down writer's block and to create really fabulous poems—ones that read like a new voice instead of two single authors.

Karla Huston and **Cathryn Cofell** collaborated on two exercises for *Wingbeats*. For Huston's biography, see page 107. For Cofell's, see page 142.

Entering the Conversation of Poetry

Donald Hall says, "Poets need other poets to talk with." In *Thirteen Ways of Looking for a Poem,* Wendy Bishop writes, "what practicing poets do: they enter the conversation of poetry, reading each other, writing back and forth." Poetry therapist Georgia Robertson describes this conversation as "a human language / to make its flying sound / across the air between us."

Hall, Bishop, and Robertson may not have had the Internet in mind, but thanks to e-mail, poets no longer need to live in each other's physical neighborhoods in order to share poems. This exercise allows poets to make a "flying sound across the air" by collaborating on the creation of poems via e-mail. Of course, the exercise may also be used between poets sitting across from each other at a table in Starbucks or in a formal workshop setting and may be modified for use with more than two poets.

Procedure

The conversation starts with one poet writing an opening line for a poem and e-mailing it to a fellow poet who adds a line and sends it back for the next line. This may sound like a version of Exquisite Corpse (see "Over My Dead Body," page 136)—passing a paper back and forth and adding lines—but in this game the participants see the whole of the emerging poem as it develops. The big difference is that when the "lid" of the collaborative poem "makes the sound of a perfectly made box clicking shut" (as Yeats described how to know when a poem was finished), the poets take their own lines out of the whole and revise them to create individual poems.

Participating in this collaborative exercise took me to places I would not have gone on my own. Something about responding to other writers' lines brought out lines I wouldn't have thought to write.

Of course, this exercise does not guarantee the creation of one, two, or three great poems, but it can produce seeds for later development. At least the poets will have had the opportunity to enter the conversation.

An Example: Working in Pairs

I asked one of my poet friends living across town from me in Ft. Lauderdale to try this exercise. We began the collaboration with the same line: "This, I must say, is the sum total of this day." A question arose: Could we vary our own lines when we took them out of the collaborative work. Of course, vary away!

That is when the poem will come—after deleting, adding, reversing, and even stealing lines from each other.

Below is the collaborative poem Blaise Allen and I wrote together. The boldface initials at the beginning of each line identify the writer.

GF This, I must say, is the sum total of this day:
BA Shower, tea, walk the dogs, e-mail, return calls, walk the dogs,
      read, nap, dinner, walk the dogs,
GF teaspoons for measuring my days.
BA The clatter of keystrokes, brush strokes a canvas, practice scales,
GF all the mundane sounds that let me know I am
BA breaking open like coastal waves, transient, wild
GF for change, for transformation.
BA Afternoon light sifts through the palms
GF striping the room with sun and shade.
BA A pot of ginger tea steeps
GF steam rises from cups.
BA I heard you call out from another room,
GF your call just one of the sounds that let me know I am
BA a thief! Stealing moments, stuffing them away like fine silver
GF I will take out and polish another day when I can enjoy their
      sheen
BA and tarnished memories.

Here are the poems we created individually from our collaboration:

Looting the Day

It starts innocently enough:
shower, walk the dogs, e-mail, return
calls, walk the dogs, read, plan dinner.
I sneak glances through windows,
notice things of value easy to pawn.
Afternoon light sifts through palms
striping the room a verdant prison.
Clocks chime, a pot of ginger tea steeps.
As night falls, my hands hail the keyboard,
I break free of my block.
Anti-muse calls out, "Stop, Thief!"

I saw you pocket moments, hide them away
like fine silver. Put them back or you'll
do time!"
I grin, and steal her last line.

Blaise Allen

Measuring Time

This, I must say, is the sum total of my days
measured by a drawerful of spoons:
I stir sugar into a succession of teacups,
the rasp of silver scraping grains against china
audible above the many mundane sounds
that let me know I am. Steam rises from my cup.
Palm fronds stripe the room with sun and shade.
You call from the other room. Your call
just another sound that lets me know I am. I will
polish the spoons some other day so I can
see the past reflected upside down in their bowls.

Gretchen Fletcher

An Example: Working in Trios

Using the same opening line, here is an example of a three-way collaborative poem I worked on with two poets from Texas, neither of whom I have met. Below is our combined poem. Again, boldface initials identify the writer of each line.

GF This, then, is the sum total of the day:
BG unexpected angry words, still vibrate within—everything else
      was lost
TB and then, oh that moon—full and smiling
GF we bathe as in a lagoon of light
BG massaged by moonbeams, taut muscles release
TB night whispers her secrets in our ears
GF secrets loves and wishes and fears
BG propel our souls to remembered dreams and laughter
TB a gentle rain spills music from the sky

GF pours in arpeggios over us, cooling hot anger
BG rewarming the day's pleasures, frozen in the fire
TB musical ice soothing the soul's fears

From that collaboration, we wrote these individual poems:

The Sum Total of the Day

It had been a day of seething heat,
of anger fueled by summer steam,
punctuated by a pizzicato of harsh words.
Until the evening when we bathed together
and the moon poured in arpeggios over us,
forming a lagoon of light around our bodies
washing away fury, revealing all our wishes.

Gretchen Fletcher

Angry Traces

This then is the sum total of the day.
Unexpected angry words, still vibrate within,
other memories were lost.
Later, taut muscles relax when massaged by moonbeams,
remembered dreams and laughter uplift our souls
to rewarm the day's pleasures, frozen in anger's fire.

Barbara Randals Gregg

Fears

Sometimes when I find myself alone
walking fearful into night's dark mouth
I look up and see that moon
plump and smiling at nocturnal secrets
whispered in his ear by the night
secrets of gentle rain about to spill
like music or musical ice to soothe and cool my soul's fears

Travis Blair

Gretchen Fletcher was a winner in the Poetry Society of America's Bright Lights/ Big Verse competition and was projected on the Jumbotron while reading her winning poem in Times Square. She was also twice awarded the Grand Prize in San Francisco's Artists Embassy International Dancing Poetry Festival, selected as a finalist for the Howard Nemerov Sonnet Award, awarded first honorable mention in Canada's *lichen literary journal* Serial Poet competition, and named a Juried Poet at the Houston Poetry Fest. Her poetry has appeared in *The Chattahoochee Review, Pacific Coast Journal, Northeast Corridor, Inkwell, Pudding Magazine,* and *Upstreet,* among others—and has been anthologized in *Poetry as Spiritual Practice, Poetic Voices Without Borders, Open Windows 2005, Proposing on the Brooklyn Bridge: Poems About Marriage,* and elsewhere. Fletcher leads poetry and creative nonfiction workshops for the Florida Center for the Book, an affiliate of the Library of Congress.

Diction Translations

If an accomplished poem can be described as a masterpiece, then the work we will produce in this exercise can be thought of as finger paintings, abstract color explorations and collages. Diction or word choice in a poem is a vitally important characteristic. This exercise provides an opportunity to explore how changes in diction can radically alter a text. Mad Lib-inspired word games, diction translations, and other devices of play and chance can provide the seeds for poems. They allow us the opportunity to roll up our sleeves and dirty our hands in all of the wonderful hues of the dictionary.

Harryette Mullen provides some remarkable models of these techniques in several poems from her collection *Sleeping with the Dictionary*. For example, in the poem "Dim Lady" she translates Shakespeare's Sonnet 130, substituting Shakespeare's formal diction with the language of 1950s slang and advertising. Shakespeare's opening line "My mistress' eyes are nothing like the sun" becomes "My honeybunch's peepers are nothing like neon" in Mullen's poem. In "European Folk Tale Variant," Mullen provides a *Law & Order* retelling of "Goldilocks and the Three Bears": "The way the story goes, a trespassing towheaded pre-teen barged into the rustic country cottage of a nuclear family of anthropomorphic bruins."

Materials

- Several non-poetry texts that use very specific types of diction, for example: excerpts from an economics textbook, the Bill of Rights, the Pledge of Allegiance, a fairy-tale or children's story, the disclaimer that appears on the back of an airline ticket, a crime novel, a recipe, etc.

- You may also want to experiment with a few classic poems that utilize antiquated diction: a Shakespearean sonnet, a Romantic ode, etc.

Procedure

- Take a look at your text—or, better yet, a couple of texts. How would you characterize the diction? Is it formal or bureaucratic? Does it employ discipline-specific jargon (terms only a specialist in a particular field would know)? Does it use legalese? Or does it use a basic, conversational—even informal—type of diction?

- What would happen if you radically changed the diction in the text?

- You may want to begin by circling every other noun in the text. Now replace them with nouns that represent a completely different kind of diction—Mad Lib style. In the beginning, use nouns that alliterate with those in the original text. If you are having trouble coming up with nouns, use a dictionary or thesaurus.

- You can do this very systematically (replacing every noun or every other verb) or very informally (substituting whatever language you would like). The more varied the diction you use, the more likely you are to hit upon really energetic language.

- Experiment until you start coming up with exciting language combinations throughout.

- Once you have completed this step, read through the piece again. How has the meaning and/or tone changed?

- You'll realize that—depending upon the original and the kind of diction you used to replace it—your "translated text" might become humorous or take on political tones. Perhaps this will feel like a finished piece unto itself. You may also end up with phrases or fragments of electrified language that will form the seeds of new poems or find their way into another work.

Variations

- This exercise can easily be done in a group or classroom situation in which you provide the initial texts. I've used it in one-day workshops with high school students and had them Mad Lib or translate their high school's mission statement. The exercise can also be done collaboratively in small groups or workshop settings.

- Individuals can build a folder of texts that they can draw from when they are stuck trying to start a new poem or jump-start a poem that has stalled. Building the folder of texts becomes fun in itself. I've collected examples from the *Ladies Birthday Almanac*, old school books, all kinds of technical pamphlets, and disclaimers found on everything from licensing agreements to credit card statements.

An Example

Here's one I came up with recently, using the text of "America the Beautiful" and mixing it with symbols from the stock market ticker:

O BTYCF for spacious SKY,
For amber WAV of GRAN,
For purple MTN MAJC
Above the fruited PLNS!
AMR! AMR!
GODIX shed his GRA on THES
And crown thy GOOD with BRO
From SEA to shining SEA!

Susan Briante is the author of *Pioneers in the Study of Motion* (Ahsahta Press, 2007) and *Utopia Minus* (Ahsahta Press, 2011). Currently, she is translating the work of Uruguayan writer Marosa di Giorgio, as well as writing about industrial ruins and abandoned buildings in American cities. Briante is an assistant professor of literature and creative writing at the University of Texas at Dallas. She lives in east Dallas with the poet Farid Matuk.

Line-Finding

Coming to understand the forces at work in lineation requires an elastic and focused mind, and a curiosity about the pleasures of building and breaking language. Students of poetry are often guided on a path from received form to free verse as if from constriction to release, and are left with their drafts to wonder why freedom feels so self-conscious.

Sometimes it's good to think we make by finding. There are many methods, of course. Each is designed to leave the writer feeling as though language has found her. Rinse the dust from two bowls and separate an egg, and you've ruined the possibility for abacormancy (the reading of patterns in dust) but you may be ripe for oomancy, which determines a truth by interpreting the patterns of an egg white mixed with water. Dactylomancy, which sounds like a friend of poetry, turns out to involve the swinging of a ring on a string. Paper geomancy asks that the eyes close while one taps the point of a pencil onto paper, making marks where, later, patterns will seem to have appeared. Sometimes, while reading sentences, a repeated misuse of the rules of capitalization warrants interpretation. Sometimes not. Either there is pleasure in the oo of oomancy or there is not, but we might agree that oomancy offers a smaller delight.

This exercise owes a debt to Tom Phillips, whose beautiful project A Humument is its inspiration. Details of his project—including a gallery of examples—can be seen at www.humument.com.

Procedure

This exercise is best done by a group. Someone should choose a page of text, preferably in prose, probably removed from the subject of poetry, and possibly removed from the contemporary vernacular. Tom Phillips took his genius to a Victorian novel. I've had interesting results using a page of text from a 1915 primer on ladyhood, *The Ideal Woman*, by Mary R. Melendy, M.D., Ph.D. Pass identical copies of the same page to all, and make colored markers available. Each student circles words and/or clauses (lines) that appeal partly because they are lifted from context, and partly because their new life gives pleasure according to the association found in logic, cadence, and/or sound (discord is also an association). The remaining text is blackened, hatched through, or drawn over, obliterated (or partly so) in a pattern of its own. The result is an object lesson in subjectivity, with the new lines wearing their limit of placement on the page while flying off the reflections of their maker.

Examples

Here are two results of a recent line-finding exercise. Aisha Sharif and Christina Wallace used the same page from *The Ideal Woman*.

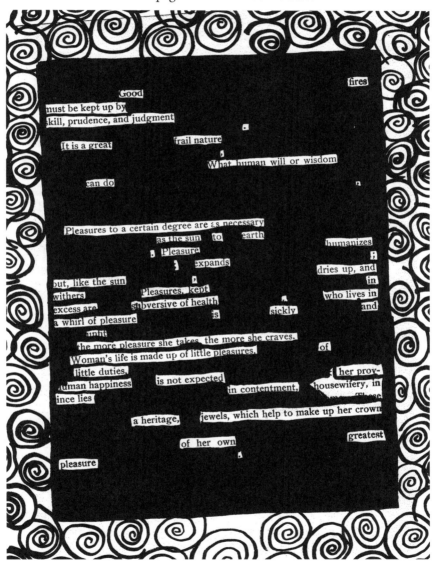

This line-finding exercise is by Kathleen Peirce's student Aisha Sharif.

This line-finding exercise is by Kathleen Peirce's student Christian Wallace.

Follow-Up

In the final step (flight?) of this exercise, everybody views all the results. The differences among the pages are often very interesting. Ask students to describe what their writing/finding/oblitering pleasures were. Ask them to find a poem in a book or anthology that shares this pleasure. This articulation and recognition of style tends to be more fruitful than obedience to the rigors of another's pleasures, and leaves the writer with something to consider adding to (or discarding) in the next writing event, when pulling words out of what we like to think of as air.

Kathleen Peirce teaches poetry in the M.F.A. program at Texas State University. She is the author of four books of poems, *Mercy* (University of Pittsburgh Press), *Divided Touch, Divided Color* (Windhover Press), *The Oval Hour* (University of Iowa Press), and *The Ardors* (Copper Canyon Press). She has won awards from the Associated Writing Programs, the National Endowment for the Arts, and the Guggenheim Foundation. She received the Presidential Award for Excellence in Teaching from Texas State University in 2010.

Two Sides of the Same Coil:
Blending Google Sculpting and Automatism

Your goal in this exercise is to produce a mid-length lyric poem, around 16-30 lines, in about six hours (including a two-hour break, but not including revisions). As you write, you'll thread together the linguistic outpourings of two very different cognitive processes—one reactive, the other generative. Spontaneity and quick reflexes will be key. Your self-critical apparatuses should be tabled throughout the process. Don't drink too much coffee beforehand, and don't bring your superego to bear too heavily upon your text.

Stylistically, this exercise is designed for you to attack a subject through two radically different techniques. The first is the neo-Dadaist, Flarf-influenced process of *Google sculpting,* or of capturing and refiguring found texts from the web. The second is *automatism,* a Surrealist technique of writing from the subconscious that was championed by André Breton and Philippe Soupault in the early 1900s. The clash of these two forms—one fundamentally destructive and the other constructive—provides a fun and radical platform to splinter then reglue an otherwise ordinary and unassuming topic.

Procedure

I. Select a topic, preferably a single word, name, or term. You might choose something such as *oranges*, for example, or *sheep* or *MIA* or *drill bits* or *Abraham Lincoln*. For my book *Glass Is Really a Liquid*, I wrote a whole sequence on individual gods from ancient myths, although only a handful made it into the final manuscript (one follows later in this essay as an example).

II. Once you've selected your keyword, proceed on your computer or iPad or smartphone to your favorite search engine. Watch out for the ones that keep track of what you search!

III. Type your keyword into your search engine and pull up ten distinct sites. By *distinct*, of course, I mean separate websites, but you might also wish to choose sites that interpret your keywords in different ways. You might be surprised by the ways in which the Internet has misread your poetic intentions. Just now, for instance, I googled *copper* and came up with not only the element, but a ski resort, a web-based graphic novel, economic news, a recipe for younger skin, an Internet provider, and a pest-control company.

IV. Click the link to the first site and select a line for your poem from the words on the webpage. You might choose to lift a sentence or phrase verbatim, or you might choose to merge a couple of half-phrases into a juicy new combination. Type or copy the line directly into your word processor rather than using the intermediating media of pen and paper. You're allowed to change verb tenses, of course, or other little grammatical features to ensure continuity within your poem. However, try not to take so many liberties as to destroy the integrity of the process.

A tangent on process: At this point, it's quite possible you're saying, "Wait just a minute! Those aren't *my* words!" To which I respond: of course they're your words. You can have any words you like. After all, every word you've ever written, unless you're very adept at coinages, appears in at least one other book. And seriously, how much of a difference is there between the process I'm outlining now and, say, the way rhyme limits one's pallette of potential word choices in the lines of a sonnet? In this exercise your word choices are delimited more by associations of content than by sound, but in either case you engage in the delightful tug of war between form and meaning that defines the very essence of poetry. Within these restrictions, your choices expand like exploding planets. From the Internet service provider site generated by my search on *copper*, for example, one might compose the line "If you have any questions, please call" or "Thanks for not shipping jobs overseas" or "Far superior to people and the disastrous zero"—three radically different ways to begin a poem!

V. Double-space (i.e., leave a blank line).

VI. Compose or choose a line from the second site and double-space again. Then create a line from the third site, double-space again, until you've selected one line per site for a total of ten double-spaced lines. Try to limit yourself to five to ten minutes per site so you don't overthink the process—the goal is to enter into dialogue with the webpages rather than beating them into submission. After you're finished, take a quick glance through your lines to make sure verb tenses and pronouns are as consistent as you want them to be. (But don't edit—either for smoothness or for clarity—yet.)

VII. This is the most important step. Rest for about two hours to reset your cognitive processes and manufacture a little distance between your thoughts and your poem. My recommendation is to watch a movie, preferably one with an engaging, action-packed, but non-challenging plot. Jet Li's *The One*? 28

Days Later? *The Chronicles of Narnia*? *Finding Nemo*? The activity you choose, in any case, should be one that doesn't permit your mind to wander—something that drives your thinking for a short time, something that acts as the equivalent of a tiny bowl of lemon sherbet to cleanse the palate between courses.

VIII. Has the movie made you a bit punch-drunk and weary? I hope so! Whenever I make one of these poems, I begin around 10:30 at night, completing Steps I to VI by around midnight. After the movie, near two a.m.— some microwave popcorn in my belly—I'm ready to begin the automatism component of this exercise. But do whatever it takes to bring you into that dreamy, susceptible, dizzy, but coherent mental space—you can even drink a single beer or glass of wine if appropriate to your age and needs. Return to your computer.

IX. Begin filling in the lines between the lines. Let the first "automatic" line (the second line of the poem) be a response to the first and a bridge to the third, but without regard for the rest of the "found" lines. Work quickly and freely. Take risks. Be absurd if you want to. Don't think about how to respond to the preceding line or what you're writing—just free-write. Work with quick associations, use the first words and images that come into your mind, let the muses pummel you with their lightning bolts. Try not to edit, although you can swish some of the words around in your mind before you write them down. Continue all the way through the poem, until all the blank lines are filled. You may end either with a found line or an automatic line.

X. You now have the raw stuff of your poem! It's late, however, so go to bed and don't think about your lines until morning.

XI. Revision. Here's where your aesthetics can shape your poem's raw material into whatever sort of surface—polished or raw—you choose. Personally, I prefer my poems to remain somewhat rough-hewn, since the purpose of this exercise isn't to produce a glittering gem so much as a chunk of gold. Still, if you prefer your poems pretty and endings tidy, indulge yourself in as much tinkering as makes you happy. Even if you prefer ragged edges, as I do, a little touching up might be called for. Depending on your end goal for your poem, you might consider rearranging lines or keeping them as they are, smoothing transitions, developing images, adjusting rhythm, etc. You could even go back to a particular site to try again, if its line doesn't fit the rest of the piece.

XII. You did it! Revel in the joy of your new poem!

Variations

- Instead of ten sites, pick eight. Or twelve.
- Reverse the order: begin with automatic writing, then search the web after your movie.
- Instead of double-spacing between lines, triple-space and auto-write two lines at a time.
- Collaborate with another poet: Have one find the web-based texts and the other perform the auto-writing.
- Write the poem from bottom to top.
- Choose another exercise in this book.

An Example

Clytemnestra

When the signal's given, her torrid affair
In white, the colorlessness beneath the maze
On mountains the next would light & so on
The rise of the bubbles to the rim of the flute
So vehemently electric, stone proceeding
In strings popping, notes carried off the margins
& easy challenges for chalk, animation, a singer
Reckless at the tips of the rope, the fiberoptics
Helped elect #61 when suitable to text, author
& wish that type might be more than a dance
On tiles, coasters, cups, & mugs—Play with me
Or its picture, lit from arrears & glittering fragility
A 14-inch minotaur stuffed, magical, stadium
90-something to vibrate, a muddled machine
On the floor placing pieces of red all around
& animating theatrical apparel, the location of
Our adding machine's dollhouse evening, 2 spiders'
Interlocking messages, engraving audible salt:
A nymph defending herself against elegy

Bruce Covey

Bruce Covey lives in Atlanta, Georgia, where he teaches at Emory University, edits *Coconut Poetry,* and curates the "What's New in Poetry" reading series. He is the author of five books of poems, including, most recently, *Glass Is Really a Liquid* (No Tell Books, 2010), *Reveal* (Black Radish, 2011), and *Elapsing Speedway Organism* (No Tell Books, 2006). His work has also appeared in *LIT, Jacket, Columbia Poetry Review, Sonora Review,* the *Best American Poetry* website, and many other journals and anthologies, including *Online Writing: The Best of the First Ten Years.* Parts of *Reveal* have been translated into Italian. Covey was selected for the 2006 edition of *Best of the Net.*

Chapter V:
Structure and Form

In poetry you have a form looking for a subject
and a subject looking for a form. When they
come together successfully you have a poem.

W. H. Auden

Rosa Alcalá

A Walking Petrarchan Sonnet

This exercise is inspired by and is an extension of Bernadette Mayer's sonnet exercise, in which she asks the poet to walk a block for each line of a sonnet, then write one.

Procedure

I. The Walk In my adaptation of Mayer's exercise for the Petrarchan sonnet, the poet is asked to walk eight blocks (for the initial octave), then return six blocks (to complete the final sestet). The physical turn and retracing of steps is meant to enact the Petrarchan sonnet's *volta,* in which the poem's premise, laid out in the initial eight-line stanza, is revisited, overturned, questioned, or reinforced in the concluding six-line stanza.

II. The Notebook This exercise requires one to carry a notebook and record what is seen, heard, touched, tasted, and smelled on each block. The observations are recorded by block, and each block becomes a line. Since blocks are often limited to urban or suburban neighborhoods, this Petrarchan sonnet exercise allows for other markers of distance or spatial divisions, such as red mailboxes, mulberry trees, etc. I encourage students to try this exercise close to home, hoping they will rediscover the places and things they walk or drive by every day in their haste to get elsewhere.

III. A Variation It is also possible to do this exercise *at home*—moving between rooms, floors, patio, and front porch.

Preparation

This exercise can be used to learn the fundamentals of the Petrarchan sonnet; students can choose to compose Petrarchan sonnets in iambic pentameter or hendecasyllables (eleven-syllable verse) that employ traditional rhyme patterns. Or students can use this exercise to write free verse or experimental sonnets. It is helpful, then, to show students a series of traditional sonnets, as well as experimental or free verse Petrarchan sonnets (such as Mayer's), and discuss how each employs the form, particularly the use of the volta.

Because this exercise requires students to enter and explore their environments, I may also assign Gaston Bachelard's *Poetics of Space*; a variety of place poems, such as those found in Federico García Lorca's *Poet in New York* or María Meléndez's *How Long She'll Last in This World*; Charles Olson's essay

"Projective Verse"; and examples of documentary or investigative poetics, such as Brenda Coultas' *A Handmade Museum*. We may also discuss the relationship of the foot to poetic measure, from the traditional iambic foot employed in the sonnet to William Carlos Williams' "variable foot."

Possibilities

When I described this exercise to a fellow poet who lives in the Midwest, she said the walk could land her students in a cornfield. Here in El Paso, on the border with Juárez, eight blocks in one direction could conceivably place you in a different social and political reality, and a six-block return might place you on a bridge between two nations. This reminder of the proximity of the border, and of the socio-economic interdependence of lives on either side, as well as the recent horror of violence that has affected Juárez, leads me to see the sonnet—and poetic form in general—as a way to engage with the physical and political complexities of the places in which we live. While I do not encourage my students to venture into territory they deem dangerous for the sake of a poem, any environment, however innocuous it may appear, can prove surprising if the poet pays attention. The walk becomes, then, a metaphor for the poem, which is always treading between the familiar and unfamiliar, the known and unknown. It transgresses, erases, and inscribes new borders; questions its original premise; moves away from the place in which it began, then returns to it, but never fully, its perspective now changed. The poem is also place-in-itself, complete with divisions, structures, inhabitants.

Examples

Sometimes students, rather than stay close to home, want to take a walk in a place they've been to many times but haven't truly seen. Or they want to visit those iconic places in their hometown they normally avoid. Miranda Smith does this, creating a free verse Petrarchan sonnet about a plaza in downtown El Paso:

Paseo de las Luces

Cigarette wedged in a grate, brown bag ghosts by, and above,
sky flies, unscathed by time. I understand the postage stamp's allure:
    Paseo de las luces,
I want to go there. Who has roped this thin, white-barked tree, to a pole?
Backward glance from a businessman, this glance is all we have, the wind
is constant now, cold, announcement from headquarters:

the city's night. Padlocked double doors, the shadows of writing on writ-
     ing.
An escape-ladder tattoos a wall, the sidewalk is closed a few feet
(Why the parenthesis?). Crocodiles, wry and hungry, blue-green fence

like a water-logged penny, fantastical cage for grass.
A tree, veined and measured by dead Christmas lights, the sound
of a man limping, stressed signal, silhouettes of aging men on benches,
waiting, homeless or heading home, I can't tell, all experts in biding
     time. Moons
of knees through blue jeans, flat exposed feet, a dreaming statue offers
     me his elbow,
giant wing, a dentist's drill rises. Sign for *ballroom,* leading nowhere.

Miranda Smith

Smith writes of this experience, particularly the effect of the volta, as part of
an ethical process:

> As I walked the first eight blocks, I noticed signs, and other demarca-
> tions of space (a tree mysteriously roped to a pole). It felt exhilarating to
> peek into the city's secret life.
>
> When I walked the six blocks back, I was forced to pay attention
> to the human presence in the city, to people trying to navigate the city
> through so many cages (and unwittingly, into the cage of the poet's pen). I
> noticed human echoes: the nostalgia of dead Christmas lights, the sound
> of a man limping.
>
> Revisiting the six blocks forced me to become a denizen of the city,
> a participant, rather than just a tourist. I was returning, not just pass-
> ing through. Perhaps this is why I experienced my alienation from the
> city most acutely during the walk back. As I speculated about the lives of
> the aging men on benches, I grew more separate from them. The second
> stanza investigates this painful psychological distance.
>
> Throughout the journey, the city seduced me with signs (*Paseo de
> las Luces*). But after the volta, the seduction exhausted itself ("sign for
> *ballroom,* leading nowhere"). The poem also switches focus at the volta,
> from urban space and language to the city's inhabitants.

Essential to this exercise, as Smith's commentary indicates, is a certain level
of awareness. What I often require, then, is a discussion of the relationship
between process and outcome, as well as between form and content.

Poet D'Arcy Randall has tried this exercise twice. In the first, printed below, she took the walk—eight blocks there and six blocks back. Unlike Miranda Smith, Randall wrote a traditional rhymed Petrarchan sonnet.

Walk with New Vision

For my new eyes, the streets show off fresh paint.
The dullard glow of old veneer is gone
and waves of coreopsis' orange tones
splash through whorls of green without restraint.
Across the stones the rose flares scarlet tints.
Above, the elms' long *ports de bras* are drawn
on skies of lapis mined at Bamiyan.
So odd to think my now-bedazzled haunts
were ever tarnished, or that I had lost
the loropetalum's myrtle, never seen
the child in saffron dance around the room
in an open limestone house, the glinting rust
of dozing trees across a silvered lawn,
the China white hit of the zoomed-in moon.

D'Arcy Randall

For Randall's second sonnet, she walked the rooms of her house—the variation suggested on page 167. Notice the shift, when the poet moves from octave to sestet. The sonnet moves from indoor rooms and the memories they evoke to a ringing doorbell and the urgency of the present.

A Walk between Worlds

The veil between our worlds grows thin, which means
I light the candles, raise the local dead.
The gold arched mirror's blind to me. Instead,
it shows the room where Grandpa's rifle leaned,
fell off the wall, fired, lit Aunt Agnes' scream
while Edna stood in her small pond of blood.
I leave her bandages, bring take-out food
to other elders waiting in their frames.

Now the doorbell rings, I hear a yell
Trick or Treat! I step outside—they dive
for candy as their dim-lit parents smile.
A skeleton and a bee queen in her hive
take my hands and lead me down the trail
to the ghoul-thronged road. We'll take the night alive.

D'Arcy Randall

Rosa Alcalá is the author of a poetry collection, *Undocumentaries* (Shearsman Books, 2010), and two chapbooks, *Some Maritime Disasters This Century* (Belladonna, 2003) and *Undocumentary* (Dos Press, 2008). Her translations include Lila Zemborain's *Guardians of the Secret* (Noemi Press, 2009), and poems for *The Oxford Book of Latin America Poetry* (2009). She teaches in the Department of Creative Writing and the Bilingual M.F.A. Program at the University of Texas at El Paso.

Barbara Hamby

The Abecedarian Corset

The most beautiful poetry comes from the deep self speaking about what it is to be human. The unconscious is always with us, but how do we grab hold of it and yank it to the surface? The abecedarian form—a 26-line poem with the first letter of each line in alphabetical order—has always been magic for me. There is something about having the whalebone corset of the alphabet on an otherwise empty page that excites my imagination. I wrote an abecedarian poem that I included in my first book *Delirium*. The poem took me to places that surprised me. I loved that feeling. I have a pretty obsessive personality. I count everything. I alphabetize everything I can. I'm a collector, so the idea of writing a series of abecedarian poems was immediately engaging.

For my second book, *The Alphabet of Desire,* I wrote a sequence of abecedarian poems. I wrote most of them over a summer, and it was one of the hardest and most thrilling things I've ever done. They say we only use 20 percent of our brain's capacity. That summer I felt as if I was pushing 27 percent. I loved the weird subjects that emerged, the gorgeous words I found, the mix of highfaluting language with slang and dialect. I made wonderful lists of words, especially for the difficult letters of our language—*j, q, x,* and *z.* Sometimes a word would open up the poem for me, for example, *zugzwang,* which is a German word meaning "move compulsion." It's a chess term—you have to move but whatever you do will hurt you. If that couldn't be translated to most of my misbegotten romantic involvements as a young woman, I wasn't the poet I thought I was. And so it went. The form forced me to make wild associations that I wouldn't have made otherwise; it is like a high-speed elevator to the deep self, at least for me. I've tried to write metered poetry, but everything I write sounds so boring and stilted. The abecedarian form was meant for me. I especially loved the language that it allowed me to use.

In my next book, *Babel,* sometimes I used the form to get a draft, and then I pulled it apart and reconfigured it as a free verse poem. "Ode to American English" had its beginnings as an abecedarian poem. The title poem of *Babel* entwines two alphabets at the beginning of the lines. In my latest book, *All-Night Lingo Tango,* I came up with two different variations on the form. I'm working with the beginning and end of the line in both forms. The first I call a double-helix abecedarian because I entwine two alphabets at the beginning of the line and two at the end. I've only written four of these, because there are so few words that end in *j* or *q*. The second form I call an abecedarian sonnet though it is only 13 lines. If only our alphabet had 28 letters; then I could be more traditional. However, I love the number 13, so I'm not complaining. The first one I wrote began with an *a* and the line ended with a word that ended in *b*. The second line started with a *c* and ended with a *d* and so on. It didn't take me long to start thinking about another sequence, but there was that *j* and *q* problem. So I came up with the idea of 26 poems, each starting with a different letter of the alphabet, so I'd only have to come up with 13 words that ended in *j* and *q* and not 26. Again, it was an all-absorbing process. I finished the first drafts in about a month, though I tinkered with them for two years.

All of this is to say that the form can be exhilarating to work with, but it also can be stilted and dry, as all formal poems can be when the writer uses abstractions instead of images.

Procedure

I think the best way to start is with the alphabet typed vertically down the left margin of the page. Start with a simple form before trying the more complex variations. You might want to make lists of words that begin with some of the more difficult letters, such as *x, z, j,* and *q*. Begin with an image. For example, you might want to use your vegetable garden as a metaphor for how hard it is to write. Then you might make an alphabetical list of vegetables and gardening terms: *artichoke, asparagus, basil, blueberries, carrots, cauliflower, dig, elephant garlic, furrow, fallow,* and so on. Don't insert them in the poem, but have them ready and waiting when you need them.

Examples

A Traditional Abecedarian

I never start a poem knowing exactly where it will take me, and that uncertainty is especially important with an abecedarian. However, it is important to have some direction or a set of images in mind. Laura Richardson's poem "Armadillo Highway" has a narrative so compelling that many readers don't realize it is an abecedarian poem. The diction and voice drive the poem, and the formal constraints aren't in the foreground. However, notice the brilliant use of the letter *x*: "X-signing" says everything about Jackson and about the kind of life the narrator is trying to leave. It fulfills the form, but it does so much more.

Armadillo Highway

Armadillos on the highway like cracked watermelons.
Baby laying on the seat. Nobody on the bus
care to hold him. Lord, sometimes I pray to
die, I get so tired. I been working since I was
eleven. Ain't nobody ever took care of me the way
family ought to. Momma shacked up with near every
grown man in town, left me at home to raise Eva. Was a
heavy load for a girl my age, but I never let on.

I guess it was my insides all bunched up that made me
jump when Jackson came calling, promising to take me to
Kansas City and make me a singer. I ain't much to
look at, but I know I can sing. Never did leave Georgia.
Maybe he never meant to take me. Anyhow, the
night I run off he took me to his place over in
Old Town, pressed himself up between my legs. I
prayed and cried, but Jackson told me to be
quiet, that he had picked me out to be his girl.
Rutting and grunting, he sounded like an old pig.
Sure enough, next thing I know I was having a baby.

Trouble is Jackson don't come home no more. Keep his
ugly self down at the bar most nights. Read me chapter and
verse like he done wrote the Bible himself, saying a
woman supposed to come unto her man. Shoot! Old
X-signing, whiskey-drinking coot. I packed my bags
yesterday, grab up my baby, and we getting out of this
zoo. Hit the road like that poor armadillo, long gone.

Laura Richardson

A Double-Helix Abecedarian

In Rob Stephens' "Ode to Old Testament Life," there is a completely different take on the form. The poet is writing a double-helix abecedarian, and though there is a narrative impulse to the poem, he is calling attention to the alphabet, the word play and the verbal pyrotechnics of the form.

Ode to Old Testament Life

Amen, let's start with a shout out to my ladies named Esther, Heph Z.
  Zibah, and Oholibamah for making this ode breathtaking like a
branch of olives or a rainbow after a flood, because when that bully
  Yahweh thinks we can't hear, he sends a plague that even Job
curses—but let's keep this poem PG, not nasty like Song of Songs sex,
  X-rated and giving studious altar boys boners for years B.C.
during ceremonies in the Holy of Holies while they kneeled in their pew
  worshipping but never touching the Holy Arc of God,
even though it was so tempting which is why Moses declared in Lev.
  verse 15:16 "be clean without semen from dreamin' of Eve."
Fellas, you want to be like David, dream interpreter, war guru,
  unlikely King, penthouse poet? Learn to use a slingshot, buy a staff,
grow your hair in golden curls and pray your ass off like Daniel in that pit
  teeming with lions because Jehovah is always recruiting
his prophets, though it's a vocation some take to extremes like when Amos
  streaked through Israel, Elijah faced 450 pagan prophets, or Jonah
immersed himself into the belly of a whale because God the Transporter
  required him to travel on a tight budget. And ladies—mini
Judiths out there—I recommend you learn to slip your foe a tranq,
  quietly hack his head off with a stake, and bask in the glory of raj
killing, or bathe where a David can see, so he'll give your hubbie the clip,
  pop a cap in his back door so that you two can enjoy a sweet fuck,
legitimate love, authorized ass, and you'll be his one in a thousand boo
  or rather one of his thousand boos, but he'll want to spill
more seed into you because he wants a son with your eyes, your skin,
  none of the flaws of a pagan ho, and this is all slim until a medium,
Nathan, has a chat with God the Prude and publicly calls your dude a ham
  maligning your beautiful name, Bathsheba, daughter of an
oath, clean one. Yep, God the Obdurate will catch you like he caught
  Samuel:
    lying in bed getting some shuteye when you'll hear someone whis-
        per, "Lo,
pagan, arise" from outside and it won't be your horny mistress or some
    crook
      keening your name, but El Shaddai interrupting your nap,

cueing you to write that chapter of the Bible he's been planning, book J,
    Jecoliah's untold tale of how she walked to the Promised Land from
        Iraq,
reared seventeen children, and bore the curse of being an Israeli
    immigrant and a woman and so the book you write will never
satisfy the chumps who sort the Dead Sea Scrolls to create the Torah.
    Heaven, you know, doesn't appear in the Old Testament books,
the dead instead plunge to the depths of Sheol, the pit of Everlasting
    Gehenna where the Serpent throws burning apples at your spirit
unprotected by the King of Kings, where "Cain and His Gang of
    Fugitives," Hell's house band, will eternally entertain you
via grunge music blaspheming the lamentably long list of names He
    expects people to call Him, but why end this ode on Destruction Av.
when we haven't mentioned Delilah who emasculated Samson or
        discussed
    Dinah who inspired an entire tribe of Hivite men to saw
extra sensitive skin from their shafts, because when you're an Isaac
    circumcision is just the first sacrifice to endure so that the hex
you receive during your Biblical life isn't from some phony god like
        Beelzebub,
    Baal, or a Golden Calf but from the real deal: God the Snazzy,
Zeba'ot, the Big Cheese, Yahweh Shalom, the Pie in the Sky, the Alpha
    and Omega, the Eternal Swag, The Wizard Who Knows His Way
        from A to Z.

    Rob Stephens

An Abecedarian Sonnet

Zeus, It's Your Leda, Sweetie Pie

Zip up your toga, thunder thighs, that's Hera
barking like Cerberus on amphetamines. I was a skeptic,
don't you know, but you've got the equipment, as the
frigging king of the gods should. All the mortal gals are agog,
hinting for an invite to our next divine date, as if I
jump in your Cadillac, and we race toward a three-star snack,
lightning bolts setting the highway ablaze miles ahead. I'm

nervous about your wife. She blinded Tiresias, and Apollo
plays possum when she's around. Zeus, that's your cue—
reassure me. Don't think I want to move to Mt. Olympus.
Those relics are a snooze. Athena, there's dust on her tutu,
Venus's, too, so get a move on, or my Helen will wow
exactly no one and his horse. Let's dillydally, Ding-Dong Daddy.

Barbara Hamby

Barbara Hamby is the author of four books of poetry: *Delirium* (1995); *The Alphabet of Desire* (1999); *Babel* (2004); and *All-Night Lingo Tango* (2009)—the latter two from the University of Pittsburgh Press. She and her husband David Kirby have edited an anthology of poetry, *Seriously Funny* (University of Georgia Press, 2010). She has received fellowships from the Florida Arts Council, the National Endowment for the Arts, and the Guggenheim Foundation. She teaches in the Creative Writing Program at Florida State University.

The Pie Plate:
Serving Up a Slice of Travel through the Haibun

Dear Reader, I am covered in ice and snow for most of the year. But summers here in western New York mean a bevy of fresh fruit from the local cherry orchards, blueberry fields, and strawberry patches. I live within five miles of several farms that allow me to pick my own fruit. And where there is a bevy of fruit, there must be pies.

*

I love travel writing, and one way to capture a "slice of travel" in a poem can be found in the haibun, a Japanese poetic form. Though not a prose poem in itself, the haibun is a slice of a journey or destination, composed of a prose poem *and* a whisper of sorts: a haiku. The result is an elegant block of text with the haiku serving as a tiny bowl or stand for the prose poem section. A whole series of them looks like neat little signs or flags. A visual delight.

*

My favorite baking accoutrement is a red ceramic pie plate made by Williams-Sonoma. It was a housewarming gift from a turtle friend and poet—a guy who has no home himself: he carries all his possessions on his back, can slip into the sea or sun himself on the beach whenever he pleases. He gave me this red shell—inverted, it's a drum—the tink-tink-tink of cold ceramic and my spoon like a calling for dinner, and especially, what comes after. I love the promise of buttery crust and scoop of fruit. I love what it smells like: home.

*

Before I had my second baby, I was often away from home—a mint green rancher with a wild and sprawling lily garden—for various visiting writer gigs or to teach poetry workshops across the country. I found that writing haibun is a way for me to record my travel in a condensed and imagistic light, that is, to record the beauty, danger, tragedy, adventure, etc., that we sometimes experience when we travel. Many writers of haibun start by keeping a daily journal of haibun, not about travel per se, but to record each day's events. Other writers of haibun use the form to re-imagine fairy tales or examine persona. Now that my husband and I are juggling a newborn and a wily three-year-old, keeping a haibun journal is a refreshing way to get some "day pages" written first thing in the morning or last thing at night. Even on the days I feel too zombie-fied from late-night feedings, I can always at least manage a draft of a haibun. I'm amazed how what may seem like an ordinary week becomes almost *magical* from recording it haibun-style.

*

I like teaching the haibun, in particular for students who claim they have never "gone anywhere interesting," or haven't traveled out of state or country. I teach haibun as the last component in a poetry course or as the last form of poetry before we turn to fiction writing in a dual-genre course. All the rules and suggestions of what to keep in mind as one crafts a haibun make it especially freeing and fun to see what innovations the students come up with by "breaking" the rules of the haibun and seeing what hybrid writing they create by doing so.

*

Some believe the turtle carries the weight of the world. I want that turtle to put down his pack and join me at the table. I promise him here and now that the next pie made from this plate will pipe hot steamsongs. I want to capture my journey in haibun, each slice of a new city or new landscape brimmed with filling and sweetness. Let the grace of my hands form a crust so flaky and fine my reader will forget his burden, his heavy step. He won't remember whether he had seconds—only the curve of his spoon, the simple lattice of berries.

Background

In 1690, Matsuo Basho is said to have initiated the travel or diary haibun genre in a letter to a friend (*Genjuan no ki, The Hut of the Phantom Dwelling*) that concluded with a haiku. The letter referred to the period when Basho lived for several months on a hill on the southern shore of Lake Biwa, east of Kyoto.

Bruce Ross in a 1997 essay entitled "North American Versions of Haiku," in *Modern Haiku*, states that haibun has "syntax that is dominated by images" and cites Makoto Ueda's four characteristics of haibun: 1) a brevity and conciseness of haiku; 2) a deliberately ambiguous use of certain particles and verb forms in places where the conjunction *and* would be used in English; 3) a dependence on imagery; and 4) the writer's detachment

The Haiku Society of America has the following definition of haibun: "A haibun is a terse, relatively short prose poem, usually including both lightly humorous and more serious elements. A haibun usually ends with a haiku." Longer haibun (200–300 words) often intersperse sections of prose and haiku, with connections that "may not be immediately obvious, or the haiku may deepen the tone, or take the work in a new direction, recasting the meaning of the foregoing prose, much as a stanza in a linked-verse poem revises the meaning of the previous verse."

Procedure

I. Prose Poems Remember that the traditional purpose of the haibun is to recreate *a travel journal* and you can be almost guaranteed that your readers will *not* have been to the place you are writing about, or, if they have, will certainly not have experienced it in the same way. When you read a piece about a place you have never traveled before, what are the elements that sink you away to a reverie, and what are the elements that make you feel like you too have traveled there? What elements make you tune out? (Try to avoid the latter, obviously).

II. The Senses Smell is generally the hardest of all the senses to capture. I tell my students that if they can capture smell in a believable way, 80% of their rendering is pretty much complete. Why do you think this is? One exercise that my students especially like is when I ask them to describe what they smell like. It's harder than you think! Go ahead and try it now in your writing notebook. BE REAL. Even if you wear vanilla mango perfume, you do NOT *just* smell like vanilla and mango. Maybe the smell of vinyl lingers in your hair from a raincoat you wore earlier in the day, or coffee, gasoline, perhaps . . . if you are stuck, lean over and ask someone to help you get started. Don't be shy! The best example came from a five-year-old, of all people. When I asked him to describe what he smelled like, he thought for a moment and said, "chicken nuggets and pencils!" I smelled the top of his head and laughed—by golly, he was right!

III. Structure When you construct the prose poem part of the haibun, this is your chance to take risks with syntax and diction that you normally wouldn't take in a lineated poem. Try repeating phrases or single words. Write a really long sentence and make your next sentence a fragment. Repeat a motif—elements of light, a color, etc.—throughout your poem. Try including an animal doing an unusual action—not one usually associated with that animal. A dog that barks? *BO-ring!* But a dog that *walks the ceiling of your hostel room*—now THAT will pique the reader's curiosity. Try to go for a tone of play, of magic, but don't go so far that the reader will be wondering if you are trying to do a bad imitation of *Alice in Wonderland*. The prose poem part of the haibun should at least have *essential* truth to it, not necessarily factual truth. In other words, it should at least *ring true* emotionally for your reader.

IV. Haiku Finally, end your haibun with a haiku, traditionally a five–seven–five syllable count, though contemporary haiku often vary in the number of syllables. Traditional haiku include a seasonal/time reference, an image or two from nature, and a flash of surprise/realization. Some haibun's haiku naturally flow from the last line of the prose poem, but you can also start your haiku as a completely new thought. I like to think of the haiku as something of a letter's postscript—a little something extra to finish the haibun with a quiet flourish.

Examples

Setagaya-ku Haibun

Fall 1982, Tokyo

Gingko trees cast off their fruit—sour stink rising from rotten ghosts. The white line dividing sidewalk from road is stained brown, stained slick by the globes. I am eight, my loafers marvelous with their fake American pennies. I crush laced exoskeletons under my soles—cicadas grown so large they burst from their skins: now shells, air. Detritus among lost bobby pins and sick, soft fruit. Since the first cold snap, the nights hang silent, gaping where they once *sh sh shimmered*, brushed by a thousand wings. On the other side of the tall wall saturated by late afternoon light, college boys laugh, bounce tennis balls against stone. The street is an empty tongue. I imagine stepping past the white line, edging into the wide, calling street.

If a car turned, would
it find my body soft, as
crushable as fruit?

Tamiko Beyer

Desert Cicadas Haibun

It's July, so the cicadas are out merrymaking in the mesquite trees off our balcony. The heat and humidity turn them into armies of disembodied electric shavers. These big handsome buzzy insects inspired poetic thoughts of immortality among the Chinese, while the Japanese came to the opposite conclusion in their haiku by equating cicadas with the fleetingness of life.

Once, I gave a buzzing flashing-eyed plastic cicada keychain to my mom, who had lived all her life in cicada-free Hawaii. The odd bug effigy delighted her and she took it on all of her trips to Las Vegas with my dad. She believed the cicada was her lucky charm that could bring forth great rivers of fat nickels pouring from the slot machines. Often it did. Her cicada vanished when she died one Vegas, twelve years ago. My own belief is that listening to cicadas mows down any bad feelings overgrown in one's heart: fear, shame, rage, grief—all cleanly weed-whacked away.

Trees trill electric
in the heavy summer heat
singing us alive.

Sharon Suzuki-Martinez

An Ode to my Hair: A Haibun

The terrain in which you open up your black mantle, dark sprouts which grow at the base you show me where the shadow transforms into the ghost of strands you ask where the change. Across, the brusque strokes, the stuck bristles of dark sprouts, a cloud of black hay rises filled with smokestains overlaid over peach in the undergrowth. Twenty-seven years have grown up, fertilized the lengths laid upon the path of my body, the knobs of my shoulders cloaked.

mother seasons pass
snowroot hidden by the black
I wonder how long

Ching-In Chen

Aimee Nezhukumatathil is the author of three poetry collections: *Lucky Fish; At the Drive-In Volcano,* winner of the Balcones Prize; and *Miracle Fruit,* named Poetry Book of the Year by *ForeWord Magazine* and winner of the Global Filipino Literary Award. Other awards for her writing include a poetry fellowship from the National Endowment for the Arts and a Pushcart Prize. She is Associate Professor of English at State University of New York, Fredonia, where she was named the Hagan Young Scholar and received the Chancellor's Award for Scholarly and Artistic Excellence. She lives in western New York with her husband and two young sons.

Circling the Pine:
Haibun and the Spiral Web

For me, the basis of all poetry writing begins in synthesis—like Indra's web. One can pluck the web of one's experience at any node, and the whole thing vibrates. A good poem connects the thing perceived with the perceiver, as does a good haiku. Basho is reputed to have said, "To write of the pine, go to the pine." In a good haibun, we go to the pine, and then through the haiku we follow the pine's roots, or needles and cones as they fall, spiraling farther and farther afield while orbiting the pine—still linked to the original image.

In *The Haiku Handbook*, which I co-authored, my late husband, William J. (Bill) Higginson, reflects on haibun written in the West: "Bringing the spareness of haiku poetry to prose gives us the best of autobiography and familiar essay—the actions, events, people, places, and recollections of life lived—without weighing them down with sentimentality, perhaps the greatest enemy of art and life."

The adding of haiku to haibun prose is akin to the experience of linking in the communal poetry called renku. I've always enjoyed writing renku, a process that requires one to come up with verses that *move away* with respect to each preceding verse, but still connect in mood, tone, image, theme. Renku writers refer to this process as *link and shift*. If the haiku in a haibun work well, they both anchor the piece and let it go. They simultaneously frame and break the frame, allowing the content to spiral outward in ripples of association.

After having deliberately written a number of original haibun, I recently decided to experiment with revising both longer narrative poems and prose poems to create haibun. I hope that sharing my process with you will encourage you to experiment in similar ways.

I. Revising a Narrative Poem Into a Haibun

When one takes a narrative poem and transforms it into a haibun, something remarkable happens to the original. A good poem may already reverberate in several directions, but recasting it into poetic prose and adding haiku might open it up further—precisely because the haiku shift the focus enough that it becomes a different work. They expand upon the original perception. Consider the following two examples from my own work.

Here is the original version of my poem "Driving Home":

Driving Home

We flash past a wreck at the road's edge—
a motor-home cracked open as it smashed
into the guard-rail and fell on its side.

Furniture has spilled from its twisted ribs
like stuffing—a bed, a dresser, and a table
pitched into the weeds.

A man and woman sit beneath the trees
in lawn chairs, staring at debris and the
red and white strobes of police cars,
the recently arrived ambulance crew.

But this has become history, this story
dwindling behind us as the road unwinds
through mountains and night begins
to fill it, falling from these hills
like skeins of purple silk.

Earlier on a more local road, we'd slowed
to pass six stags arrayed in a meadow
like figures from a medieval frieze,
full-blown velvet racks upon their heads.

As we drew abreast of them, they turned
to run into the forest beyond, vanishing
so quickly that they seemed a dream,
sacred stags sent to lead the hunt,
and faintly I heard horns on the wind
and the distant baying of hounds.

Behind the man and woman by the road
another woods begins, another dream,
and from those trees the branches bend
to pull them in so swiftly that they never
crashed at all, never sat in canvas chairs

beside the ruins of their home at that
random intersection with our lives—
though now we meet again.

In the haibun version of the poem above, I found myself making changes in the prose, particularly in the first and third paragraphs of the haibun versus the first and fifth stanzas of the poem. I combined the first two stanzas of the poem into one prose paragraph, and in the third stanza, I deleted some words and recast others to achieve a more straightforward version of the lines.

Also in the haibun, I combined stanzas five and six of the poem, cutting as I did so. I found myself wanting to combine verse stanzas here and there because the rhythms of the prose seemed to demand that. The interspersed haiku are based on memories. They shift away from the narrative, but connect in image, mood, and theme—especially the theme of time passing.

Driving Home

We flash past a wreck at the road's edge—a motor-home cracked open as it smashed into the guard-rail and fell on its side. Furniture has spilled from its twisted ribs like stuffing—a bed, a dresser, and a table pitched into the weeds. A man and woman sit beneath the roadside trees in lawn chairs, illuminated by the red and white strobes of police cars and the recently arrived ambulance crew.

storage unit—
after your death, I discard
box after box

But this has become history, this story dwindling behind us as the road unwinds through mountains, and night begins to fill it, falling from these hills like skeins of purple silk.

grandmother's shawl—
sunset filters through
the frayed fabric

Earlier on a more local road, we'd slowed to pass six stags in a meadow. Poised like figures in a medieval frieze, they bore full velvet racks on their heads. As we drew abreast of them, they turned to run into the forest beyond, vanishing so quickly that they seemed a dream, sacred stags sent to lead the hunt, and faintly I heard horns on the wind and the distant baying of hounds.

she plucks feathers
from the just-killed hen—
blood in the sink

Behind the man and woman by the road, another woods begins, another dream, and from that woods green branches bend to pull them in so swiftly that they never crashed at all, never sat in canvas chairs beside the ruins of their home at that random intersection with our lives.

milkweed pods—still
spilling seeds into the sky
of my childhood

The following is another example of the benefit gained when revising a free-verse poem into a haibun. Even in what I considered its final draft, the original poem felt unfinished, lacking enough *punch* to capture my experience.

Estell Manor State Park

That gray day, wind soughed in the pines,
and oaks arced full over trails that faded
into green or snaked into a density
of swamp and lichened trunks.

We walked a narrow road around
the wooded heart, wondering which trail
would claim us first until the wind
caught a dead limb and tossed it
down before us—the loud crack
fusing with its swift descent.

We said the usual things: what if
we'd been a few yards further along,
or a car had been there—then cautiously
pressed on, although we stopped
to drag the heavy branch aside

before we left the loop road for a trail
that led us deeper in.

Framing the poem in haiku gave me a chance to pick up on both the harsh shock of the limb falling and the lingering fear in the wake of the experience.

Estell Manor State Park

turkey buzzard—
red beak into its own
black wing

That gray day, wind soughed in the pines, and oaks arced full over trails that faded into green or snaked into a density of swamp and lichened trunks.

We walked a narrow road around the wooded heart, wondering which trail would claim us first until the wind caught a dead limb and tossed that full weight down before us—the loud crack fused with its swift descent.

We said the usual things: what if we'd been a few yards further along . . . or if a car . . . then cautiously pressed on, although we stopped to drag the heavy branch aside before we left the loop road for a trail.

night thoughts—
my heartbeat quickens
in this dark

In the first draft, this poem-turned-haibun included only the last haiku. However, a friend suggested it needed something more at the beginning. I added the opening haiku because I had seen that turkey buzzard in the park, and the irony of the fact that it usually sinks its red beak into carrion struck me at the time. Thinking about how close my friend and I had come to being seriously injured, or even killed, that harsh image seemed a fitting introduction to the mood and content of the haibun. The closing haiku, although amplifying the earlier fear, can also be a universal experience. We all have experienced those thoughts that can visit us in the pre-dawn hours.

II. Turning a Prose Poem into a Haibun

The same reverberating circles of meaning can happen when haiku are added to a prose poem. I wrote "Voices in the Rain" on a chilly November night and "After the Blizzard" a few hours after a fierce February blizzard had dumped several feet of snow on southern New Jersey. Both pieces began as prose poems and then wanted that expansion that adding haiku can offer.

Voices in the Rain

Thinned by running water, blown on a thawing wind, distant voices drift through bare branches, waver like flickering stars. Between us and those galaxies, someone slams a window. A dog barks. A faint train whistle rides the clouds, going somewhere. Riddles rise and spill onto the blacktop in the parking lot out back. Mother has been dead five years.

antique store—
the doll carriage holds
costume jewelry

The haiku following "Voices in the Rain" echoes memories of visiting antique stores with my mother, and shifts to her love of costume jewelry. For me, it reverberates with a kind of nostalgia—the distance of time echoing the distance in the prose images of the haibun.

After the Blizzard

They say when one is dying, one's whole life runs through the mind, a kind of rapid-transit time-travel. But this can happen anytime. Having lost my husband, I stare out at drifting snow while memories slip through my fingers like rosary beads.

back-yard clothesline—
diaper by diaper she grasps
the weathered pins

Now locks of all the hair I've ever cut are falling around me—snippets from the album of my past. Baby bits my mother trimmed held traces of my first birthday cake. The full-length strands my scalp lets go each day chart months of me. The two most recent inches held the sad chemistry of a year ago. I watched a young girl sweep them away.

we count the rings
in a fallen tree trunk—
how green the lichen

Tonight, as deep snow presses against my windows, I remember slow-dancing, my head leaning on my love's shoulder, our arms wrapped around each other. I want to dance that way again.

mating, the monarchs
seem one butterfly—
wings upon wings

As a prose poem, "After the Blizzard" didn't do enough to really capture my emotions that bitter night. When I added the clothesline (remembering when my children were little), the fallen tree trunk (and yes, we did count those rings), and the butterflies (an image from a documentary), the poem really opened up to absorb my mix of feelings.

In the first haiku, grasping the weathered pins echoes the rosary beads. In the second, the many rings echo the falling hair and left-behind years. The third haiku speaks for itself. As you can see from the above, combining haiku and prose makes haibun a very effective genre for capturing deep emotion.

I encourage you to try taking narrative poems, or prose poems that you're not sure work the way you want them to, and explore the possibility of revising them into haibun. You may also fall under haibun's spell. It can be an exciting and rewarding process

---

Penny Harter is published widely in journals and anthologies, and her literary autobiography appears as an extended essay in *Contemporary Authors.* Her books include *Recycling Starlight* (2010), *The Night Marsh* (2008), *Along River Road* (2005), *Buried in the Sky* (2002), *Lizard Light: Poems from the Earth* (1998), and *Turtle Blessing* (1996). With her late husband, William J. Higginson, she co-authored *The Haiku Handbook* (Kodansha International, 25th anniversary edition, 2010). Her illustrated children's alphabestiary, *The Beastie Book,* came out in 2009. A Dodge poet, Harter read at the 2010 Dodge Poetry Festival. She has received three poetry fellowships from the New Jersey State Council on the Arts, as well as the Mary Carolyn Davies Award from the Poetry Society of America, the William O. Douglas Nature Writing Award for poems in *American Nature Writing,* 2002, and a 2011 fellowship from the Virginia Center for the Creative Arts.

Afaa Michael Weaver

The Bop

The *bop* is a poetic form I created as a writing exercise for my Cave Canem students during the time I served as a member of Cave Canem's first faculty in 1997, one year after the founding of the organization. It is a form that progresses along three stanzas of free verse with a refrain either taken from popular music or created by the poet.

The bop allows the poet the space to work through an issue or to celebrate an event, person, etc. In working through an issue, the bop is argumentative, and, of course, it may also be argumentative in celebration. The form is named after a vernacular term in use in Baltimore during my upbringing; *bop* referred to the way a man in particular walked down the street. It was his signature in the world. As a poetic form the bop may be seen as the way a poet presents himself or herself to the world as performance. To write a bop means to play the score of what it means for the poet to *be*. In that way the two words *be* and *bop* may be joined to form *bebop* as interesting wordplay, but the poetic form I created uses music only as part of the structure. The bop did not originate in music, but in the manner in which a person—originally a man—walks.

Procedure

I. In its original form the bop's first and last stanzas contain six lines each, while the second stanza contains seven lines. A refrain follows each stanza. The example on the facing page adheres strictly to the original form so that teachers and students may know the point of departure.

II. The first stanza states the issue or subject. The second treats the issue or subject. The third stanza is a resolution and/or act of celebration, to one degree or another. For example, to resolve the question of one's obsession with ice cream could end in a celebration. What is implied in the progression of the poem is transcendence, whether the issue or subject be obsession with ice cream, impulsive spending, or climate change.

III. If the refrain is taken from popular music, the poet should adhere to copyright restrictions, and if necessary pursue permission. If the refrain is from music in the public domain, there should be no problem. If the refrain is the poet's own creation, the poet not only avoids copyright issues but provides himself or herself with a fresh, added challenge.

IV. The bop may be written as a group exercise. A workshop class can be divided into groups, one or more to create the stanzas and another to create the musical refrain. As a text for performance, the bop has many possibilities. The form is meant to be an enjoyable experience. The operative bop word is fun.

The Standard Bop: An Example

BP

a bop for the dinosaurs

A bubbling crude from below,
a lava spewing up, vomiting
a goo beyond petroleum
to dollar signs from memories
of dinosaurs dead and gone,
pumped now at the gas stations.

Drill, baby, drill until I'm gone—

Bosses hit the side of the rig
outside their offices miles away,
spreadsheets, bonds, calculators,
profit indicators, bank vaults
betting on futures, pensions lost
on roulette, promises, promises,
but no love where barrels count
the bubbly black power as gold.

Drill, baby, drill until I'm gone—

The uncounted fossil hearts
of reptiles and those they ate,
baby reptiles, mama and daddy,
all the scaly ancestors of birds,
brown pelicans shrouded in oil,
the precious juice of our cities.

Drill, baby, drill until I'm gone—

Afaa Michael Weaver

Variation on the Bop: An Example

"A Little Salt" uses a short quotation from the subject of the poem as the refrain, and the refrain itself varies in structure throughout. There are more than the three stanzas called for in the original form, and the poem itself is more narrative. The larger theme of complex familial love is not resolved so much as lamented in the lyrical manner and structure that the bop allows.

A Little Salt

My grandmother snuck it into every bite
It simmered down under cabbage and likker
Soakin my tongue, puckerin my cheeks
Even after the gout came knockin like a
Neighbor askin for a cup of . . .

A little salt won't hurt nobody

Grandma piled extra butter, pinch a salt,
Some more sugar whenever she could
Sour cream joined the pineapples
Teasin mandarin oranges with heart stoppin taste
She made salads for church, for my brothers, me
Greens with fatback simmered onion-skin thin

I heard people say it's food for the soul
My hesitance stares into the bowl
Wonderin if food makes you whole

A little salt won't hurt nobody

Grandma, maybe you were wrong
About food and other things
You always hushed the howlin stomach
My trips to the full freezer safe
Until the stroke, a little bit a salt was sweet

A little salt seeps into the tongue
Salt dissolves, yet it lingers
A little salt won't hurt nobody

Tara Betts

Additional Bop Poems:

- Honorée Fanonne Jeffers, "Bop: To Know You Is to Love You" in *The Gospel of Barbecue*
- Evie Shockley, "double bop for ntozake shange" and "the last temptation: a 21st century bop odyssey" in *a half-red sea*
- Tara Betts, "Bowery" and "Escape of Choice" in *Arc & Hue*
- Lyrae Van Clief-Stefanon, "Bop: The North Star" in *]Open Interval[*
- G. E. Patterson, "Green: A Bop" in *Tug*

Afaa Michael Weaver (Michael S. Weaver) is the author of eleven books of poetry. The most recent is *Like the Wind,* a translation of his work into Arabic. His twelfth collection, *The Government of Nature,* is forthcoming. He is currently editing an anthology of bop poems, *Bop, Strut, and Dance: A Post-Blues Form for New Generations.*

Paren(t)hesis

During the early 1960's, while I was teaching at what is now Cleveland State University, a student named Russell Salamon walked into my office to show me a poem titled "She" in a repeating form that he had invented. In this poem Salamon began by taking a set of parentheses as his center:

( )

He then took a sentence, "my hands cup her cup," broke it after the subject, and inserted the set of parentheses into the break (the technical term for a break in a line of verse is *caesura*):

my hands ( ) cup her cup

This is a metaphor: *My hands are a set of parentheses.* Next, Salamon bracketed the line thus:

[my hands ( ) cup her cup]

Then he added two clauses: "Her face, her arms, her thighs, all parentheses in which I am warm drizzle-rain inside her. Forests full of soundless flowers waited once unseen, translucid." These he broke, framing the center line with them, thus:

{Her face, her arms, her thighs,
all parentheses in which I am
[my hands ( ) cup her cup]
warm drizzle-rain inside her.
Forests full of soundless flowers
waited once unseen, translucid.}

Next, a new clause: "sizzling on snowscapes of her skin, she carries rain constellations to fill flute basins where." Again, Salamon arranges the new material to frame the poem's growing center:

sizzling on snowscapes of her skin.
{Her face, her arms, her thighs,
all parentheses in which I am
[my hands ( ) cup her cup]
warm drizzle-rain inside her.
Forests full of soundless flowers

waited once unseen, translucid}.
She carries rain constellations
to fill flute basins where

Finally, Salamon wrote the poem's enclosing frame: "My finger touch dissolves into a shiverlong echo of rains / we wash our morning faces off." In place, these lines serve as the poem's first and last:

She

My finger touch dissolves
into a shiverlong echo of rains/
sizzling on snowscapes of her skin.
{Her face, her arms, her thighs,
all parentheses in which I am
[my hands ( ) cup her cup]
warm drizzle-rain inside her.
Forests full of soundless flowers
waited once unseen, translucid.}
She carries rain constellations
to fill flute basins where
/we wash our morning faces off

Russell Salamon

You can read this poem from top to bottom, in standard order, but notice how the eye is drawn to the empty set of parentheses at its center. You can start there and read the poem from the inside out, moving from the typographical parentheses at the poem's center to the metaphorical parentheses of cups and cupped hands, and from there to the embracing parentheses of arms and thighs, of "forests full of soundless flowers," and so on until you arrive at the outer edges of the poem.

When I first encountered Russell Salamon's poem, after thinking about it for a while, I recalled E. E. Cummings' poem titled "l(a"—also built of parentheses, though all he did was to take the word *loneliness,* insert into it a single sentence, "a leaf falls," and sprinkle it down the page. More to the point, though, I remembered a poem I had myself written when I was a G.I. Bill undergraduate student at the University of Connecticut only two or three years earlier—a five-stanza poem with a strict form, "Time Goes Down in Mirrors."

Procedure

I. I began by taking the title sentence, "Time goes down in mirrors," and writing a sentence in two equal parts to serve as a parenthesis around it. The two parts of the sentence rhyme, and they have the same meter:

U / U / U   soPHIa CHATters
U / U / U   for NOTHing MATters

Placing the two parts of the new sentence before and after the title—as a parenthesis—creates the first stanza:

> Sophia chatters.
>> Time goes down in mirrors,
> For nothing matters.

II. The second stanza adds two more rhyming lines with the opposite meter—a mirror image:

/ U / U /   HORace LIStens WHILE
/ U / U /   HENCE his WORLDly SMILE

These lines form another parenthesis, surrounding the poem's previous stanza:

> Horace listens while
>> Sophia chatters.
>>> Time goes down in mirrors,
>> For nothing matters;
> Hence, his worldly smile.

III. For the third stanza I decided that this time the meter would be standard iambic tetrameter for both lines of the new parenthesis:

U / U / U / U /   the PHOnoGRAPH spins OUT its TUNE
U / U / U / U /   the PAIR will LOVE each OTHer SOON

Again, the new lines form a parenthesis around the poem's previous lines:

> The phonograph spins out its tune.
>> Horace listens while
>>> Sophia chatters.
>>>> Time goes down in mirrors,
>>> For nothing matters.
>> Hence, his worldly smile:
> The pair will love each other soon.

IV. The fourth stanza adds another pair of rhyming parentheses, again in iambic tetrameter:

| $\cup / \cup / \cup / \cup /$ | outDOORS the SHADows LISten AS |
| $\cup / \cup / \cup / \cup /$ | their MOVEments METroNOMED by JAZZ |

    a.   Outdoors, the shadows listen as
    b.   The phonograph spins out its tune.
    c.   Horace listens while
    d.   Sophia chatters.
    e.   Time goes down in mirrors,
    f.   For nothing matters.
    g.   Hence, his worldly smile:
    h.   The pair will love each other soon,
    i.   Their movements metronomed by jazz.

The same lines will be used in the fifth and final stanza. Their order has been labeled here to help you see how the re-ordering works in the last stanza.

V. For the fifth stanza, there are no new lines, but the arrangement changes. The central line—*Time goes down in mirrors*—remains in the center of the poem. The lines above and below are inverted.

    d.   Sophia chatters.
    c.   Horace listens while
    b.   The phonograph spins out its tune.
    a.   Outdoors the shadows listen as
    e. Time goes down in mirrors.
    i.   Their movements metronomed by jazz,
    h.   The pair will love each other soon.
    g.   Hence his worldly smile . . . ,
    f.   For nothing matters.

An Example

Here is the poem, from beginning to end:

Time Goes Down in Mirrors

Sophia chatters.
    Time goes down in mirrors,
For nothing matters.

Horace listens while
    Sophia chatters.
        Time goes down in mirrors,
    For nothing matters;
Hence, his worldly smile.

The phonograph spins out its tune.
    Horace listens while
        Sophia chatters.
            Time goes down in mirrors,
        For nothing matters.
    Hence, his worldly smile:
The pair will love each other soon.

Outdoors, the shadows listen as
    The phonograph spins out its tune.
        Horace listens while
            Sophia chatters.
                Time goes down in mirrors,
        For nothing matters.
        Hence, his worldly smile:
    The pair will love each other soon,
Their movements metronomed by jazz.

        Sophia chatters.
      Horace listens while
    The phonograph spins out its tune.
  Outdoors the shadows listen as
Time goes down in mirrors.
  Their movements metronomed by jazz,
    The pair will love each other soon.
      Hence his worldly smile . . . ,
        For nothing matters.

Both Russell Salamon's poem (page 195) and my own (above) are rather complicated structures, although both were written by undergraduates. As an exercise in repetition and in syntax rearrangement, however, parenthetics need not be so difficult, and I used it in class for decades.

Variation

Here is a brief exercise poem I wrote. Notice how the typefaces differ. The center line is in boldface, sandwiched between two lines in all-caps. These three lines are sandwiched by two lines in italics. The poem's first and last lines—in standard typeface—make up the final parenthesis.

Pines

They are the pines
I have seen them standing
IN THE HILLS WHERE STONE DWELLS
the wind shifts among their needles
ROOTS TOUCH TOWARD SILENCE IN THE EARTH
as though they have always been
strength drawn out of darkness.

Although it's built of uncomplicated elements, notice that the poem can be read from top to bottom, from bottom to top, from the middle out, or from the outside to the middle, and it still makes sense.

Note from Russell Salamon: Think of this kind of poem as a pebble dropped into a pool. You read the normal text from top to bottom, or from bottom to top, then from the first outside ring following the rings to the middle, then from the first inside ring back out along the rings to the first one, and you can pick any of these possible ways to start with. The idea is to avoid an enforced linear logic. You see that reading the poem in four different ways gives the material a richer, more spherical feel—a kind of resonance.

Lewis Turco is the author of *The Book of Forms: A Handbook of Poetics,* "the poet's Bible" (a fourth edition is forthcoming) and two companion volumes, *The Book of Literary Terms* and *The Book of Dialogue,* all three published by the University Press of New England. Turco has published dozens of other books, including poetry as well as scholarly work. His most recent book is *The Gathering of the Elders and Other Poems* (Star Cloud Press, 2010), written under the anagram pen name Wesli Court, under which Lewis Turco writes traditionally formal poems.

The Postcard Poem

T he Postcard Poem is an assignment I first invented for myself after spending concentrated work with issues of form, line, and image. Brevity and concision are not identical, but I find that the latter often rises when I impel students to write brief poems that are nevertheless saturated with detail. Casting such a poem in the form of a postcard adds the ingredients of direction, location, and personae (a postcard must be *from* someone and *to* someone else).

Resulting poems express sentiment (quite often, longing) in a variety of different ways, and they are fun to write.

I begin by having students read such postcard poems as Greg Williamson's "Belvedere Marittimo" from *The Silent Partner* (Story Line Press, 1995); Mary Oliver's "Postcard from Flamingo" from *American Primitive* (Little Brown, 1983); and my own "Postcard from Taos" (following page).

Procedure

I. Write a postcard poem in any form and observe all of the following guidelines:
1. The speaker is *not* you.
2. You create a palpable landscape.
3. Someone you do not know (but whom you describe) appears.
4. You include at least one noun that is new to you.
5. You include at least one metaphor.
6. You incorporate three pairs of pure rhymes or homonyms placed internally, *not* as end rhymes (as in "he *wore* the *more* brittle smile of a troubled suitor").
7. Your verbs are alive. (Mary Oliver uses *sidled, bounced, thudded*, and she speaks of "a forest that *tickled* and *spoke*.")

II. As you revise, make sure to pay attention to:
1. the line as an entity
2. the usefulness of enjambment
3. the senses—images of the actual, recognizable world that shake us to life, not vague, abstract descriptions. For example, compare "Downstairs // spiders had wrapped up / the crystal chandelier" (Oliver, "An Old Whorehouse") with "It was beautiful and scary."

III. Keep in mind this useful quotation from William Blake: "To generalize is to be an idiot. To particularize is the great distinction of merit."

An Example

Postcard from Taos

Here the sky's so big, so wide, so blue. It's true
for years I begged to come, unplug myself
from television, kids, that humdrum man
who lived only for sports. I should say *lives*.
This week he's strapped with all three girls I know
he wished we hadn't had.

Last night I danced till two at the Big Dipper—
and under it, too. The bar opens
to a courtyard where only stars care
if you dance or schmooze. The way I moved!
The first guy who led me to the makeshift floor
smelled of pine trees or cedar. Another,
the bayberry soap I haven't had a whiff of
since I was a teen and prepped myself
for dates with you-know-who.

For the first time in years I wore my hair
pinned up. And heels. In that red sequined dress
I bought the day the papers were final
I almost believed I might be beautiful again.
The stars, when you dance beneath the Taos sky,
seem to multiply. And the men.

Andrea Hollander Budy

Andrea Hollander Budy is the author of three full-length poetry collections: *Woman in the Painting, The Other Life,* and *House Without a Dreamer,* which won the Nicholas Roerich Poetry Prize. Other honors include the D. H. Lawrence Fellowship, a Pushcart Prize for prose memoir, the Runes Poetry Award, two poetry fellowships from the National Endowment for the Arts, and two from the Arkansas Arts Council. Budy's poems and essays have appeared in numerous anthologies, college textbooks, and literary journals. Since 1991 she has been the Writer-in-Residence at Lyon College, where she was awarded the Lamar Williamson Prize for Excellence in Teaching.

Seven (or Ten) Line Poem

You can do this exercise by yourself, but it's a great group activity—simple, quick, and fun.

Procedure

1. Write down your phone number with or without the area code.
2. Exchange phone numbers with the person next to you. If you do this exercise by yourself, write down the phone number of a family member or friend, or try one of the 800 numbers that interrupt your dinner.
3. Use the numerals of the phone number you receive (or choose) to determine the number of *words* in each line of the seven or ten line poem. If there is a zero, use it as a stanza break.

For example, if you write to the phone number 124-5637, your poem would look like this:

line 1:	one word
line 2:	two words
line 3:	four words
line 4:	five words
line 5:	six words
line 6:	three words
line 7:	seven words

On the other hand, if you receive 120-5607, your poem would look like this:

line 1:	one word
line 2:	two words
	(stanza break)
line 3:	five words
line 4:	six words
	(stanza break)
line 5:	seven words

Example

The following poem was written to this phone number: (512) 467-0678. Note that if you include the area code for this exercise, you'll write a ten-line poem. You could even include the 1 that initiates a long-distance call and write an eleven-line poem—or use all the numbers you'd dial for an international call.

Freightliner West on I-40

So twilight at world's edge
gloaming
glowing taillights
drag this truck further
speedometer needle might as well be
clock hand ticking out distance over time

Cargo's momentum pushes, the sun's descent
pulls these rolling tires westward into the
soft pink oblivion where the highway fades away

W. Joe Hoppe

Variations

- Use the numerals in a phone number to determine the number of *syllables* in each line of your poem. Again, a zero indicates a stanza break.

- Add a vocabulary component. If you're conducting a workshop, give participants a poetry book and have them use a set number of words from it, randomly selected. Solitary writers: if you're in a motel or hotel, use the travel magazines for words. If you're on an airplane, use articles from the in-flight publication. On a bus or subway? Use the ads for vocabulary. The possibilities are endless.

- Once the form starts to work in your head, you no longer need an actual phone number to write it. Even non-poets enjoy this exercise. Have fun!

Examples

I did a whole chapbook of seven-line poems called *Poetic License* (Adastra Press, 2004). Each of the forty poems was titled with the first name of a well-known poet. For each, I also used eight to ten words from the vocabulary of the poet, though I did not attempt to copy the poet's style. For another chapbook, *Double-Edged* (Finishing Line Press, 2009), a series of love poems, I used a similar format of eight to ten pre-selected vocabulary words, one to nine words per line, and seven lines. The poems on the following page are from *Double-Edged*.

The Horizon as Razor

Your craft is heavy
With other women's dreams.
Before day's blade glints,
Before blood beads:
Tender this thin edge,
Cut words and knots,
Leave no prints behind.

Susan Terris

Solstice Song

Lend me hot blood.
Lend me the sweet-gold of bees
And the sharp edge of sting.
Lend me rills of darkness
And rivers of light,
Bass and treble
For our solstice song.

Susan Terris

Susan Terris contributed two exercises to *Wingbeats*. See page 33 for her biography.

Rebirthing the Words:
Crafting a Cento

Most often a found poem is based on fairly mundane materials—advertisements in a newspaper or magazine, documents from the Internal Revenue Service, directions on a can of Drano, the fine print on the side of a cereal box. A more sophisticated type of found poem uses actual lines of poetry as its base, and this type is known as a cento. The cento, from the Latin for *patchwork,* appropriates lines from poetry, lyrics, and even nursery rhymes and rearranges the individual lines into a new patchwork of sense and meaning. Sometimes the lines come from different works by one poet, but just as often they're from several works by multiple poets. The craft of the cento comes in how you arrange someone else's lines to create a coherent new piece of writing.

The cento is the perfect form poem for those who don't like to write form poems. It doesn't have a set number of lines. It doesn't have a set number of stanzas. It doesn't have a rhyme scheme, although it may have rhyme. It doesn't have a set meter, although it may exhibit a general metrical pattern. Everything comes down to which lines are selected and how they are arranged!

Though the cento has been around for centuries, it seems to have found new popularity lately, including fine examples by John Ashbery ("The Dong with the Luminous Nose"), Bob Holman ("SemiCento"), and David Lehman ("The Oxford Cento"). The latter, for example, is a poem composed of lines from dozens of nineteenth- and twentieth-century American poets, all of whose poems appear in the recent *Oxford Book of American Poetry,* which Lehman selected and edited. "After editing this new anthology," says Lehman, "I felt inevitably drawn to the idea of forging a cento from its pages, in honor of the poets and as a souvenir of the experience of working on the project."

I also felt a sense of homage when I created my cento, "Because the Night," composed in 22 lines from 22 different poems by rock star/poet Patti Smith, whom I was ecstatic to see represented in the *Oxford Book of American Poetry*.

Procedure

1. Choose your source or sources for lines. If you're going to focus on a single author, a collected or selected works compilation is ideal (I used *Patti Smith Complete: Lyrics, Reflections, and Notes for the Future).* If you're planning to include multiple authors, an anthology, such as the *Oxford* or *Norton,* works best, although a smaller anthology might work even better—think *Poetry 180, The World in Us,* or a volume of the *Best American Poetry.*

II. Read through the collection, reacquainting yourself with lines you'd forgotten or discovering new ones. Allow yourself at least a couple of hours. Scan poems for those lines that jump out at you, that really blow you away. Try to limit yourself to no more than one or two lines per poem, as usually a cento includes no more than one line from any one source poem. I find it useful, however, if you find you cannot limit yourself to selecting only one line, to go ahead and choose a second (or third) because you never know which of the lines will work best as the cento starts developing.

III. The key here is to keep track of which lines come from which poems! I find it easiest to have a computer at hand to type the lines that speak to me *and* to identify by title the source poem immediately after the line. You'll want to include the author as well, if you're using multiple authors (or at least the page number the line can be found on in the anthology). I also set the spacing at 1.5 (or higher) so that there's plenty of room between typed lines.

IV. Keep reading, keep enjoying, keep typing lines until you come up with 2–3 pages of them; the more lines you choose, the more options you'll have (but more options can also complicate matters). Print out the pages, and then cut out the separate lines, so that you'll end up with a number of strips with lines of poetry. Spread these out (see illustration on facing page) on a large table so that you can read all the separate strips. Don't worry about trying to keep any sense of order!

V. Now the fun of the cento begins. Read through the lines before you several times and you'll start to see patterns—lines that go together thematically, lines that sound good together, lines which surprise when butted up against each other. Pull these lines out and start arranging them on an open space on the table. (This is why I strongly suggest typing the lines and cutting them into strips—it makes moving the lines around extremely easy.) It's rather like playing with a magnetic poetry kit, only instead of words there are whole lines (well, and no magnetism). Try this, try that—look for the perfect combinations of lines. The success of the cento lies in the sequencing!

When I was writing "Because the Night," as I started playing with lines, I also noticed a repetition of certain key words (*sky, throat, cry, star, dream*), unexpected rhymes between lines (*sky/cry, you/rendezvous*), surprisingly simi-

For I was undulating in the lewd impostered night ("Seven Ways of Going"

Each dream of life I'll share with you (Dream of Life)

And we conceived it to be a beautiful thing (Momento Mori")

And the sky was open/ Like a valentine ("Looking for You (I Was)")

Well I built my dreams on your empty scenes ("Dead City")

That I'll never end transcend transcend ("Ain't It Strange")

I put my fingers through her silken hair ("Land")

Some strange music draws me in ("Dancing Barefoot")

I'm here a whisper you summoned I called ("Dead to the World")]

A silk of souls/ That whispers to me ("Paths That Cross")

We'll bare our arms as wings ("Ravens")

Upset total abandon you know I love you so ("Pumping (My Heart)")

Maybe it's time to break on through ("Don't Say Nothing")

My soul surrenders astonished to death ("Frederick")

I implore thee come explore me ("Ain't It Strange")

I could feel my heart it was melting ("Break It Up")

This maze of being ("Beneath the Southern Cross")

Till I lose my sense of gravity ("Dancing Barefoot")

The Lights like some switched-on Mondrian ("Up There Down There")

Break it up, oh, please take me with you ("Break It Up")

Ah I knew your youth was for the taking ("Kimberly")

lar assonance between lines (*moves/you, music/smooth, through/lewd*), and unforeseen anaphora (*I felt/I could feel/I was*). Not only did the night become the focus of the poem's imagery, but the imagery helped lend a shape to the poem. I began to see a beginning, a middle, and an end. I even started to feel the poem move into a structure of tercets. But none of this happened until I tried out dozens of different lines in different locations.

VI. When you reach a point where you're fairly content with the cento, take a quick look to make sure that you don't have more than one line from any one poem (if you do, keep trying lines from the spread). Read the lines together as a whole and see if they work together orally. Some poets might want to change a word here or there (e.g., a tense), but try to resist the temptation to alter the original lines. On the other hand, if there are words at the front of the line that don't work, feel free to use part of the line—just don't add any words or change any. For example, I dropped "And," which would have started the line "And the sky was open like a valentine." If you're not happy, keep trying different sequences or substitutions. Or let the lines sit for an hour or two and come back to them (repeat as necessary). You do want the poem to flow, not to read as a random assortment of single lines; your arrangement should not be purely arbitrary or accidental.

VII. If you are happy, write a small number at the end of each strip to indicate their order in the cento—see example below. These will be helpful if the lines get out of order. Then keyboard the poem. When you type the lines, do feel free to alter punctuation and/or capitalization, as well as create stanza breaks. These will help the flow of the lines in many cases, and they are part of what makes the cento your poem. After I had my first draft of "Because the Night" printed out (but after numerous temporary "table" drafts), I let it sit for a night and went back to work the next day making further changes to the

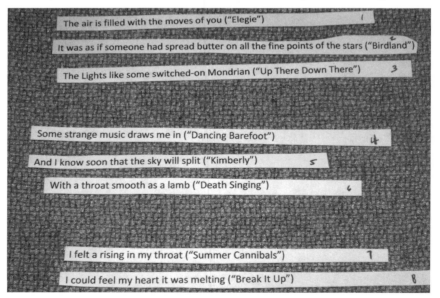

The air is filled with the moves of you ("Elegie")   *1*

It was as if someone had spread butter on all the fine points of the stars ("Birdland")   *2*

The Lights like some switched-on Mondrian ("Up There Down There")   *3*

Some strange music draws me in ("Dancing Barefoot")   *4*

And I know soon that the sky will split ("Kimberly")   *5*

With a throat smooth as a lamb ("Death Singing")   *6*

I felt a rising in my throat ("Summer Cannibals")   *7*

I could feel my heart it was melting ("Break It Up")   *8*

lines and order. At the point I reached my final draft, I made the edits on the computer, typed it out, and started on the final step of a cento, the gloss.

VIII. That's right, authors of centos are expected to create a gloss, or a key to the poems that they've used. If all the poems are by the same poet, the gloss is a line-by-line list of poem titles only; if the poems come from many different poets and poems, the gloss consists of a line-by-line list of poets and poem titles (e.g., 38. Wallace Stevens, "Sunday Morning"). Part of the joy of reading the cento is trying to figure out who wrote the source lines and which poems they come from; the gloss serves as a means of verification.

An Example

Because the Night

a cento in homage to Patti Smith,
using 22 lines from 22 of her poems/lyrics

The air is filled with the moves of you,
as if someone had spread butter on all the fine points of the stars,
the lights like some switched-on Mondrian.

Some strange music draws me in,
and I know soon that the sky will split
with a throat smooth as a lamb.

I felt a rising in my throat.
I could feel my heart (it was melting).
I was a wing in heaven blue.

The sky was open like a valentine,
a silk of souls that whispers to me.
My senses newly opened, I awakened to the cry.

Maybe it's time to break on through,
for I was undulating in the lewd impostered night
toward a dream that dreams itself.

You are the adrenaline rushing through my veins.
Each way I turn, the sense of you surrounds,
knowing no end to our rendezvous.

No star is too far with you.
Every word that's spoken, every word decreed,
word of your word, cry of your cry,
all I ever wanted, I wanted from you.

Because the Night: Gloss

1. "Elegie"
2. "Birdland"
3. "Up There Down There"

4. "Dancing Barefoot"
5. "Kimberly"
6. "Death Singing"

7. "Summer Cannibals"
8. "Break It Up"
9. "Wing"

10. "Looking for You (I Was)"
11. "Paths that Cross"
12. "People Have the Power"

13. "Don't Say Nothing"
14. "Seven Ways of Going"
15. "About a Boy"

16. "Godspeed"
17. "Dream of Life"
18. "My Madrigal"

19. "Distant Fingers"
20. "Wild Leaves"
21. "Ghost Dance"
22. "Fireflies"

Scott Wiggerman contributed two exercises to *Wingbeats*. See page 135 for his biography.

Chapter VI:
Going Difficult Places

If we had to say what writing is, we would
define it essentially as an act of courage.

Cynthia Ozick

Speaking the Unspoken

Writing poetry often feels like a solitary endeavor. As consolation, Philip Gross said, "We're never alone when writing a poem. Pick up your pen, and you're in dialogue with all the writing you've been touched by."

One way to enjoy that poetic dialogue is to write intentionally in response to other poems. Just as everyday conversation can take off in unexpected directions, writing in conversation with other poets can lead us to spontaneously speak the unspoken thoughts hidden in our hearts.

Consider this poem, one of my favorites by Angela O'Donnell, a fine poet and professor at Fordham University–Rose Hill. Here, O'Donnell shares a poignant memory, as she speaks the unspoken.

Other Mothers

Other girls' mothers
sold *Avon, Bee-line, Tupperware.*

My mother took lovers.
Young ones. Dark ones. True ones,

the kind that came back,
parked their cars in the drive,

and slept in our house
night after night after night.

Other girls' mothers
wore aprons, baked bread.

My mother slipped on stockings,
stepped into heels, and went to work

late evenings while we'd lie
half-awake in our beds.

We'd hope for peanuts, chips, mints,
small signs she'd remembered us.

Other girls' mothers
didn't like my mother,

grew green-eyed in the grocery,
cold-shouldered us at Mass

where she'd stay in the pew,
marooned, at Communion,

her black mantilla
shadowing her black eyes.

Other girls' mothers
liked their daughters,

asked them questions,
listened for replies.

My mother would have thought
them amusing

had she thought
of other mothers at all.

Angela O'Donnell

What a compelling poetry conversation starter!

Procedure

Consider your own unspoken memories. Who in your family was confusing
or peculiar or difficult? Let your mind wander back to your experiences with
them. What scenes, images, conversations, and events do they bring to mind?
How did you feel about those persons in the past? How do you feel about
them now? Is there something about your relationship with them that you
have never told anyone?

With those thoughts as inspiration and in dialogue with Angela
O'Donnell's poem "Other Mothers," compose your own poem about your
mother or father or extended family member, an "About Other _____" poem.
Take O'Donnell's lead; be specific with imagery and careful with commentary.
Use the distance of time to write objectively about your subject, but allow
yourself authentic feelings, so that the reader can empathize with you.

Ralph Waldo Emerson, attributing Plato, said that poetry is nearer to vital truth than history. That is certainly true when we write about family and childhood; poems of remembrance are more than just the facts. Because birth, not choice, determines the people who are our parents, siblings, sons, and daughters, our experiences of family are often conflicted. Many people recall wondering, as children, if they might be adopted or wishing for another family. Others remember feeling that everyone else's family was normal except theirs. Some admit difficulties but revel in the blessing of their heritage.

Another reason our family memories are so complicated is that our true feelings about our closest relationships can be suppressed for years and years. The stability of families often depends on each person's tolerance of difference at the expense of honesty. There may be grudges, disappointments, and, in the worst of cases, scars that we conceal into adulthood. On the other hand, we may have been so blessed that we long for a way to adequately say, "I love you."

An Example

At a conference where I used this exercise based on O'Donnell's poem, participants immediately identified with the uncomfortable experience of an unusual family member. One workshop poet wrote a lovely piece about her own mother, who was an immigrant. Another described a sibling whose competition she endured all her life. Someone else admitted to strong feelings about an alcoholic father; another had a sister whose lifelong illness was a burden. Some poems were more positive and focused on enduring family relationships.

One intriguing poem written in response to "Other Mothers" came from Texas Poet Laureate Karla K. Morton. Morton was led to consider her own role as a mother. It was a reminder that self-examination can also be what we keep unspoken. Here is her poem:

I *Am* the Other Mother

She waited at the bank's door, in labor,

but in his rush to pick her up,
he died in a traffic accident on the way;

ah, but then, I was a false alarm. . . .

She married again when I was two,
but never fully relied on him—

working every day, cooking every night;
cleaning, sewing, ironing, devoting her life to us. . . .

I never even had a store-bought dress
until I was a senior in high school.

I *am* the other mother;

unworthy of her blood, with no domestic gifts—
a life of roads and take-out for *my* children. . . .

But when I come home, I sit with my daughter
on the sofa, her favorite show on TV;

and I wrap my arm around her shoulders,
and whisper *all* my love.

Karla K. Morton

In this poem, as in O'Donnell's, Morton opens with a compelling narrative, then offers us her contemplations. In Morton's case, that includes her mother and also her daughter. Whatever you choose for a topic, consider several points of view as you write:

- Your *vital truth*—the past, as you remember it
- The actual facts about your childhood or family
- Your own suppressed or carefully managed feelings
- Your family member's perspective or experience
- Your situation now, years later

One of the joys of poetry writing is that, as we lead readers to new realizations, we are changed ourselves. As you delve into this exercise, you may experience Frost's "lump in the throat"; writing honestly is transformational. If you can be gentle with yourself and those about whom you write, this can be a chance for the balm of self-recognition to heal you and your reader.

Using another metaphor, in exploring intimate feelings about your family, you may finally be able to open the suitcase you have been carrying all these years—the one full of unspoken pain or confusion. Once you have unloaded your proverbial *baggage,* you won't have to carry the weight of it around with you anymore, because you have finally been able to speak the unspoken!

Additional "Other" Poems

- "My Life among the Birds" by Alan Bereka, from *The Comic Flaw*
- "Simile" by Barbara Crooker, from *Line Dance*
- "The Price of Perfection" by Cleatus Rattan, from *The Border*
- "Parents" by Robert Wrigley, from *Earthly Meditations*
- "Daddy" by Sylvia Plath, from *Ariel*
- "The Boy" by Marie Howe, from *What the Living Do*

Anne McCrady has published poetry online and in literary journals, magazines, and anthologies. Her poetry collection *Along Greathouse Road* won the 2003 Edwin M. Eakin Memorial Book Publication Award from the Poetry Society of Texas, and her chapbook *Under a Blameless Moon* won the 2007 Pudding House Chapbook Prize. McCrady has also published fiction, creative nonfiction, and spiritual materials and has recorded much of her writing. Online, she offers monthly poetry lessons and literary commentary and also posts a daily online prompt, the *InSpiritry Question for the Day.* As the founder of *InSpiritry*, an endeavor to *Put Words to Work for the Greater Good,* McCrady is a writer and presenter for literary, spiritual, educational, and community groups. The mother of three adult children, McCrady lives in East Texas with her husband, Mike.

Finding Voice

It has been a paradox for me that workshops always leave me wishing for more time. If I have a week, I wish it was a month; if I have a semester, I wish I had a year; and if I had a year, I'd probably want to marry the group and live happily ever after. I've stopped doing workshops that give me less than a weekend with a group. I don't feel it's safe, responsible, or right to ask people to be vulnerable and open, and then leave them too quickly. However, there are people that I long to somehow connect with who may not be able to take a workshop with me. Therefore, I am completing an Artist's Manual, meant to serve as a workbook for individuals interested in the Finding Voice Method. The work shared here is excerpted from my forthcoming Artist's Manual.

I don't believe that writers have to write the personal all the time. I don't think that we have to wallow in our pain or repeatedly return to our traumas. However, I know that stuck places rob us of time. The sadness, resentment, shame, guilt, fear, hurt, and anger that we don't examine and release lives in our bodies. The stories we don't tell weigh heavily on our spirits. Our child within is captain of our subconscious until we make the well within safe and clear enough for that child to play and dance and run and laugh freely. No matter your genre, form, or aesthetic, it remains true that examining, articulating, practicing, and experimenting with your personal rhythms, traditions, cultural sensibilities, and identity accelerates and magnifies the power of your artistic voice.

Procedure

I. When facilitating, I like to start by offering questions.

Exercise Questions

1. What is your race/ethnicity?
2. Where were you born?
3. When where you born?
4. What was your first language(s)?
5. What was your class when you were growing up?
6. What physical challenges/abilities did you have as a child?
7. What was your gender identity growing up?
8. What was your sexual orientation when you were young?

9. Who raised you?
10. Who loved you?
11. Who did you love growing up?
12. Where was your (birth) mother when you were growing up?
13. Where was your (birth) father when you were growing up?

II. Locate a picture of yourself as a child, a picture that moves your heart. If you can't locate a picture, create one in your mind. Sit with the picture. Let the child speak to you. Write in stream of consciousness.

III. Looking at the picture, see your neighborhood. See yourself and your mother in your home (even if you didn't live together).

- What is the family lie that shaped your life?

- What is the family truth that shaped your life?

- Say something to your mother. Have her say something to you.

In a workshop I expand this line of questioning to include fathers and both sets of grandparents. Since it is impossible for me to include all the questions that might come up in this unit of a workshop, I've chosen questions that have been key in my own artistic development. The excerpt from my creative writing shared here was born from the embodied questions.

IV. Create a timeline. Make the start date the date that your oldest grandparent was born (if you don't know, imagine it), and make the end date your date of birth. Fill the timeline in with local, national, and international events. How did the context of the times inform and affect your mother, your family history? How did the context impact your life?

An Example

love/rituals & rage, an excerpt

performed by The root wy'mn Theatre Company.

home.
they filled
the room
with laughter
hot-sauce-craklin'-pig-skins
and bid wisk.
they filled the room

with bourbon
estée lauder
and Aretha/baby
baby sweet
baby
they filled the room
bosoms   rocking
hips/heated hearts and
laughter/they
filled the room
with hugs
and lipstick
smooching cheeks/they
smiled at me
with smothered porkchops
greens and rice/and
"i heard it through the grapevine"
from velvet chairs
next to large lamps
neath velvet pictures
where they
played games with male visitors/and
i don't remember
what they said/i
remember
that they filled the room   and
smiled at me

and i have since
been searching
for wy'mn to
smile at me
and fill
my room.

Sharon Bridgforth

Sharon Bridgforth, a resident playwright at New Dramatists since 2009, is a writer working in the Theatrical Jazz Aesthetic. She is the 2010–2011 Visiting Multicultural Faculty member at DePaul University's Theatre School. Her piece *blood pudding* was in the 2010 New York SummerStage Festival. Bridgforth is author of the Lambda Literary Award–winning title *the bull-jean stories* and *love conjure/blues,* a performance/novel. Both books are published by Red-Bone Press. Her work has received support from The National Endowment For The Arts/Theatre Communications Group Playwright in Residence Program and the National Performance Network Commissioning Fund. She is an affiliate of The Austin Project, sponsored by The John L. Warfield Center for African and African American Studies, University of Texas at Austin. Bridgforth's *Finding Voice Facilitation Manual* is published in *Experiments in a Jazz Aesthetic: Art, Activism, Academia, and the Austin Project,* edited by Dr. Omi Osun Joni L. Jones, Dr. Lisa L. Moore, and Bridgforth (University of Texas Press, 2010).

Hand and Divination

T he following exercise is a variation on an object exercise inspired by grief worker and author Virginia Fry, author of *Part of Me Died Too: Stories of Creative Survival among Bereaved Children and Teenagers.* I met Fry during a volunteer training at The Children's Room, a grief support center for children, teens, and their families in Massachusetts. Fry, a hospice worker and grief counselor, had us trace our hands and respond to several questions: *What is in your hands? What are you trying to handle? What hurts your heart? What heals your heart?* The warm-up inspired me to consider the emotional connections to all that our hands touch and feel, as well as the finiteness of our aging bodies. When I first did the exercise, I could not help but consider the mystical associations of palmistry and divination, so I added this component to the exercise.

Phase I: The Warm-Up

For the steps below consult the illustration on the facing page—a tracing I made of my own hands, including my answers to the questions in the exercise.

Directions

1. Outline your right and left hand on a sheet of blank paper.
2. Inside the outline of your right hand, answer these questions: *What hurts your heart? What is in your hands? What are you trying to handle?* Be sure to write in the palm and fingers, however you see fit.
3. Inside the outline of your left hand, answer this question: *What heals your heart?* Write all the things that help your heart, that comfort you. You might include things you like to do (e.g., running, drawing, baking) or even people you like to talk to.
4. Now, take some time just to observe your hands. You might want to focus on one hand. Aim to bring in your senses: what you see, smell, feel, or even what your hands are so often feeling, touching, etc.

According to Virginia Fry, there is a correlation between the two hands. Things written on the *hurt* fingers and palm may be healed by the things written on the *help* fingers and palm. While some might be skeptical, I was amazed by how accurate these correlations were for me. Inside my right index finger, for example, I wrote *passive aggressive silence,* while inside the left index finger, I wrote *Yoga,* a practice that could help heal passive aggressive silence.

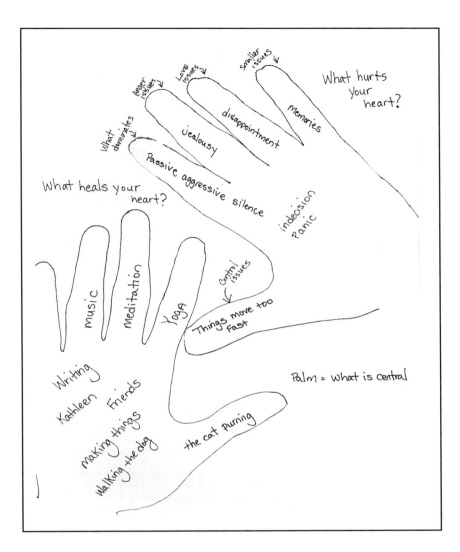

From Virginia Fry: What is in your hands? What are you trying to handle? What hurts your heart? What helps your heart?

Pointer finger: What dominates your thoughts

Middle finger: Anger issues

Ring finger: Love issues

Pinky: Smaller issues

Thumb: Control issues

Phase II: The Tarot Card

I. Have participants choose one Tarot card. I find the Major Arcana work best, as the images are archetypal and generally more layered and detailed.

II. After studying the card, have participants write a word list based on a sensory description of the card. Encourage the use of strong, active verbs and concrete nouns, as well as the inclusion of textures, smells, and sounds.

III. Once participants generate their word lists, have them take time observing their hands and taking notes about their hands.

IV. Using both word lists as inspiration, have students write from there. They may choose to write a narrative poem, the story of their hands and/or the card they drew; a lyric poem about their hands or card; or even a persona poem, writing in the voice of their hands or the figure on the card they drew. If either the hands or the card dominates the exercise, follow that inspiration. Let the poem lead.

An Example

The poem that follows grew out of this exercise. For Steps I and II above, the first card I tried was the Chariot. The word list I developed is below. Later, however, I thought of the Death card, which gave rise to the poem's skeletal material. Much of what was on the original word list got revised out.

Word List for the Chariot

carriage, reins, bounce, pulled, torn, two horses, direction, landscape, solace, dirt, earth, water, ground, chains, terse, reins, slack, fertile, sea, salt, roar, crush

First Draft

I make a fist and then release it
reins now slack in my palms
the horses run in two directions
I bounce along in the carriage—
There is no peace here
but my hands dig in the dirt
and find solace in the ground
digging deep—skeletal bones
moving in their time on earth
before they lie down and return to it

before they lie still for good
nervous hands, digging down
into the earth, planting a seed and then withdrawing
from that dark soil
patting it down, alkaline and fertile
the hands tending to the watering can
watching as they move
so separate from me—alive as if to say
some part of me in spite of this lives

After a Sudden Sorrow

My hands find solace in the ground
Bones and skin dig in dirt
It is their time on earth
before they lie down and return to it
before they lie still for good
Nervous hands stirring
plunge down into the earth
plant a seed and then emerge
from that dark soil
patting it down
alkaline and fertile
and I watch as they move
so separate so alive as if to say
some part of you in spite of this lives—

Alison T. Cimino received her M.F.A. in poetry at Texas State University–San Marcos and her B.A. in English at Trinity College, Hartford, Connecticut. Her poems have appeared in many journals as well as *The Cambridge Codex Project,* a visual art installation to promote literacy in Cambridge, Massachusetts. Cimino serves as an artist-in-residence teaching poetry through arts integration to teachers and administrators and writing poetry with students in middle and elementary schools. In Fall 2006 she worked as an artist-in-residence for Attleboro middle schools through the ABC 1 and the National Endowment for the Arts' Big Read projects. She teaches a poetry class for educators at Lesley University.

Tales from the Bathroom:
The Curious Path to a Poem

In the early stages of a workshop, establishing trust among participants is crucial, but spending workshop time to share personal histories can run the risk of being more waste than asset if the stories get too long. It is also important to start with an engaging, even surprising prompt that will inspire participants with an immediate response and encourage them to return the following session.

Procedure

Over the years, my favorite trigger has been a very simple declaration: *Write about the bathroom of the home you grew up in.* Oh my, the pained faces, the audible gasps! How can we possibly write about the bathroom?! What is there to say about a bathroom?! The key is not to limit the possibilities of the prompt, not to overthink it. Start with the very first thought and let the pen take over. A flood of images will inundate the page.

But what if you lived in more than one place? American families move often, particularly in the mobile society of the past fifty years. In the case that there were multiple houses in which you lived as a young person, rely upon the first memory that comes to you or the bathroom that stands out the most when you consider the task at hand.

Don't panic. Just write.

I never reveal my rationale for this prompt until after responses are shared, which is generally a week or so later, when workshop participants reconvene. In the case of a single workshop, the process accelerates, with participants completing final revisions on their own. I will share my thoughts about this prompt, but I suggest that you stop reading now and try the exercise first for an untainted first response before you read my reasoning.

Rationale

The bathroom represents a taboo. In general, we do not discuss bathrooms, although they are common to our daily experience. We commonly read poems about other rooms in the house—for example, Gwendolyn Brooks' "Kitchenette Building" or Ted Kooser's kitchen portrait, "A Room in the Past." Li-Young Lee peeks into his parents' bedroom in "Early in the Morning." Some take steps similar to Elizabeth Bishop's "In the Waiting Room," a poem that moves far beyond the front porch to join an aunt waiting for her dental appointment. Randall Horton's "The Card Game" provides a chilling fly-on-the-wall view of the cell block of an American prison. With the shift in focus to the very private space of the bathroom, you can access memories, images, and reactions that you likely have not visited in a long time and can perhaps craft a poem unique in tone and voice.

The bathroom trigger offers a keen view of family relationships. As poets respond, the reader holds a periscope to a private view of family rituals, sibling relationships, parental expectations, and personal behavior. The single child has a much different experience from the poet who grew up one of seven children. Dad's shaving ritual or Mom's bi-monthly hair coloring may reveal much more than a memoir drawn from the usual script for sharing the past.

A bathroom's décor reflects much about family cycles as well as eras of interior design and plumbing technology. Some of us may have grown up without indoor plumbing. Some have not had the experience of a home with a single bath, while others have experienced the highest of Kohler opulence. Many middle-aged writers remember pink wall tiles and swans on the wallpaper. Some poets may remember the little slot in the medicine chest for used ejector razor blades or a clawfoot tub perfect for a bubble bath. Others may remember shag carpet of the 1970s or the white octagonal floor tiles of the Depression or the red hot-water bottle hanging on a hook on the back of the door.

Examples

Kyla Town, a Syracuse-based poet and fiction writer, delivers a complex emotional tone in very accessible, yet carefully crafted language in this poem:

Mom and Superman, circa 1972

With the gloaming, my mother woke,
shook sleep and rum from her brain,
took the coffee I brought her, shuffled
into our bathroom. In slippered feet
and nightgown, cheek against
vanity, I watched this woman
who was Mom, Mommy, Margaret become
who she was to everyone else lurking
at the hospital where she worked
in the growing umbra beyond our yellow light.

In this room, where everything was blue,
I watched her daub on foundation,
paint her lips Hard Candy red, spread
Revlon Riviera Blue across
each sleep-deprived lid, glue
on her lashes and line
her eyes with Flashy Black, and finally
rouge the apple of her cheeks
in Asian Sunrise. With each stroke,
my mother erased her usual face,
but furrows still carried the current
of disappointment through her skin,
her eyes still hazed by
cigarette smoke and booze.

She cursed as she pinned
on her winged nurse's cap, origami
bird tethered to her hair.
Each night, I watched my mother change
like Superman in a phone booth.

Kyla Town

In the following excerpt by a poet from central New York, who has participated in many of my workshops, we recognize that no matter the poet's age when the poem is written, teen angst and self-consciousness transcend generations:

from What the Lilac Knew: A Memoir

We had no indoor bathroom until I turned thirteen.
On nice days, we used an outdoor privy, otherwise,
a commode housed in a dark out-of-the-way corner.
I remember washing up at the kitchen sink,
baths taken in a tin tub on the kitchen floor,
the pleasure of a tub bath on summer grass.

The privy was a sturdy little building, pitch-roofed,
walls of weather-beaten barn wood, a small window.
It stood behind a lilac tree where robins nested
every year. Weeds and grass grew up at the door,

wild strawberries and Queen Anne's lace, as well.
Inside, a covered seat and holes, a bag of lime dust
to douse offensive odors. I loved the quiet there,
listening to crickets, critters chasing each other,
the robins, just thinking.

Mary L. Gardner

As Gardner's poem illustrates, another reason for the prompt is to examine issues of privacy and the search for self in family community. Parents have been known to lock themselves in the bathroom for a moment's peace. Children often do the same, although sometimes they get stuck. Large families may have practiced communal bathing. We come of age in the bathroom, and privacy becomes even more important. These are all ample occasions for a poem that is unique to your own voice and experience and to which readers may relate.

Humor is totally acceptable. Funny things happen in bathrooms. One poet wrote that he was the youngest of his family and everyone doted on him until the inevitable day that no one arrived to help him clean himself after a trip to the commode. It was a very funny piece about a four-year-old sitting stranded in the bathroom, calling out to each family member in succession and, finally, the rite of passage that the event became in his personal independence. Another example of a mirthful yet telling response to the prompt is the following poem by painter and poet Michael A. Sickler.

Bathing a Tiny Dog in a Very Large Bathroom

for Paul Blackburn

It had a cathedral's intimacy
Could have been rented
2 big to lose your virginity

A bathroom accountant's wish
So builder's-choice white
every hair showed

Tile bird-egg speckled sink
tub and commode chosen
from a 1960 Red Devil color chart

Mirror big as an
XXL so big How big Sooo
big too embarrassed to pee
so big others can watch

Saturday ritual: imagine
a toy dog in the sink
so so suburban

All that [   ] cornered
Shampoo like a rabid smile
Dog shrinks

under the Kohler bubble-stream
snapping as if you were his dentist
So sewn cutely

in a towel like a diaper
you want to rinse him
in the toilet.

Michael A. Sickler

I committed myself to respond to this same assignment during the first work-
shop in which I employed the bathroom prompt. After many false starts,
failed attempts, and numerous revisions, the resulting poem appeared in my
first collection, *Coaxing Nectar from Longing*.

Ugly Duckling

Indifferent swans floated pointless
among the pink and gray cattails
of our bathroom walls.

Porcelain honeycombed the territory
between toilet and tub,
Italian-ice cool beneath bare feet.
In the middle of a fitful night,
this was both oasis and cell.

The mirror initiated its lying habit early,
back licked by a silver-tongued devil.

Bathing could not dispense dread.
Bubbles held no consequence.
Dreams turned rancid
and parents fell deaf to sobbing.

The steam hasn't cleared.
It obscures this nightmare face.

No towel absorbs the night sweats
well enough to stop them.
Nothing squelches the callous silence of swans.

An autobiographical poem can be self-indulgent, self-deprecating, self-congratulatory. It can also be typical. Given that the human experience is repetitive and that the themes available to us may not vary that much from writer to writer, this trigger is an unusual approach to the poetic self-portrait. It is also a challenge to change the angle of self-examination. There is tremendous personal value in accepting this prompt, even if it never leaves the pages of your journal. Try it and push yourself to detach from your own myths to create the memoir poem that heralds all you are as a human, starting in that room that, until now, was referenced in whispers and euphemisms.

Georgia A. Popoff is a community poet, educator, spoken word producer, and managing editor of *The Comstock Review.* A teaching poet in schools and community settings, Popoff is writer-in-residence to several school districts in New York State. She also provides professional development to schools and community-based organizations and has presented at numerous conferences both nationally and abroad. Her poetry collections include *Coaxing Nectar from Longing* (Hale Mary Press, 1997) and *The Doom Weaver* (Main Street Rag Publications, 2008). Currently, she is on the faculty of the Downtown Writer's Center, the Syracuse chapter of the YMCA national Writers Voice program. In addition to creative writing, she has published critical writing in *The Comstock Review,* New York Foundation for the Arts "Chalkboard," and the *Teaching Artist Journal.* Her collaboration with Quraysh Ali Lansana, *Our Difficult Sunlight: A Guide to Poetry, Literacy, and Social Justice in Classrooms and Community,* was released by Teachers & Writers Collaborative in early 2011.

Jane Hilberry

My Mother's Clothes

My all-time favorite writing exercise is a simple prompt for a Natalie Goldberg–style freewrite: write about your mother's clothes. The poem below is one of many I've written on this subject.

Driving

About to step out of the sleeve of her body,
my mother wants to keep all of her clothes.
She thinks she'll wear the fuchsia shirt again.
She says she wants to start driving. In truth,
she never liked to drive, pushing the wheel
one way or the other in tiny increments.
The speeds on the highway scared her.

It's a simple topic, but incredibly powerful. It's a short cut to good writing because it gets students to use specific images without any lectures about concrete and abstract language. (You can discuss that afterwards.)

It also bonds a class very quickly. Without being confessional, the pieces reveal a tremendous amount about each student's family life and background, about the texture of their upbringings. And it touches on that very central piece of the psyche, the relationship with the mother.

I used to use this exercise on the first day of a class just because it did such a powerful job of introducing students to one another. I've backed away from that a bit because sometimes the material can be too emotional for a first class, especially if someone has lost a mother. Now I tend to wait until there's some safety established in the group before bringing in this exercise.

Procedure

I. The Set-Up You can set up the usual Goldberg guidelines for freewriting—write for ten minutes, keep your pen moving, try not to censor yourself. It's also not necessary to stay on the given topic. I make it clear ahead of time that students will have the opportunity to read aloud but that no one is required to; one's primary loyalty is to the writing, so if it's a choice between writing something you can read aloud and writing what you need to write, always write what you need to.

Since some students may not have grown up with their mothers, it's important to qualify the topic by saying "your mother—or whoever played the role of mother in your life."

II. The Follow-Up Once students have finished the timed ten-minute writing, I give guidelines (still following Goldberg) for listening to or receiving the pieces: listen from the heart, suspend criticism, don't comment on one another's freewrites.

If there's time (this might take 30–35 minutes in a group of twelve), you can have students "give back" phrases from the writings. For example, immediately after Joe reads his piece, the other students simply say words and phrases they remember from the writing. They don't say "the part about the brown shoes" or (worse) "I like the part about the brown shoes." Instead, they just say the *exact words* they remember: "the worn-down heel." This is a nice non-judgmental form of feedback. The writer feels heard, and the listeners tune in better while each piece is being read. The remembered phrases will usually be the strongest parts of the piece.

III. Revision After students read their pieces out loud, you can do an in-class revision. A strict and arbitrary constraint works best: take your freewrite and turn it into a twelve-line poem made up of three four-line stanzas. If time permits, it's fun to hear the revisions as well.

Otherwise, students can take the freewrites home and revise them using their own methods.

An Example

Here's an example of a freewrite and the poem (revised on her own) that resulted, written by a student, Rachel Feder.

> **Original Freewrite:** Write About Your Mother's Clothes
>
> My mom and I *share* clothes. It's not a generation thing or a small thing or a memory thing. It's a sisterly thing, but no it isn't. It's a cloth thing, a curves thing, a paper-cut-out-of-you-a-little-larger thing, a can I steal this thing, a pearls thing, a grandmother thing.
>
> My gold necklace is my mother's and is one hundred years old and once when I made it blush she told me only to think of how much it has seen. I want to be a necklace for a hundred years and press myself to soft skin and watch nights and lives and get kissed so, so many times by accident. I want to be wrought with secrets, I want my clasp to be tricky, I want to be a necklace for one hundred years

and fall onto soft earth and be lost and be found. But mostly I want to be found. I want to be found and clasped and told that I am gold. I want it to be true. I want to be tucked away and given. I want everyone who holds me to look in my eyes and say *Oh, to think what she has seen.*

Thing

Once, I made a necklace blush.
You told me, *think of how much it has seen:*

one hundred years of skin,
accidental kiss, the neck

metal-blocked, the truth-touched
blush. I want

to be wrought with secrets like that fallen
filigree, that tricky clasp tricking

and clasping. I want to be a necklace
for one hundred golden years.

Look into my eyes.
Think what I have seen.

Rachel Feder

Jane Hilberry contributed two exercises to *Wingbeats*. See page 11 for her biography.

Love Letter to a Stranger

The San Antonio-based creative collaborative Refarm Spectacle recently asked me, along with a number of other writers and artists, to write a "love letter to a stranger." The resulting one hundred-plus letters were then distributed, anonymously, to people on the street during a city-wide arts festival.

One day, mid-semester, feeling fresh out of original ideas, I spontaneously gave this assignment to my undergraduate poetry class. The poems—some of the best written all year—that resulted from this relatively simple prompt confused, surprised, and delighted me, kind of like love.

I've since given some thought to why the exercise worked so well, as well as created a few variations.

Rationale

This is, at its core, an exercise on writing an epistle. *Epistola* is Latin for *letter,* and an epistle is simply a poem that is a also a letter to someone. From Horace addressing Augustus, to Paul in the Bible, to Ezra Pound's wonderful "River-Merchant's Wife," to Lucille Clifton chatting up Clark Kent, the epistolary form has proven diverse and timeless. I've long found that asking students to write a poem to someone helps focus their images, tighten language, and establish strong tone. But sometimes these poems can be all back-story reportage about the time we did this and the time we did that, or dissolve into rants about how you did me wrong. Writing a love letter to a stranger takes the innate intimacy of an epistle a step further, requiring invention of an imagined other, and creation of details about why we might find ourselves loving them, which is sort of like writing towards, and trying to love, the strangers that live inside each of us.

Procedure

I've had the most success keeping this exercise straightforward, basically walking into a room, and saying, "Write a love letter to a stranger. Now. Go." But this exercise can also be done in two parts:

1. Students look at some epistles from a wide range of poets and discuss how the poems express emotion and/or tension between speaker and recipient. Epistle poems for this discussion might include:

- "The River-Merchant's Wife: A Letter" —Ezra Pound
- "note, passed to superman" —Lucille Clifton
- "Letter to Simic from Boulder" —Richard Hugo
- "The going. The letters. The staying." —Joshua Beckman
- "As Children Together" —Carolyn Forché

II. Depending on the model poems, students can then imitate the relationship, say a letter-poem to someone they can't talk to because the person is far away or deceased. Or perhaps a letter to someone they can't talk to because the person is famous, or even a letter-poem to someone they know intimately but for some reason can't tell what they need to say in real life.

Examples

Love Letter to a Stranger

We could sit through the morning
feeding off the land
and discuss the disappointment
of a fallen orange,
the flexibility of a stick,
the tune of a rippled pond edge.
We could forget about every piece
of time, and try to map the horizons
in our skin, the setting lights
creased within our hands.
We could let the night wade in
drunk off the sun
and stumble home on a different road
with the buzzings and stirrings
of a time when we realized
that all we need lies within
the friction between
the hands of a fellow wanderer.

Megan Peak

love letter to a stranger

the definition of insanity
is doing the same thing
    over & over
expecting different results.

there is a man i always see
on the street or near a booth
inside the whataburger
on san pedro. he wears the
same dark brown pants,
hole showing a hint of
billfold beneath his right
pocket & a navy sweater
(even in the summertime).

he either looks a little
like karl marx,
or
karl marx looks
a little like
a homeless man.
    i write poems
    over and over
even my friends
& family
can barely   decipher
them
so it's not really a
stretch to write
to a stranger.

i can't pick my stranger,
or karl marx's doppleganger
might be reading this.

i think i could admit to him
that i've run out of ideas.

i could tell him that i fill
empty spaces with line
breaks
&
ampersands.

i could tell him that i love him.

that i love everyone. but only
from the blissful anonymity
of this page
without feeling shame.

but i hesitate to say anything
to an unknown stranger. i
am only willing to report
that my orange & white
triangle had a number five
on it today & my dog hates
when i listen to daniel johnston.

Clint Robertson

Variations

One variation on this exercise is to focus on the "stranger" you know well, a former self you'd like to leave behind, or a self uncovered in someone you thought you knew intimately. I've included two poems of my own generated from this variation, "Love Letter to a Stranger (Girl)" being a former self and "Love Letter to a Stranger (Suicide)" being a hidden self in someone else. Both poems are efforts at giving voice to those sorts of strangers.

Love Letter to a Stranger (Girl)

Blood warmed the green
stones around your neck.

Closer to it, the moon
smells like gunpowder.

The man who last
walked there would

now erase his steps.
All night our beach

tumbles pieces of broken
wine bottle soft

enough for a hand
reaching down.

In junior high,
I rubbed an eraser

on the back of mine
until the skin ripped—

we called this
the sissy test.

Love Letter to a Stranger (Suicide)

Of all the creatures, it's said there are those
best defined by what they escape from,
and those who are always escaping;
the mice worrying our walls, loud

as bartime Harleys chucking gravel
up and down 2 a.m., seem to be both,
while your chatter what sounds loudest
when the wheels and claws stop.

Hello, my name is Wynn, and I'll be your
customer tonight. Why yes, I'd love to try
the new green tea frappie frappie. Oh yippee!
Brother, I would want to sing of your

driving gloves and two-dollar bills,
of bubble tea and bitter pills, all choice,
but your mother's voice gnaws the wires,
pure and trapped, and I can't escape that.

Something has to happen next to make a story.
Were this forest, we'd say birds
ate your path back from the dark rooms
where you hid, practicing.

On the prairie, crowds of dandelions
return first after the long summer fires.
But this is Houston, city of closed doors,
and your profile rises from every key I try.

Someone else sees the molars of a distant
mountain range. If we become people because
of what we want, and nights I wish the quick
and painless demise of living things,

kicking the mousetraps, upside down
and empty at dawn, then what? Red eyes
can now be removed from the photographs.
You see how they run? And just because

I might really have liked you to move somewhere
warm and far as Molokai, holidaying there
with nice people unrelated to mine,
doesn't mean I wanted you to die.

Jenny Browne was a James Michener Fellow in Poetry at the University of Texas–Austin, 2004–06 and now teaches creative writing at Trinity University in San Antonio. She's the author of two collections, *At Once* and *The Second Reason,* both from the University of Tampa Press, and has received literature grants from the San Antonio Artist Foundation, the Writers' League of Texas, and The Writer's Center in Washington, D.C. Her poems have appeared in numerous journals, including *American Poetry Review, AGNI, Bat City Review, Gulf Coast, Measure, Puerto del Sol,* and the *Southeast Review.*

Dressing

Whenever I write, I always envision myself writing toward a wall. Sometimes the wall is formidable, utterly imposing, with a height, breadth and depth I can't fathom. Sometimes it's hardly a wall at all—it's fluttering and practically transparent, looking as if I could simply poke a finger through to let light tumble in from the other side.

These flimsier walls are the ones I confront and conquer. For instance, I worry constantly about my granddaughter—her bouts with moodiness, skin that won't clear, skirts that are arguably too short, whispered phone conversations I find myself straining to hear, and the way she's buffeted about by her friendships—in the bosom of popularity one moment, ostracized the next.

But after I consulted with the harried and equally confounded guardians of other adolescent girls, I knew I could write my way into and through what had frightened me. I wasn't alone. Every morning, in households all over the world, other perfectly sane adults cowered in front of a closed bedroom door, wondering who, or what, would emerge. I'm not alone. And my fifteen-year-old is not an anguished misguided rebel on the verge of heroin addiction, self-mutilation, and a snickering, bejeweled boyfriend nicknamed Thug. She's just a teenager.

The walls that appear impenetrable present the greatest challenge. I see myself getting closer and closer to them as I write. Often I turn back after I've barely glanced the impossibility of the wall. Other times, some combination of verb and noun, hard and whispered rhyme, pushes me right up to the iron chill of the barrier. I touch it. Emboldened, I shove a little, then a little harder, only to feel the wall reassert itself and grow steely with resolve.

There's a wall with the face of my son, the muttering and brooding stranger who was imprisoned for two years, whose name I buried while my friends' overachieving offspring were snagging their Ph.D.s, considering a run for office, or touring Europe with their jazz bands. Another wall is shaped exactly like my estranged mother, stubbornly clinging to my fallibilities as her own, approaching death still numbed and bitter about my singular obsession with my father, who was murdered during a robbery more than thirty years ago.

Then there's the wall I've built myself, bricked with scarlet moments of public humiliation—a soul-draining and regrettable first marriage, a fight for a child, and a bout with depression so debilitating I purchased a gun.

On the other side of these high, wide walls, poems live. I have no doubt that they're the best poems I've never written. These are the stanzas that stubbornly elude me—words, plump with revelation and discovery.

This exercise addresses the problem of tackling tough emotional content. I couldn't write about my mother because of all the guilt, anger, and fear that churned from every first attempted line. I couldn't write about my son because the shame resurrects. I couldn't write about how my shortcomings have changed me because it required a public admission of being less than perfect. Although actually no one is. Perfect.

I've come to believe that the secret lies in accessing that space beyond the wall just once, even if you have to trick yourself into the trip. I designed this exercise to do just that. If you can do this, if you can write into and past what evades you, the wall flashes thin and you see clearly what taunts you on the other side. You can reach it. You can write it.

Procedure

I. We begin with a general discussion of poems that *have* been successful, usually poems of friendship or family. Then I indulge in a bit of diversion by asking participants to name the one person they love most in the world. At this point, guards are down, and the expectation is that we're about to trudge some oft-traveled route—penning an epistle, perhaps, or a persona poem, or a poem about some particular aspect of their relationship with the person they've named.

II. Instead I say: Imagine you have walked into a room. The room, scrubbed raw and spotless, is almost entirely white—white walls, a white ceiling, white floors. Whatever is not white is a glaring, medicinal silver. In the exact center of the room is a steel slab. Upon that slab is the naked lifeless form of the person you love most in this world.

It is your job to dress this person for burial.

At this point, I leave time for incredulous groans, wide-eyed stupor, and fierce signs of resistance. The writers will feel duped, as if they've been forced into their own impossibility. Some will immediately attempt to soften the blow: "Can I do my best friend instead? Yeah, I love him more than I love my mother." *Sure, you do.*

Stand firm. You are urging them toward the dark place on the other side of the wall. If they can claw their way through this exercise, nothing will seem unreachable.

III. What makes this impossible possible? What makes this poem the one that just may begin to break the brick?

I instruct the participants to think of this as a *process* poem—*First I do A, then I do B, and when I'm done with that, it's on to C.* Slow the process down as much as you can. Instead of saying "Then I put on his pants," imagine the initial touching, the lifting of the foot. Which leg first? Why? Do you notice old injuries, moles, scars, clipped or overgrown toenails, a big toe that has always rested high upon its neighbor? Which particular pair of pants? Why? Or you begin by brushing the hair, perhaps applying make-up. You consider bruises, imperfections. You lift the head to ease a blouse over, guide arms through resistant sleeves. You think about jewelry, maybe see the person naked for the first time. Make the process, the step-by-step, the core of the poem—until it's no longer the core of the poem.

It's okay to veer off into memory, to imagine how the death came about or reminisce about remembered moments, but you must *always* return to the table and your task. I've had students never get any further than the closet and the selection of the clothes, hours before entering the room. Some just freeze in the room, drifting into an easy nostalgia ("I remember the days we used to . . .") without ever stepping any closer to the body. Poetic though they may be, these are all diversions. This is what it means to write towards a wall. To get past the wall, you must go on with the task at hand. Be frustratingly slow and deliberate. Get the job done. When the poem is finished, you'll realize that you've dwelled for quite some time on the other side of that wall. And you've survived.

Once we get past the inevitable "You gotta be kidding" phase, responses to this exercise have never failed to amaze me. Once participants realize where they are, and that—at least temporarily—they're going to have to stay there, they draw from the deep well of their creative selves to keep from going crazy. In short, they remember that they are poets.

Examples

Pedicure

No one remembers your feet.
After they leave, I linger
remembering how you used to
run around with chipped toenail polish
in flip-flops all summer and I suspect

someone has just slid socks and flats over
these same undone toes.

I am your sister.
I cannot let you be buried
in ashy ankles and flecked paint.
Never could figure out why
you liked your polish in shades of bruise:
eggplant, navy, hunter green.
Maybe it had something to do with
how much you hated feet.
Hated people touching your feet,
hated anyone else's feet coming near you.

I perch on the wheeled stool
and get to work on your left foot first,
lifting the patent black flat and rolling down
the sheer dress sock, slow—slow.
Your foot feels too light,
and I half expect you to wake up
and slam it back down or yank it away
complaining how your sole is ticklish.

But you don't.

So I get the right foot ready too.
Patent flat off.
Sheer sock off.
And I was right.
Your toes are a hot mess.
What is left of a shade that looks
like a cross between raspberry and mocha,
like it would have made a better coffee drink
than a color, mottles your toenails, so I pull out
the blue remover, the cotton balls,
and start rubbing away the polish
one toe at a time.

Your ankles are smooth and dry; the skin looks cracked
and all I have is a little bit left of Mom's blessed oil
in my purse to rub into them.
So I do, sealing the rifts in your skin with olive oil
brimming with gold flakes and myrrh and her prayers.

And it is too quiet, too cold.
And I imagine if it was just us, really us,
and not Death too, there would be music,
so I start singing, and you and I both know
I can't carry a tune to save my life,
and the only song that comes
to mind is by Frankie Valli.
And I hope you're somewhere laughing at me,
picking up the chorus I'm dropping all over the floor.

When your toenails are clean, I pull out dark
platinum polish called Mithril from my purse.
You were always a little bit razor blade,
a little bit shooting star.
The polish, as its name promises,
shines like nothing could chip it, not a jackhammer,
not some hero's mythic blade.
I finish the first and begin a second coat,
getting into it now, the back and forth of the little brush
coloring in your nail, I forget for the most part your skin
feels like the outside of an ice cooler.
And this is my last memory of us:
me, you, and your bony, yella', size 11 feet.

Somewhere, I imagine you are singing too.
The polish is all on now, but still mostly wet—
I lean forward and begin
to blow.

Bianca Spriggs

Sweet Silver

Goddamnit, Sadie. You would have it cold in here. Always, that AC cranked so high I can't bend my fingers, always that air through the vent misting like ghosts coming down from that stucco ceiling, and me, bundled up in a hoodie and fleece blanket on your white leather couch.

Oh, Sadie. It's *Florida* outside, and I can't bend my fingers, they're all bent up, just like Martha Rose used to do when she contorted her hands each night showing me just how bad she needed her arthritis medicine, which meant I needed to stop and get her a case of Old Milwaukee on the way home. You remember that? Rose and her arthritis medicine? You remember her? Do you? Do you remember? Fuck, well, I suppose you do. Either that or you've gone and

forgot everything
by now, who knows.
And here I am
with what's left

trying to figure out how to warm my hands enough even to get started. But I've brought what I needed, don't you worry none—I've got your double-starched white button-down with the collar cut off like you like. I've got your pink fluffy sweatpants with the elastic pulled. I've got your tiny house shoes, right here, curled into two letter *C*s, still hot from the dryer. And yes, ma'am, your Norell too, a fresh bottle, and your fake lashes, and Lord knows we gotta do something with that stringy hair of yours, so here's your Clairol Sweet Silver and your pink popcorn bowl full of hair rollers. . . . don't worry, I found the German luger at the bottom and left that at home with Frankie, wasn't no need for me to bring that in here,

ain't nobody but me
and you, ain't no body left
to shoot

or perhaps maybe you think you could sit up from that concrete slab and wave that gun at me, dyke that I've become, yes, nobody can't say you didn't call it—all those years back when I was going through my divorce and you said, *Shit, Coey, you ain't no lesbian are you?* And I said, *Sadie, please. Besides. Why does a grandmother got to go such places?* And you said, *Well, if that man was touching you right, you might not feel like you do,* and we laughed it up, laughed all the while about him not having nothing even to diddle with, *like a hot tootsie roll in the sun,* you said, and we laughing

and dyeing your roots, back when you felt good enough to let me at it with a rat comb and a bottle of peroxide, back when you had your walker but we could still get you to the sink, you yelling and cussing that the water was too one way or the other, too hot or too cold, the water pressure about to blow your scalp off or like a monkey pissing from a high tree, yes, those were good times, Sadie. But now you're going to sit still,

sit
perfectly
still
for me, this time.

Nickole Brown

Ursa Minor

I can tell you, I've loved him each day:
the birth of him, that wet, red work—
to the death of him, the death of him.
As his sister, I dress him for incineration
not burial, because he was Buddhist and a
growing theist and a boy who marveled.

So I run my hands the length of his body,
the miraculous bone and muscle: feet scarred
and trained to dig in hard those 90 feet from home
to first—so here are your cleats, tied and tanned.
Then his thighs, tree trunks of sinew and bone—
jeans for these because he liked comfort, all the time.
Even at the lake: whittling a pointy stick because

he was young and inexperienced, in jeans and sweater.
I teased him, then, touching his back with my fingertips
but he just smiled.

Then torso: sculpted just these last two years out of a
doughy boy into an athlete. And those broad shoulders
so unlike mine. I choose a blue t-shirt because his eyes
were that spidered blue of a cracked open star.
Our mother: *my blue-eyed boy, my green-eyed girl.*
And his arms: thick and strong like cut limestone;
left tattooed, like his sister's—Sanskrit prayer in fat
black ink. That day: he held my hand as the needle sank
into him, smiling to make me feel better, telling
me that it wasn't as bad as it sounded.
Then face: same sloped forehead, nose, mouth, ears. In life,
smiles the same with that wobble. And I smooth
my fingers over his eyebrows—a leftover game from
childhood—and send my palm over his hair to the crown
and it's all joy from here on out because we were so
disarming, the pair of us. We swaggered, we swayed.

Jenny McDougal

Patricia Smith is the author of *Blood Dazzler* (Coffee House Press, 2008), a National Book Award finalist; *Teahouse of the Almighty* (Coffee House Press, 2006), a National Poetry Series winner; *Big Towns, Big Talk* (Zoland Books, 2002); *Close to Death* (Zoland Books, 1998); and *Life According to Motown* (Tia Chucha, 1991). She also penned the groundbreaking history *Africans in America* (Harcourt Brace, 1998) and the children's book *Janna and the Kings* (Lee and Low, 2003). Her poems have appeared in *Poetry, The Paris Review, Tin House, Callaloo, TriQuarterly,* and other journals, as well as many anthologies—most recently *The 100 Best African-American Poems, Black Nature, Word Warriors, The Spoken Word Revolution, The Oxford Anthology of African-American Poetry,* and *Best American Poetry 2011.* Smith, recognized as one of the world's most formidable performers, is also a four-time national individual champion of the notorious and wildly popular poetry slam, the most successful competitor in slam history. She is a professor of creative writing at the City University of New York, and is on the faculty of both Cave Canem and the Stonecoast M.F.A. program at the University of Southern Maine.

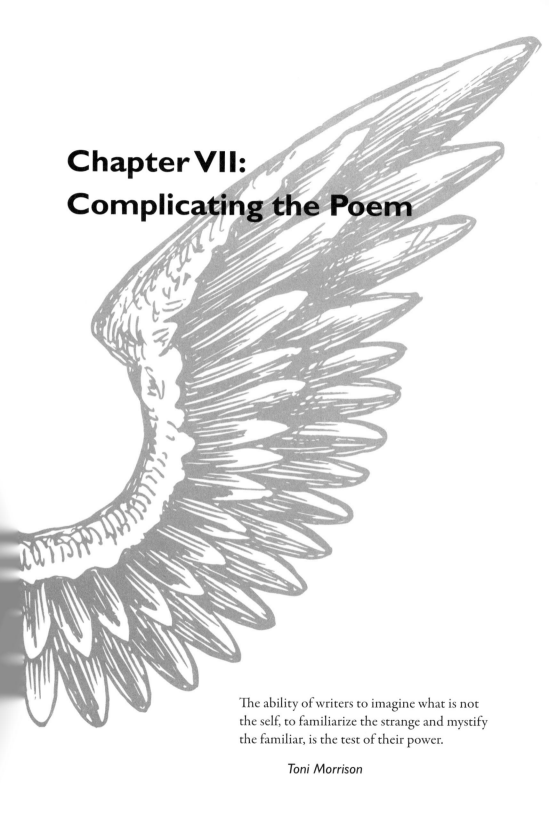

Chapter VII:
Complicating the Poem

The ability of writers to imagine what is not
the self, to familiarize the strange and mystify
the familiar, is the test of their power.

Toni Morrison

Teaching Imagination

In his essay "Four Temperaments and the Forms of Poetry," Gregory Orr defines imagination as "the flow of image to image or thought to thought. It moves as a stream of associations, either concretely (the flow of image) or abstractly (the flow of thought)." This exercise is designed to help writers who rely on narrative or structure at the expense of the imagination of the poem. It encourages students to take risks, to trust their intuition, to explore new subject matter and language styles.

Procedure

I. Reading It is helpful for students to examine poems that privilege imagination as a primary device and to discuss how imagination complicates a poem, how it adds another dimension to the persona or the speaker. Students might benefit from reading any number of poems easily found online. Specific poems that I recommend include:

- Paul Celan's "Corona"
- Emily Dickinson's "I felt a cleaving in my mind"
- Thomas James' "Mummy of a Lady Named Jemutesonekh"
- Rainer Maria Rilke's "Lament"
- César Vallejo's "Black Stone Lying on a White Stone" (see page 105 for a translation of Vallejo's poem).

II. Index Cards Distribute packets of fifty small index cards or slips of paper to each student. If you are working alone for this exercise, have a supply of index cards or slips of paper ready.

III. Fifty Questions I ask students a series of questions (see pages 252–53 for examples). They anwer each question on a separate index card, each answer in a complete sentence. I ask them to answer quickly, without over-thinking. I assure students that no one will look at their answers unless they decide to share them. Students should feel comfortable answering questions honestly and without worry. They can decide what is appropriate for a poem later.

IV. Selection and Arrangement After students have answered at least fifty questions, they look through their answers amd compose poems by arranging at least ten of the index cards in a particular order. Once they have selected the cards they want to use, they are encouraged to try various orders—to make surprising leaps. Writers may revise or polish to compose the best poem possible; however, they should resist trying to write connective tissue between cards/answers, as doing so defeats the purpose.

Variations

There are a couple of ways that one might expand on the exercise. First, I like to give students a chance to read and discuss Gregory Orr's essay from which the definition of *imagination* comes. Orr's essay succinctly defines the poetic imagination and its importance. Second, sometimes I let students submit their own questions. Teachers might ask each student to compose one or more questions and add them to the teacher's list. Writers who work alone might reach out to a network of friends or fellow writers, asking them to compose questions for one or more lists.

Tips for Your List of Questions

I'm including a list of sample questions that have proven successful for my students, but I encourage writers to add, delete, and edit as they see fit. It's good to choose several questions that might draw out similar themes while resisting a logical progression. For example, in the list that follows, there are questions about sleep, about the writer's bedroom, and about dreams, among other subjects. I also recommend questions that force writers to write different kinds of sentences as well as to draw on different topics, such as science or mathematics or history.

Sample Questions

1. When and where were you born?
2. Tell me something unique about your mother.
3. When it's quiet, what don't you want to think about?
4. Describe something in the room.
5. Tell me a secret.
6. Describe a disaster without naming it.
7. What's the most important date of the year and why?
8. Describe a historical event.
9. What are you scared of? Why? Be specific.
10. Describe how a dream plays out in your mind.
11. If you could be anywhere right now, where would you be and what would you do?

12. Write a command.
13. Who are you closest to and why?
14. What do you regret?
15. What are you most proud of?
16. Describe the last time that you felt joy.
17. Who put you to sleep as a child and how?
18. How do you fall asleep now?
19. How well do you sleep?
20. What do you find vulgar?
21. What has changed that you wish hadn't?
22. What do you want to change?
23. Describe your bedroom.
24. Describe the taste in your mouth.
25. Describe what the blind see in their dreams.
26. Describe a happy moment. Begin with "Once. . . ."
27. Describe a sad moment. Begin with "Once. . . ."
28. Write a sentence that begins, "I'd be lying if I said. . . ."
29. Quote the punch line of a joke.
30. Paraphrase the end of a story.
31. What are your favorite flowers and why?
32. Describe love in concrete terms.
33. Describe anger in concrete terms.
34. Rewrite one of your answers in a completely new syntax.
35. Say something in another language.
36. Describe a scientific principle.
37. What fills you with fear?
38. What fills you with awe?
39. What is the difference between fear and awe?
40. Define madness.
41. Define grace.
42. Ask me a question.
43. Write down two things that you miss.
44. Write a list of four things you hope never to see again.
45. Finish this sentence: "My name means. . . ."
46. Finish this sentence: "Back then. . . ."
47. Finish this sentence: "Once and only once. . . ."
48. Finish this sentence: "Never. . . ."
49. Finish this sentence: "I cannot. . . ."
50. Finish this sentence: "I wish. . . ."

An Example

Lullaby

I envy the cats
and their perpetual sleep.

My mother is descended of Charlemagne
And several King Edwards and
Her own mom, with her scattered mind.
Mama put me to bed each night
Intoxicating blonde hair and lotioned skin
But I would not go down—
Awake, under blankets
Imagining myself a kitten in its mother's womb.

I slept deeply for years
In New Orleans
Crescent mama
Now the city sleeps
Without me.
The day she drowned was thick and red
And all the way in Texas
I couldn't breathe.

If god came back
He'd have to tell us
He's sorry.

Katherine Morrow Jones DePalma

Blas Falconer is the author of *A Question of Gravity and Light* (University of Arizona Press, 2007) and the co-editor of *Mentor and Muse: Essays from Poets to Poets* (Southern Illinois University Press, 2010). His second full-length collection of poems, *The Foundling Wheel,* is forthcoming from Four Way Books. He teaches poetry and coordinates creative writing at Austin Peay State University, in Clarksville, Tennessee, where he is the poetry editor of *Zone 3: A Literary Journal* and Zone 3 Press.

The Bermuda Triangle

would like to offer a simple exercise in kick-starting the imagination, a means to gently ambush the censoring mind in order to arrive at the more nimble, multi-layered realms of the unexpected. Tricking past linear thinking can be difficult on days we can't get going, flooded and distracted with the daily detritus, filled with past and present obligations—or just faced with the anxiety of the empty page. This exercise is a form of play and a strategy that brings spontaneity to the process of writing poems.

Following the instructions below, you can write a decent working draft of a poem in thirty to forty-five minutes—or at the very least generate enough material for several poems to come. Through whiplash leaping juxtapositions, combining opposites, and nonlinear navigation, this is an exercise in surprise and most of all in surprising yourself. In Robert Frost's famous introduction "The Figure a Poem Makes," he says, "No tears in the writer, no tears in the reader. No surprise for the writer, no surprise for the reader. For me the initial delight is in the surprise of remembering something I didn't know I knew."

Frost also says about the poem, "It begins in delight and ends in wisdom." Who knows what your poem will begin and end with in this exercise, as it is a journey into the unknown? I call this exercise the Bermuda Triangle for two reasons. The first is that you will be venturing into the unknown, into the possibly threatening and uncanny territory that is your mind and imagination. Second the mode of composition and construction of the poem is a kind of triangulation. The poem will ultimately move quickly to weave and juxtapose the three points of our triangle, but first we have to generate these three points.

I: Generating the Triangle

Point A: The Fear List To begin this exercise, take a sheet of paper and write on the page from left to right all the things that you fear—from the little mundane things to the biggies. These can be forgotten fears from the past to projected future fears, both real and imaginary. (Once someone wrote that she was terrified of butterflies.) Write quickly, and try to capture whatever pops into your mind. It is important to write from left to right across the page rather than as a list down the page, as you want one image or phrase to flow into the next, to see how one thought becomes the inspiration for the next. After about five but not more than ten minutes, stop writing.

Point B: The Desire List For this list, write all that you desire or have desired, from the everyday to the sublime. (In this exercise the sublime, the mundane, the profane, and the sacred often become interchangeable.) Write from the past, the present, and the future. As with your list of fears, write across the page from left to right instead of making a vertical list. Try to be as specific as possible. After free-writing for five but no more than ten minutes, you are ready for the third list.

Point C: The Image List Here you are invited to write a list of sensory images, fragments, and little word pictures of colors, sounds, smells, textures—a blue bicycle, a half-socked foot on an olive oil–stained floor, a red wheelbarrow beside the white chickens, a dog snoring, rain on a swimming pool. These can be invented or remembered. Think of them as little sensory snapshots. Try to incorporate all the five senses and again be as specific and concrete as possible. Again, as with the previous, steps, link your images left to right across the page instead of making a vertical list.

The Completed Triangle By the end of this writing period you have generated three substantial lists—fears, desires, images—the three points of your triangle. If you are working with a group, you might read snippets of your lists aloud to each other; if you are alone, read them to yourself or to your pet. Notice how these lists alone are poems in the making. If you are in a group, notice the similarities and the particularities in the lists, what we share and what remains stubbornly our own. We can think of poems as navigation between the particular and the communal. Also notice how the sounds of the words often propel us to the next entry or memory or thought, reminding us that sound in poetry is often the thread through the labyrinth.

II: Creating the Poem

Now we are ready to start the triangulating process. Look over your three lists and either randomly or purposefully circle three entries in each. Don't think about it too long. Now take ten but no more than fifteen minutes to interweave and construct a poem of ten to fifteen lines that draws from the three entries circled from each of your lists. That means you have nine elements to work from. You don't have to use them all—just make sure the poem draws at least once from each list. Find a way to jumble these elements—to meld and mesh entries from your fear, desire, and image lists. The only restriction is that you cannot use the words *fear* and *desire*. When you are finished, you will surprise yourself with your self and with what you have created.

One theory states that the Bermuda Triangle is the home of a magnetic anomaly, so that you can no longer depend on a compass for accessing true north; this is the metaphor at work in this exercise, in that we are operating without stable polarities and so opposites are rendered ambiguous. The entries from the fear, desire, and image lists often become indistinguishable from one another, showing how opposites attract and create excitement and energy on the page. If you want, you can fine-tune your quick draft of the poem, bringing in the conscious level of the revision process. This exercise can work with other combinations of three. The first two should be opposites; the third, a list derived from the sensory world.

An Example

Here is an example of this exercise from Kaitlyn Owens—her three lists, her quick draft, and her final revised poem. Notice which fragments she took from each list and the way she created her surprising and engaging poem based on the lists.

Fears clowns, balloons, umbrellas, fire, drowning, aneurisms, even numbers, being pinned under a car, throwing up, finding a dead body, tidal waves, hurricanes, tsunamis, flash floods, tornadoes, someone stealing my blanket, strokes, airplanes, fireworks, having a bone pop out of my skin, people I love dying, me dying in a painful way, being homeless, going on Welfare, getting pregnant, not being able to get pregnant, miscarriages, asteroids, the dark

Desires a dog, a large paycheck, rich parents, the ability to become invisible, time travel, quiet home with a bay window, my own library with shelves so tall I need a rolling ladder to reach all the books, healing powers, the ability to breathe underwater, a Jiffy Treat Banana Split Cyclone, to play professional football, to be a man, to not have to work and get everything, a hound's-tooth print dress, an owl tattoo, a pet pot-bellied pig, a new laptop, someone to clean my house, someone to organize my closet, the innate ability to be organized, not to be allergic to cats, tangerines, taffy, some Chapstick

Image Snapshots giant amber beer bottle statue submerged in the front yard, a dog's leg popping out of socket under the car's crunch, the crackle of Cocoa Krispies in a coffee mug, underwater diving dogs barking SOS, steamed broccoli burning mama's hands as she pours the water out, the creak of cicadas, tracing your name with a pen cap on my thigh, goose bumps from whispers, morning hair after taking Tylenol PM,

black licorice stuck to dad's fingers, an exploded pen stain on my back-
pack, a broken caterpillar leg stuck to your panty hose, August at 6 a.m.
before the school bus comes, an orange-checkered flannel shirt covered
with back sweat, the smell of donuts frying at the county fair, a carnie
with no teeth and two black eyes, midnight laundry machine buzzing off

Draft Poem:

A miscarriage occurs when you pick
a centipede off your pantyhose,
his wiggly legs will get stuck
to the nylon fibers and pop off
even if you mean to be gentle,
me docked down at the bay
in disbelief that the waves will make
my bones crackle like Cocoa Krispies in a coffee mug.
I think hurricanes look prettier in a hound's-tooth print dress.
I think your answers are taffy and the weight
of the water won't drown me, won't fill my lungs
with salt but instead will make things mirror bright enough
so that I can see the centipede on a fish hook
being cast out into the ocean
so it can catch a meal big enough
to feed an entire grinning family

Revised Poem:

At the Clinic

A little miscarriage occurs
when you pick a centipede
off of your pantyhose.
In the process, his legs
are sure to gel to the nylon
and even if you tug him
real gentle, one's bound
to pop off. The tiny green thing
will stop wiggling
in a few seconds. I can see the doctor

through the windows
of the Hilton Head Prompt Care
scratching the stubs of his beard
and rehearsing breaking bad news
in front of a mirror. I think
he learned how to do all this
in med school, learned how a young girl
bleeding needs to be dealt with
softly, needs to be asked
where her mother is,
needs to be told that maybe
this is best for everyone
and that it can stay her own secret,
that ectopic is another word
for being in the wrong place
at the wrong time. But when
he comes traipsing in,
his words glug like ocean water.
And underneath his white jacket,
he's wearing his Sunday best,
smug as Moses parting the Red Sea.
He offers to have a nurse hold my hand,
but I shake my head. I think hurricanes
look prettier when wearing a hound's-tooth dress.
I think the answers are salt water taffy.
        I think that if I smile when the waves
hit, they won't sting. They won't
make my hips crackle
like Cocoa Krispies in a coffee mug.
The weight of the water won't
drown me. It won't fill my lungs
with salt but will instead reflect
sunlight, make things mirror bright
enough that I can see a centipede
on a fish hook being cast out
into the ocean so it can catch
a meal big enough to feed

an entire grinning family,
the water left only with a few air bubbles
from where that fish had been.

Kaitlyn Owens

Catherine Bowman teaches at Indiana University and is the author of the poetry collections *The Plath Cabinet* (Four Way Books), *Notarikon* (Four Way Books), *Rock Farm* (Gibbs Smith), and *1-800-HOT-RIBS* (Gibbs Smith), which was reissued by Carnegie-Mellon University Press as part of its Classic Contemporaries Series. She is the editor of *Word of Mouth: Poems Featured on NPR's "All Things Considered."* Her poems have appeared in *The New Yorker, The Paris Review, Ploughshares, the Harvard Review,* and *The Best American Poetry Series.*

Lisa D. Chavez

Shapeshifting Poems:
The Power of Transformation

We all know how poetry can transform the ordinary into the extraordinary, but sometimes poems themselves get stuck and need some magic to transform them. This exercise, which I've used several times in graduate poetry workshops, focuses on radical revision—a true re-seeing (and re-writing!) of the poem. While I focus on poetry here, it would work just as well in another genre, and while I've always done it in a group, it's also an exercise that a writer could do alone.

I: The Original

I ask students to bring a piece of writing they feel strongly about—something that obsesses them but that for whatever reason is simply not working in its current form. In a workshop setting, we all read the piece ahead of time, and in class the writers tell us something about the poem or story or essay they've brought: how they came to write it, what they like about it, what they believe is not working, or what is causing the piece to be stuck. Then we discuss the piece, focusing on things we find intriguing and also things we thought we needed more information about or were confused by. It's a not a typical workshop critique: we don't expect the writer to revise by making changes to the piece as it is, so we refrain from giving editing suggestions. Instead, I ask everyone to think of ways a piece could be radically revised: would the poem we're looking at be interesting as a short story from another character's point of view? What would the poem look like if it were a lyrical essay? We try to make our suggestions as open as possible—what we're looking for here is possibility.

II: Transformation to Another Literary Genre

I send everyone home and tell them they must completely transform the piece. When we see it next (I usually give a class two weeks for this) the poem must be in prose, or the prose must now be a poem. The goal is to make the new piece as unlike the original as possible. I suggest that people rewrite without looking at the original piece so they can get as far away from it as possible. I also suggest people try a genre they are less—rather than more—comfortable with. Students have told me that when they "cheated" and transformed, say, a poem to a prose poem, they felt they didn't get as much out of the exercise as they would have if they had tried a truly different genre.

In class, we then look at this totally new piece and discuss it in much the same way we did the first time: our discussion focuses around what is intriguing to us in this new transformation and what we might miss from the earlier version. We also make suggestions for the next transformation, which is into another artistic medium altogether.

III: Transformation to Another Art Form

It has been easiest, and the most fun, to have the entire group do the third transformation—from writing to another art form—in the same art form and do it in class. This exercise could also work with everyone choosing a preferred art form, though.

I ask everyone to take their second written piece and make it something that does not contain words. In various classes, we've made masks or dioramas or collages. I simply pick a form, and we all transform our piece into that artistic medium. The masks—molds of our own faces, which we made in class with strips of plaster cast material—were possibly the most fun, but also the messiest and most labor-intensive. The diorama idea started as a joke. When I asked students in a graduate class what they would like our art project to be, someone said that it would be fun to make dioramas, the little three-dimensional scenes housed in shoe boxes that many of us remembered from elementary school. We decided to go with the joke, and we had a lot of fun with it, ending up with some really intriguing mixed-media art projects!

I believe the transformation to an artistic medium works best if it is not a medium that the writer is already quite good at; part of my idea with this stage is to make it feel like play and also to have us as writers return to the earlier stages of trying to master a craft, when we were, perhaps, more interested in process then we were in trying to produce a "work of art." I also think it is freeing to work in a totally different art form, especially in a form we may not be quite as skilled at. It can also be frustrating, but when we are freed from the need to produce a polished final product, our minds are able to take more playful leaps, and we may gain some insights from this process. At the very least, we have fun!

Usually, we spend a class period working on the art project together, and then I ask everyone to finish it at home, and to bring it to our final class, where they will present both the art piece and the final transformation.

IV: Transformation Back to the Original Genre

The final transformation is to rewrite the piece back in its original genre. The poem becomes a poem again—but very different! We've been on a journey with our poems, and they are forever changed. In the final class, I ask writers to present to us their final transformation back to the original form, to share their art piece with us, and also to talk to us about what they learned during their journey of transformation.

Rationale

What I like best about this exercise—and what others have also told me they enjoyed—is that often a writer comes up with more than one piece of writing that is interesting and workable. Perhaps the original poem did not work, but the final one often does, and in between, the writer may have created a story or essay that is also worth working on. Some writers choose to keep something close to the original poem but are happy to discover they now have a story or essay to work on as well. Some like the final piece best. I've done this exercise along with a class several times, and I often end up keeping the middle step, the piece that is transformed into another literary genre. Whatever the end result, transforming a piece through different genres and art forms forces us to examine an original idea in an entirely different light, and it often regenerates the initial excitement and energy that were lost in the drafting process.

We can always learn something from working in a different genre—for example, prose writers can learn more about concise language and precision from poets; poets can learn about character development and setting of scene from prose writers. The forced journey into another form will transform not only the writing, but perhaps the writer too, as he or she learns to move out of the familiar landscape of one genre into the dark woods of another.

An Example

The poem I've included, by Samantha Tetangco, was not her final transformation. She came to the workshop with the first chapter of her novel, which she transformed into a poem, then back to prose, though by the time she'd made the transformational journey, her novel's point of view had shifted, and the opening chapter was now quite different. This is what Sam said of the project:

> Having worked on my novel for over two years now, the first chapters were frustrating me so much that I was unable to write. I couldn't see it anymore. When I transformed it into a poem, however, I was able to access it in a different way. . . . What I got was an emotional core that was lacking

from the original piece. Later, I decided to change the point of view.

The poem, which she wrote from the point of view of her narrator, helped her consider point of view in the novel, and helped her re-see her entire project. Interestingly, her point of view in the novel did not shift to first person, as you might suspect, but began in first person, continued in first person as a persona poem, and then she revised her entire novel into third person! Regardless, the poem works independently of the novel.

To Shannon,
Upon News of Her Engagement (to Someone Else)

While you plant roots, I man the ship
of this hotel lobby and think of the way
you'd call it all a wash. I imagine you
beside the Old Dutch windmill, poking fun
of how it no longer spins. Behind you,
time passes in four different zones
while here, in this city of lost angels,
the second hand has already stopped.

If you were here, I'd tell you how
I hate this city with its purple hued skies
and my doomsday morning drive home.
I spend my nights nestled inside a fountain
amidst pennies cast by a married woman
who sits naked on the ledge of a seventh story
window. She drowns herself in gin—
while I just drown.

This is the City of Angels, after all,
and it doesn't take God to know it isn't heaven.

Samantha Tetangco

Lisa D. Chavez has been teaching creative writing for over twenty-five years. She lives in the mountains of New Mexico with her husband and three dogs. She has published two books of poetry, *In an Angry Season* and *Destruction Bay,* and has also had nonfiction and poetry published in a variety of literary magazines and anthologies.

Rube Goldberg Poems

The idea for these poetry exercises came from watching a video of a Rube Goldberg machine in action. It's a marvelous thing to behold. In this particular video, a ball bearing falls into a bucket. The bucket, once delicately counterbalanced, descends with the new weight of the ball bearing onto a catapult-like device. The catapult fires a wet sponge onto a sheath of paper towels hanging from a toy car. . . .

The genius of the Rube Goldberg machine is its complex machinations in order to achieve a menial task. In this example, the task was to feed a parrot a cracker. What a marvelous metaphor for the process of writing. There are complex rituals that a writer must perform in order to convey a thought, an idea, an emotion.

At about the midpoint of the academic session, I like to give my students an assignment based on Rube Goldberg machines. It's a good assignment to spring on students when they are in the doldrums of the academic session. I change the parameters for this assignment from year to year, but the spirit of the assignment remains consistent—it's a problem-solving/critical-thinking task. What follows are two variations on the Rube Goldberg exercise.

Variation I

Students must write a narrative poem with the following components:

1. The poem must be about a memory or event from childhood.

The structural scaffolding of the poem is the first component. The memory becomes the task that needs to be achieved like the goal of a Rube Goldberg machine. All the other components are devious instruments that slow down the process but eventually become integral moments. When you watch a Rube Goldberg at work, you remember the catapult firing, or the ball bearing weighting down the bucket, but you don't necessarily remember there's a parrot at the end of the machine awaiting his cracker.

2. The poem must contain a scent that speaks.

The second component is an interchangeable one. I suggest using some type of prompt that provides students the opportunity to use synesthesia—the mixing of senses. I've used "a color that sings" in the past, for example.

3. The poem must have the color teal.

The third component is usually a color, but an unusual color. It's far too easy for students to lay claim to colors like red, gold, or blue, so provide them with an uncommon color.

4. The poem must include a kitchen tool.

I like to have a tangible object as the fourth item. Mind you, all of these components are interchangeable with the exception of the first component.

5. The poem must include a neighborhood dog.

The fifth component would not have to be a neighborhood dog. I include one in the requirements here because my memories of childhood are filled with neighborhood dogs. If you can think of a suitable substitute, by all means, provide one for your students.

6. The poem must contain a lyric from a popular song.

The final component provides a type of temporal marker. Students often reflect on what songs were popular at the time of their specific childhood memory.

Variation II

Students must write a narrative poem with the following components:

1. The poem must be about a memory or event from childhood.

Again, the first component is the aim or the goal of the poem. All the other components are there to delay the process.

2. The poem must have the title "Self-Portrait with _____ "

The second component in this example is a leading title. I've often found that with these exercises, if you assist the students with their titles, the rest of the poem seems to have more breathing room. (See also Lisa Russ Spaar's "The Self-Portrait Poem," page 277.)

3. The poem must contain a protractor.

As in the previous example, I like to have a tangible object present in the poem. It forces the poem to maintain its bearings in reality.

4. The poem must have a mythological figure.

The mythological figure in this example can be used as an allusion, or it can be an actual character in the narrative. I leave that up to the writers.

5. The poem must have the color camouflage.

The fifth component in this case is an unusual color, similar to the third component of the previous example.

6. The dead must speak in the poem.

Finally, the sixth component in this exercise is the supernatural element of the dead speaking.

Rationale

This is a good exercise for students at the intermediate to advanced levels in a poetry workshop. It's a challenging assignment that requires students to work on transitions between images. It invites students to explore the possibilities of personal narrative. And it also creates opportunities for problem-solving and critical analysis.

While some students may not be pleased with the results of their poems, it is a good community-building exercise in that it facilitates strong workshop discussions and camaraderie.

An Example

I've provided an example of a Rube Goldberg poem using the second variation. It was written by Phayvanh Luekhamhan, a student I had for a brief workshop.

Self-Portrait with Icarus

Richmond Greyhound Station

Gary, you should have been in the Air Force,
as your dead father's summoned voice demanded.
Now you're 34. I am 34, too. We're strangers awaiting a bus
discussing early retirement and life (if you're lucky) after that.
How many men have you blindfolded or shot?
Being a foot soldier is not all you thought.
What he tried to do: steer you clear of regret.
But you would not be Laika, eternally voided.
No, you wanted homecoming's burning off.

You're heading back to your sister's house.
Colorado City, the old Pontiac, its green paint crusting.

Green: the dress of uniform, of lies, the monochrome of stealth vision,
of *Oh, please, dear God, no. . . .* The future is the dozen more years
        you'll pack
into your parti-colored duffel, alongside your toothbrush and Bible.
My hair is all kinds of grey. Yours will be too.
You're holding a map of Virginia, its accordion pages wilting.
Attractions bleed into roads you will not take.

They treat you like real people, you say, *not like the Army.*
USAF. Shrug and say *it don't matter now.* Your voice
making precious jewels of your vowels. Both wings and guns extract
different kinds of freedom. Gary, your father knew
the exact measure of mistakes. He has set compass and protractor
to the parabola of your spirit, found your melting point.

    Phayvanh Luekhamhan

Oliver de la Paz is the author of three collections of poetry, *Names Above Houses, Furious Lullaby* (Southern Illinois University Press, 2001, 2007), and *Requiem for the Orchard* (University of Akron Press, 2010), winner of the Akron Prize for poetry chosen by Martín Espada. He co-chairs the advisory board of Kundiman, a not-for-profit organization dedicated to the promotion of Asian American Poetry. A recipient of a Fellowship Award from the New York Foundation for the Arts and a GAP Grant from Artist Trust, he has had poems in journals such as *Virginia Quarterly Review, North American Review, Tin House,* and *Chattahoochee Review,* as well as anthologies such as *Asian American Poetry: The Next Generation.* He teaches at Western Washington University.

A Manipulated Fourteen-Line Poem

This exercise was designed to help stimulate the imagination and provide a launching pad for a potential poem—also to introduce poets to some of the basic techniques of prosody and poetic composition, including metaphor, sensory imagery, off-rhyme, alliteration, syntax, personification, enjambment, allusion, and form. Finally, the exercise aims to show poets that form can be generative, that sometimes having multiple constraints can actually be liberating and allow the writer to discover something unexpected, to push in a direction that might be unfamiliar or surprising.

Procedure

Read and reflect on the following Stravinsky quotation before beginning:

> The more constraints one imposes, the more one frees one's self of the chains that shackle the spirit. . . . the arbitrariness of the constraint serves only to obtain precision of execution.

Follow the guidelines below exactly and without deviation, trying your best to fulfill the requirement of each line before moving on to the next one.

Line 1: Write a line that has a smell in it.

Line 2: Make a one-line, end-stopped statement about a city.

Line 3: Comment on the time of year, the season, or the weather.

Line 4: Use an internal off-rhyme.

Line 5: Use syntax in an unexpected way.

Line 6: Write a line with personification(s) and color(s) in it.

Line 7: Finish a sentence that begins: "Next year at this time . . ."

Line 8: Make an allusion to a book, movie, or artwork.

Line 9: Be sure this line includes a metaphor *and* enjambs.

Line 10: Make this line a question.

Line 11: Alliterate at least three words in this line.

Line 12: Make this line shorter or longer than the previous one by no fewer than five words.

Line 13: Write whatever you like!

Line 14: End on an image.

Of course, *before* you begin, you should familiarize yourself with all of the terms that the exercise asks that you use; so find out for yourself what *off-rhyme* and *enjambment* are and then start the poem. The more familiar you are with using these elements of poetry, the more natural and fluent the end-product will be. The final caveat is to make a poem that makes some kind of lyric or narrative sense, however you define that. The finished poem will be fourteen lines in length, comprising a species of American sonnet.

Variations

This exercise can be turned into a variation on Exquisite Corpse (see page 136), with each member of a group taking one of the imperatives and then putting them together to see what transpires. It can also be turned into an exercise between two people, in which one of them writes the first line and sends it to the second, who writes the next line, and so on. The exercise can explore other terrain as well. For example, in an exercise in dramatic monologue, each line can be written in the voice of a persona, rather than the poet. The template of this exercise is supple enough that more rules can be added or subtracted and other rules substituted, depending on the goals of a given workshop.

Tips

Faced with such strict adherence to a form, be flexible. Allow your mind to wander, to let in elements at the periphery that might not seem at first like they belong. The first time through, you might simply be trying to fulfill each rule with little sense of how the lines hold together, but after writing a draft, you can go back and try to make the pieces cohere. It's often useful to have a subject in mind that you want to encircle, to write around, to use as a tool to get at the poem—obliquely—something you've wanted to write about for a while but have been unable to approach. Remember that the poem is a success if it gets you to write something you normally wouldn't have written. Even if you are left with only one usable phrase or memorable image, the exercise has more than fulfilled its purpose. You can always use the end-result as the basis or direction for another poem.

Examples

Weeping Iris

Stale cigarettes and rotting sausage links should make them cringe,
But Paris tourists pay no heed to dumpsters.

Nor do they notice the figure lying in the rain:
He dreams about a distant time, of grand châteaux, pinot noir wine,
Rich mahogany.
Purple and blue iris hues dance in outdoor gardens.
Next year at this time I will reclaim my place,
Where strokes of Monet line hallways.

How does a man whose thoughts are endless streams
Of luxuries appear like this,
Mumbling memories?
His teeth chatter—clothes soaked beneath last week's gazette.
Tourists walk on.
The rain drips purples and blues.

Magdalena Kinga

Foreign Exchange

"His right nipple smells like his left nipple, which smells like his
        navel. Every
hairless body smells the same in cities like Cambodia," the British
        tourist concludes.
There's no season, but one kind of weather here: the sun always cop-
        per, casting its
colour onto the topless boys whose shoulders are crushed by the
        shrewd British pounds.
Crushed not by armies, but arms of those who suck nothing but
the third-world juice with their white lips, dancing tongue and
        whiter skin.
Next year at this time, this boy will see the same daddy, same cur-
        rency.
He will be worshipped as *David*, but fondled again like a dildo in a
        cheap hotel bed,
in which dignity is dust. With just a soft sudden blow, it dis-
appears like a shadow in darkness. But would he open his eyes?
        Would he
be able to see he's rolled over by a hairy bear born to break bones?
All eyes can be blinded by the dollar sign.

Back home, the boy will wash his body, soapless and not sobbing,
     while
his daddy will count the stamps in his wrinkled burgundy passport.

Nicholas Y.B. Wong

Beyond the Pond House

Astringent and pithy as vermouth reducing in a pan,
Elizabeth Park at night gathers up the best of Hartford.
In early winter, after the roses have stopped blooming,
the snarl of frost-covered lawns, under pinprick of stars
could farms, as once, be again a tract of land to work
with harrow and riddle until pumpkins gloated tan.
Next year at this time, even more credit default swaps
could turn wives of insurance men into Emma Bovary.
But out here, the tops of buildings are trees in a thick
wood, irrelevant. What could be further from the mind?
Along this curve of earth, the city drops away, a cinder
in the wind when nothingness begins.
Not Wallace Stevens' nothing that is and is not here,
but the shadow of a newly dead branch too dark to see.

Ravi Shankar

Ravi Shankar is co-Director of the Creative Writing Program at Central Connecticut State University and the founding editor of *Drunken Boat.* He has published four books of poems: *Seamless Matter, Voluptuous Bristle, Wanton Textiles,* and *Instrumentality.* Along with Tina Chang and Nathalie Handal, he edited *Language for a New Century: Contemporary Poetry from the Middle East, Asia, and Beyond,* called "a beautiful achievement for world literature" by Nadine Gordimer. He has won a Pushcart Prize, been featured in *The New York Times* and *The Chronicle of Higher Education,* appeared on the BBC and NPR, received fellowships from the MacDowell Colony, Djerassi, and the Connecticut Commission on Arts & Culture, and has performed his work around the world. He is currently on the faculty of the first international M.F.A. Program at City University of Hong Kong. Norah Jones is not among his daughters.

Three-Day Defamiliarization

Defamiliarization is a concept invented by the Russian theorist Viktor Shklovsky. Basically, the idea is that the purpose of literature is to take objects that have become familiar and rote, and to make them, through the act of writing, strange again. Reading and writing therefore help us once again to fully experience and feel the things in our lives to which we have become numb. "Art," Shklovsky says, "makes the stone stony." By writing down what we typically see and come into contact with, and performing some rhetorical operations on those words, and then thinking about how those sentences will go together, we will write something that is both strange and familiar, that is, a poem.

Procedure

Day One (30 minutes)

1. Go for a ten-minute walk outside, and while you are walking, write down ten phrases of things you actually see and/or think.
2. Go for a ten-minute walk inside your house and do the same thing.
3. Type the twenty phrases out on your computer.

Day Two (30 minutes)

1. Write twenty new lines, each of which incorporates one of the phrases you generated from your ten-minute walks on Day One.
2. Now write a new line in response to each of those twenty lines. Each new line will argue with, question, contradict, or elaborate on the line to which it responds.
3. Try to write some of the lines in the form of questions, some in the form of negations, some in the form of speculations, some in the form of advice, etc.

Day Three (one hour)

1. Draft a poem using the twenty responding—not original—lines from Day Two.
2. Add as much additional material as you like.
3. Title the poem, using one of the original phrases or lines.

Rationale

I like this exercise first of all because it creates several conditions for things to happen that are worthwhile for me as a poet and person, and which I might not otherwise be inclined to do. Perhaps most important, it gets me outdoors. Sometimes when I am trying really hard to write I spend a lot of time reading, thinking, staring—and it all happens inside. In the abstract it seems like a great idea to go outside, but doing so often leads to goofing off, which is not necessarily bad and might ultimately lead to something good. But it's nice to have a specific poetry task, a kind of research project.

The second thing I like about this exercise is that it takes place in three relatively short bursts of activity, spread out over three days. This has the advantage of making the writing process feel manageable and also sustained. This is especially good if I haven't been writing a lot recently or have been feeling overwhelmed by life and its endless demands.

Third, the task to take phrases and modify them rhetorically—by arguing with them, responding to them, contradicting them, turning them into a questions—forces me out of the rut of writing the same kind of sentence again and again. Poems can gain momentum and energy and life from lines that vary. Plus, forcing myself to write a question, a negation, an elaboration, leads me to say things that surprise me.

The unspecified part of this exercise, the part that will be the most interesting and personal, is how each poet will weave together these lines/sentences. Merely stringing them together in some kind of unassociated order is likely not going to be interesting. Thinking about how the phrases and sentences connect, and making them do so in a way that feels authentically strange but not strange is the poetic task. Each poet will solve it for him- or herself.

An Example

In the poem below you can see lots of objects that come from going for short walks, both in the neighborhood and inside my apartment. I ended up using some of the sentences that contained concrete objects—the dead spider, the paint cans, pieces of paper—to set up an initial situation. Once I had that, I just moved through the other lines, fitting them into the growing mood/situation of the poem. The title comes from the word *happiness,* which, for whatever reason, popped into my head during one of the short walks. It's not a particularly interesting word in isolation, but in the context of the poem, it becomes activated, defamiliarized.

Phrases from Day One:

old paint cans
undefinable wind
sunny bridge
chrome
beautiful blue fire escape
old gray warehouse
ugly water feature
yellow Kawasaki
serious yoga student
long sunny avenue
pink umbrella
dead spider
lighter than anything
orange tulips
old yellow candles
empty jackets
drawings of Barcelona
our suitcases
ironing board
blue gloves

Not all my phrases made it into the final version, but for the first draft I used them all, without exception. This is a very important step in the process: by forcing myself to use certain words or phrases that I ordinarily wouldn't, the poem was led in a completely unexpected direction. In fact, it is the words and phrases that I might in a different poem have found more natural or easier to use that I ultimately discarded, as the poem moved in a different direction.

Poem for Happiness

the dead spider rested on my windowsill
using one piece of paper I pushed it
onto another piece of paper
then dropped it accidentally
behind some old paint cans next to the door
the orange tulips you gave me
for a second seemed to be in a mostly nice way
laughing as I bent down

wearing dishwashing gloves a blue
color not found in nature
in order to find the little brown body
that was for primal reasons
horrifying me and stand in the doorway
and hold it out in front of me
to the wind which even if everywhere else
in the city it is calm
rushes down our street
where the yellow Kawasaki
is always parked next to the green bin
I threw the candles we can't light anymore
into because their wicks are gone
and you cried because
I had thrown out the beautiful candles
the sun turns in a different direction
everything becomes suddenly chrome
and now I am thinking on a hillside
where the wind is blowing very strongly
we will get married
our future a long sunny avenue
we have already walked part way down
or a pink umbrella
or a very loud water feature
in the middle of the city
around it on a concrete ledge
the workers sit next to each other
even though they do not know each other
and read silently together and alone

Matthew Zapruder is the author of three collections of poetry: *American Linden, The Pajamaist,* and *Come On All You Ghosts* (Copper Canyon), named by *Publishers Weekly* as one of the top five poetry books of 2010. Co-translator from Romanian, along with historian Radu Ioanid, of *Secret Weapon: Selected Late Poems of Eugen Jebeleanu*—he has received a William Carlos Williams Award, a May Sarton Award from the Academy of American Arts and Sciences, and a Lannan Literary Fellowship. An editor for Wave Books and a member of the permanent faculty in the low-residency M.F.A. program at the University of California, Riverside-Palm Desert, Zapruder lives in San Francisco.

Lisa Russ Spaar

The Self-Portrait Poem:
Facebooking in the Vale of Soul-Making

We live in an age of easy and ubiquitous self-portrayal. Blogs, Facebook, Skype, YouTube, and other digital and cellular "galleries" (whose technologies are developing so rapidly that by the time this entry appears in print some may already be obsolete) allow individuals a protean array of venues in which to post, curate, manipulate, and remove visual images and verbal profiles of themselves with what seems like a faster than real-time alacrity. This proliferation of self-portraiture is so rampant that it's possible for viewers and readers to become inured to its magic, craft, and power.

Self-portrayal is not new. Since antiquity, visual and spatial artists have depicted themselves in their productions—tangentially, allegorically, masked, or with bold psychological forthrightness. This practice burgeoned in the mid-fifteenth century with the availability of more and cheaper mirrors and looking glasses (and what model, after all, is as affordable and readily available as the artist?). This interest in self-portraiture has continued unabated into the twenty-first century, spurred by advances in photography, imaging, digitalization, communication, information systems, and the widespread availability of the Internet. Rembrandt, Dürer, Vigée-Lebrun, Kahlo, Van Gogh, Picasso, Munch, Sherman, Bacon, and Morimura are famous for their serial work in visual self-portraiture, revisiting the self as model over time, persona, and space. The result, often with a great deal of what Emily Dickinson called "veil," is, for the viewer as well as the artist, an excitingly vexed and fluid engagement with what it means to be a self, an artist, a maker.

The self-portrait as a conscious mode comes relatively later in poetry than it does in visual art. It's true that in ancient poems from all cultures, a poet as a discrete, private entity burns through the stock or universal *I* that characterizes anonymous or dialogic lyrics like the *Song of Songs* or the Psalms, and speaks across the centuries with an individual urgency—the voice of Sappho, Dante, Mirabai, or Tu Fu, for instance—traveling great distances to articulate with prescient freshness a subjective loneliness, God-hunger, or desire. And while it's certainly possible among the Modern poets to feel a ghost of Eliot in his Prufrock, Yeats in "Among Schoolchildren," Mew in any of her ballads, it is with the postmodern poets, borrowing largely from ekphrastic examples, that the self-portrait as a formal, aesthetic approach emerges. Ever since Walt

Whitman began "Song of Myself" with *I* and ended it with *you*—and Emily Dickinson coyly asked "I'm Nobody, who are you?"—American poetry in particular has been stalked by issues of personal as well as national identity (one wonders what experiments the Modernists might have undertaken had they had access to these two extraordinary nineteenth-century American innovators, who worked largely below the radar and essentially rolled their own poems in a century not quite ready to receive their experiments). Late-twentieth– and early twenty-first–century poets such as John Ashbery, Charles Wright, Mary Ann Samyn, Jorie Graham, Lucie Brock-Broido, and others have made a serial and deliberate practice of working in self-portraiture, often achieving their most powerful effects through indirection and effacement as they sojourn through what John Keats called poetry's most singularizing province, "the vale of Soul-making."

What follows are three self-portrait exercises that invite the practicing poet to investigate and portray the self through manifold lenses, indirection, and what Anne Carson would call poetic "ruses." These études, taking as their ostensible subject the poet him- or herself, are designed (like all good writing exercises) with the hope of foregrounding the processes by which and the reasons why we make poems.

Exercise I: Self-Portrait

Write a poem using the following guidelines or obstructions:

1. Your poem may be no longer than thirty lines.
2. The title of your piece must contain the word *self-portrait* (e.g., "Self-Portrait as Detested Writing Assignment" or "Self-Portrait with Sigmund Freud" or "Exit 9, Jersey Turnpike: A Self-Portrait").
3. You must use the following words: *gill, toxic, lambent*.
4. The poem must contain a piece of small machinery.
5. The poem must ask at least one question.
6. The poem must end with a concrete image.

An Example

I tried this exercise myself:

Self-Portrait in Summer
with Grim Reaper, Glimpsed from a Bus

The local public ride, a bus in trolley trappings,
lumbers past lambent 18th-century brick with a faux Disney optimism
I can't muster, the green of pool tables or old newsroom lamps,

brass fixings, a smart whistle.
I'm blue with toxic fumes. What is my destination?
A stoplight. I stare out at a heavily hooded man
scything weeds beside the road. The gill-slits
of the orange whacker emit a low drone behind glass.
He's nicking lilies, too, wilted crimson stars
sprawled out with grass-flecks on the sidewalk.
Relief as we pull away. Perhaps some gelato, I think,
as the pane flares with amnesia, a sun-blinding glare.

Lisa Russ Spaar

Exercise II: Self-Portrait as Place

Write a fifteen-line poem using the following guidelines:

1. Your poem will be titled "Self-Portrait in/as _____," filling in the blank with your hometown or state.
2. Incorporate an interesting detail or fact about this place (e.g., "Two-thirds of the world's eggplant is grown in New Jersey" or "It's illegal to pump your own gas in New Jersey" or "New Jersey has a spoon museum displaying over 5,400 spoons from all 50 states" or "New Jersey is home to the Mystery Port Parts Club" or "There are more diners per square mile in New Jersey than anywhere else in the world").
3. Use the following words in some form: *choke, mizzle, flock*.
4. Include an erotic moment.
5. Use one of the following epigraphs:
   "Ruin is formal." – Emily Dickinson
   "This heaven gives me migraine." – Gang of Four
   "In the late entranceway the desert rhymed." – Paul McCormick

An Example

Allison Geller wrote the following poem in response to this exercise in an advanced poetry writing workshop:

Self-Portrait as L.A.

> *In the late entranceway the desert rhymed.*
> Paul McCormick

The flocks follow the roots of their own Pacific Flyway
over the paved veins of the city,

turning phrases in the smog-choked sky.

Hush of dusk. Owl hoots and coyote cries
give wasted answer to lizards' whispered
scuttle over lamp-lit stucco walls.

Through the dawn's acid mizzle a rabbit floats
in the pool. No one can say what chased it,
if it was chased at all.

Under the tree, plum-heavy, lapped with bees,
the humid morning wilts a book,
one sting spent before it died.

Below the hill the valley opens up,
daily migration begun again, a headlight V
pointed down the natal highway.

Allison Geller

Exercise III: Self-Portrait as Persona/Object

Write a poem using the following guidelines:

1. Portray yourself as and through **the persona** of someone real, liter-
   ary, or historical (e.g., Yogi Berra, John Cage, Murasaki Shikibu, Isado-
   ra Duncan, the Biblical Adam, Dr. Seuss, Jackson Pollock, Diane Arbus,
   Michael Jackson, St. Teresa of Ávila, Marquis de Sade, Alice B. Toklas,
   Louis Armstrong, Vishnu, Issa)—or as **an object** (e.g., a high-heeled
   shoe, lighter, coffee cup, turntable, rain barrel, eight-track player).
2. The title must contain the following format: "Self-Portrait as _____"
   or "Portrait of the Artist as _____."
3. This assignment may require that you do some research in order to
   animate your poem with the bright particulars (biographical details,
   settings, physical attributes) that make a world credible.

Examples

Sarah Wade wrote the poem on the opposite page in a workshop with me. Fol-
lowing her poem, I offer my own attempt at this exercise.

Self-Portrait as Issa's Cabinets of Wonder

> *the image of a simple house . . .*
> *Mankind's nest . . . is never finished.*
> Gaston Bachelard

Shell of snail,
cup of thorns,
echo of mountains

   in a tea leaf.
   The instant of
   the memory of
   the sting of,
   breath of.

Meaning of man,
matter of one moment
gathered into syllables.
Given weight and seed.

   Poet, gatherer of.

                 ~

Nothing is more dignified
than deliberate poverty—
a robe, a lone word, a walking stick.
The universe, *uchuu*, perches
on the simplest blooms.

   He wanders Japan collecting singularities,
   enclosing each one in ink,
   a dark edifice.

Places to shelter when poverty
is not deliberate:
three children (one a daughter)
and two wives carried into death.

   And when a fire flees into the ground,

Carrying his house on the back,
lie down in the granary,
moving permanently into poetry.

~   ~   ~

Vast. Vast. Vast. A microwave sings.
Issa, cup-of-tea, steaming.
Sip, open the old book of *haiku*:
hear him, still sleeping within
twenty thousand drawers of himself.

Sarah Wade

Self-Portrait as Blue Boot

> *the same thing I want from you today,*
> *I would want from you tomorrow . . .*
> Bob Dylan, "Boots of Spanish Leather"

Running as repining. Blackberries scatting the lane,
        moreen dapple, sea-green coppice,

soles slapping gravel, a blue hunch underfoot
        & a louvred purr as from across that lonesome—

Is there something you can send to me? A token?
        Two rabbit ears tense,

shimmer in sun, pink uterine flags in the bamboo.
        Blunt sparrow, wing-rush, at my forehead

a flung shard of shade, a spadeful chucked at the grave.
        I never know what to do

with my hands at such moments, missing you, moving:
        useless hooks unfisted now,

sprung creels, unshod spurs, open to all tempest,
        distances, oceans, boon.

Lisa Russ Spaar

Additional Self-Portrait Poems

- "Self-Portrait with Her Hair on Fire" and "Self-Portrait on the Grassy Knoll" by Lucie Brock-Broido

- "Portrait of the Artist with Li Po" and "Portrait of the Artist with Hart Crane," as well as five poems called "Self-Portrait" by Charles Wright in *The Southern Cross*

- "Self-Portrait as Wall Paper with Little Stoves," "Self-Portrait with Taxidermy," and "Self-Portrait as an Animal, Skinned and Hung" by Mary Ann Samyn

- "Self-Portrait, Jackson" and "Self-Portrait, Leakesville" by Jimmy Kimbrell

- "Self-Portrait in a Convex Mirror" by John Ashbery

- "Self-Portrait" by Linda Pastan

- "Self-Portrait" by Robert Creeley

- "Self-Portrait as Brigitte Bardot in Contempt" by Alex Dimitrov

- "Self-Portrait: Red Chalk on Laid Paper" and "Self-Portrait with Crayon" by Allison Benis White

- "Self-portrait As Apollo And Daphne," "Self-portrait As Both Parties," "Self-portrait As Demeter And Persephone," "Self-portrait As Hurry And Delay," and "Self-portrait As The Gesture Between Them" by Jorie Graham

Lisa Russ Spaar is the author of *Satin Cash* (Persea Books, 2008), *Blue Venus* (Persea Books, 2004), and *Glass Town* (Red Hen Press, 1999), for which she received a Rona Jaffe Award for Emerging Women Writers in 2000. She is the author of two chapbooks of poems, *Blind Boy on Skates* (University of North Texas Press, 1988) and *Cellar* (Alderman Press, 1983), and is editor of *Acquainted With the Night: Insomnia Poems* (Columbia University Press, 1999) and *All That Mighty Heart: London Poems* (University of Virginia Press, 2008). Her work has appeared in numerous journals and anthologies, including *The Paris Review, Ploughshares, Poetry,* and *Best American Poetry 2008.* Her reviews and essays have appeared in *The New York Times, The Chronicle of Higher Education,* and elsewhere. She is the poetry editor of the Arts & Academe blog of *The Chronicle of Higher Education.* The recipient of awards from the Academy of American Poets, the Virginia Commission for the Arts, and the Guggenheim, Spaar directs the Area Program in Poetry Writing at the University of Virginia.

Mind Is Shapely

Allen Ginsberg famously wrote, "Mind is shapely, Art is shapely." As a poet, I've often thought about this statement and wondered how does one transfer the shapeliness of Mind to Art? I consider this question when I design the ongoing workshop I currently teach in Austin, Texas.

I love shapes. I sometimes wonder whether poetry, like life, is the eternal part of becoming, expressed mathematically as a returning series of ones and zeroes that forms a nautilus spiral or the helix of DNA. It seems to me that poetry is about opposites and complements, sound designs and sense correspondences. Patterns like these are shapely.

I find it useful and important to bring attention to the poems of other poets. Poems written by others inform the pattern and spectrum of one's study. Study must be applied to the writing as this approach rhymes with our purpose: a pattern is based on a correspondence. These patterns require attention, to see how—in language—previous poets addressed states of experience, both interior and external, and how these speak to their audiences across time.

So I suggest this as prelude to one's writing: to physically engage a book of poems. This is especially useful if the poems of a single poet are read aloud for an hour. However one performs the poems, this is where the cadences of language, the twists of syntax, the evocative call from inside to outside, are voiced. These form a place from which a poet can perform another basic maneuver of writing, that of mimesis—an act of mirror representation.

As the facilitator to such an experience in my poetry workshops, I ask that the participants read a text of a single author aloud by turns. To contextualize the volume of poetry, I provide the writer's social/historical circumstances and we take notes on textual relationships. We then dedicate an hour to writing, during which I note writing strategies drawn from the poems.

Repetition—the drawing from patterns—is recognized in all of the poems we engage. Repetition is an ancient technique in poetry, tracing poetry's origin to incantation and song. Something happens when you repeat a word, phrase or line; maybe this can be called shapeliness. When repeated, words or phrases can take on new dimensions, subtleties, and connotations. Repetition lets a reader recognize and experience words newly.

Procedure

Here is a sample repetition exercise I might assign my workshop.

I. Listing I ask participants to begin by making a list of the following:

- Somewhere you went today
- An observation of the weather
- An article of clothing
- A meal
- Ten randomly selected nouns (avoiding abstract notions such as *loneliness* or *hope* in favor of the more concrete person, place, or thing) for which one generates a complementary pair of words that are slant or off-rhymed (e.g., *line/time, window/finger, cinnamon/uterine, red juice/furious*). Note that this guideline introduces occasions for assonance, alliteration, and consonance.

II. Drafting I then invite the poets to write freely, using as many of the words/phrases from this list as possible and ask that whenever they encounter a phrase, word, or line that feels evocative, to repeat it.

III. Crafting Once the raw writing is complete, crafting is in order to further carve out shapeliness. I might suggest that the poets read the results aloud to cull any awkward phrases and eliminate abstractions such as *forever, peace,* or *humility* (such words often lack immediacy when they appear in poems).

Tips

Rewriting and rearranging the text differently can mean discovering corresponding and compelling patterns. I encourage poets to think of visual interests in the resulting text by considering how lines are broken, asking where caesura might lend clues to a reader's understanding. This process can mean the scoring of a poem on the page in such a way that it allows the eye to take up the visual field of language and participate in the creation of meaning. Another favorite suggestion of mine is to re-imagine the poem by rewriting it from the last line to the first. Often one finds that energy patterns emerge with maps to shapeliness.

An Example

In preparation for this exercise, Cindy Huyser read from Denise Levertov's *Overland to the Islands* and *With Eyes at the Back of our Heads.*

Ten pairs of rhymes / slant rhymes:

creek / deep
rumor / murmur
cement / lament
hedge / sedge
branch / crouch
rage / guage
foam / known
hawk / stalk
secrets / crickets
oil / alloy

The poem that developed from Huyser's list is a study in sound, beginning with the sibilance of *suspicions, scurry, swath, grass, stroke, cement.* The first pair of slant rhymes sounds the long *e—deep, creek, creek—*alternating with the short *e* sound in *empty, cement, hedge, lament, sedge, never,* and so on. Throughout, sound works hand in hand with image. Consider just one example: "A lone hawk scans / the field, talons tight on a craggy branch." We *see* the hawk here, the turning head, the talons, the branch. But listen to the words—the alliteration of *talons tight,* the hard *k* in *hawk* and *craggy,* set against the lilt in *lone* and *talons,* the short *a* of *scans, craggy, branch.*

The Garden of Misunderstanding

Suspicions scurry deep in the thicket.
Here is a creek, and a swath of tall,
bearded grass. The creek is empty,
a stroke of cement.

There is a hedge here called *Always,*
and a tall, dry stump, *Lament.* A stubborn sedge
is named *Never.* A lone hawk scans
the field, talons tight on a craggy branch.

Murmurs and rumors crouch in the grass
amid the *crick-crick* of secrets.
The hawk's eyes glint like oiled alloy beads,
bright with rage, twin gauges of grief.

The hawk feels its hunger, also known
as *Blame.* It keens into an empty sky.
Brittle stalks whisper and shift, nodding heads
adrift on a faded, dry sea.

Cindy Huyser

Note from Cindy Huyser: Throughout this exercise I kept in mind Levertov's use of alliteration, e.g., "Two bean-fed boys set bottles on the wall / yesterday, and shied at them for a half-hour / with desperate energy, taking their stand / back a way in the rubbled lot" (from "Broken Glass"); "What a sweet smell rises / when you lay the dust— / bucket after bucket of water thrown / on the yellow grass" (from "Laying the Dust"). I was a little stuck for generating the word pairs, so I used an online random noun generator to create the base list of nouns. My first draft did not contain all of the pairs, but as I revised the poem, I began to see how to employ them to work with the poem's theme.

Hoa Nguyen was born in the Mekong Delta, grew up in the Washington, D.C., area, and studied poetics in San Francisco. She is the author of eight books and chapbooks, most recently *Hecate Lochia* (Hot Whiskey, 2009) and *Chinaberry* (Fact Simile, 2010). Her work has appeared in numerous anthologies, including *Black Dog Black Night* (Milkweed, 2007) and *Best of Fence* (Fence Books, 2009). She is co-editor of the small press and poetry journal *Skanky Possum* from which Robert Creeley selected poems for inclusion in *Best American Poetry 2002.* Based in Austin, Texas, Nguyen curates a reading series and leads a creative writing workshop.

William Wenthe

Stretching the Sentence

ecause *verse* means writing in lines, discussions of poetic form tend to focus more on versification than on an equally important formal aspect of poetry—namely, sentences. Teachers, editors, and poets alike share in this relative neglect of the sentence; as a result, much of contemporary poetry employs sentences that are sometimes rather dull, sometimes affected and imitative in their patterns, and sometimes downright poorly written. This isn't only a contemporary problem, by the way. Ezra Pound made this point in 1913, when he wrote in "A Few Don'ts": "Do not think any intelligent person is going to be deceived when you try to shirk all the difficulties of the unspeakably difficult art of good prose by chopping your composition into line lengths."

Many people are put off by technical descriptions of sentences. For me it brings back memories of standing at the blackboard, a frowning nun with folded arms standing behind me, as I try to diagram a sentence that seems to have been composed for no purpose other than tormenting schoolchildren. (Any serious poet, though, should be fluent in the terminology of syntax, as a sculptor should know stone—for it is the poet's *material*.) Instead of analyzing sentence structure, then, let's just jump into this exercise, which is really quite simple. It requires no preparation and no materials but your normal writing tools (I love a fine pen on the lined page of a sturdy journal).

Procedure

1. Write a poem of at least 100 words.

2. Let the poem be a single sentence.

3. Let the poem be at least 14 lines long.

Rationale

When I assign this exercise in poetry workshops, two things invariably happen: the students protest what they think is going to be an extremely difficult task, and the students discover a further range and intensity in their writing. In this regard I can't help but think of William Butler Yeats, who said that he sought for his poetry a "passionate syntax." The phrase can mean a number of things, but for Yeats, it also means the way that a sentence can demonstrate the "quarrel with ourselves"—Yeats' term—out of which we make poetry.

The aim of this exercise is, simply, to enhance one's fluency in sentence writing. It's an exercise in technique, but it may very well serve as an exercise in invention—the generation of new material. The demands of this sentence will require you to invent, and this literal stretching of the sentence requires you to stretch your mind; you may be saying new things, in finding new ways to say them.

Most exercises—I mean, physical exercises—require you to work against some sort of restraint. In this poetic exercise, let your restraint be the standard rules of syntax and punctuation. If you want to write poems without punctuation, that's fine; but again, this should be a freedom that is achieved *after* you have understood what punctuation is, and—more important—what it can do in a poem. For the purpose of the exercise, then, I would urge you to punctuate accordingly. Of course, try not to cheat: don't just write a sentence that begins, "The suitcase contained," and then list 97 items. (The "list" is another exercise, altogether.) The burden of trying to make this sentence a *poem* is to make the sentence itself be interesting, formally. Try different sentence structures: try putting the subject and verb in different places in the sentence; try using one subject/verb combination—or several; try different kinds of parallelism and/or suspension. After writing this exercise, try rewriting it, starting from a different place in the sentence.

Why fourteen lines? I'm being arbitrary, but I choose that number because it's the length of a sonnet, and since that length has served so many poets in so many languages for a good 800 years, I think it's certainly good enough for our purposes here. The point, regardless of the poem's length, it to remind ourselves that this is still an exercise in verse, and that we should, then, be mindful of lineation as we craft the syntax.

Of course this exercise can be written in meter as well, but since the aim of the exercise is to foreground syntax, my sense is that it's best to try it in free verse. An extraordinary metrical example, by the way, is Robert Frost's single-sentence sonnet, "The Silken Tent" (104 words, 14 lines). This is a poem worth studying for its syntax, whether one aims to write in metered or free verse. In your reading, keep an eye out for single-sentence poems—there are more than you might think, and it may be that some poems you've been reading for a long time are, when you look back at them, single sentences. Jeffrey Harrison's remarkable "Swifts at Evening" comes to mind here (151 words). But the ultimate aim of this exercise—the purpose that the exercise serves, beyond itself—isn't only to write sentences that are *entire* poems, but to write sentences that are worthy *parts* of our poems. What finer example than the wonderful opening sentence of Elizabeth Bishop's "The Moose" (148 words, 36 lines, accentual trimeter)? Or the 108-word third sentence in Henry Taylor's mysterious and bittersweet "Night Search for Lost Dog."

An Example

Here's an example from one of my own poems, which, having been in on the writing of it, I can talk about in terms of its composition. This is the first stanza of a poem titled "Goldsmith and Charity":

> This modest print by Rembrandt
> of a goldsmith finishing a statue
> of a woman and two children
> is nothing like the great portraits
> that move me, move most of us, I think;
> and yet it draws me in—by the way
> the goldsmith's arm supports
> the statue against his hip, exactly
> as the woman in the statue holds
> a child to her own;
> how his other arm curves down
> to the hammer in his hand, working
> some obscure but necessary matter
> of the sculpture's base; a motion matched
> by her hand reaching down to stroke
> the naked child who stands,
> face in the folds of her robe.

I recall that fairly early in the drafting stage, I wanted this stanza to be one sentence. The reason is that I wanted a structure that would *draw in* the reader in the way that the symmetrical arrangement of Rembrandt's engraving draws in the speaker of the poem. Composing this 107-word sentence was very difficult; and reading it, too, requires a strong act of attention. But these qualities contribute to the feeling of the poem, which is in large part an homage to the difficulty, the quality of attention, and reverence toward the world I find in Rembrandt's own art. Maybe I fail my readers, or a lot of them; doubtless I've failed Rembrandt; but if nothing else, writing this stanza satisfied my own sense of the difficult pleasure in the craft of poetry—a craft that, I'm saying, is also a matter of crafting sentences.

This exercise will force you to argue with yourself, to stretch the mind and imagination between the possibilities and restraints of English syntax. There is no single correct kind of syntax that is appropriate for poetry—poets have shown that so-called "incorrect" grammar can work quite effectively. (The 64-word last sentence of Henry Taylor's above-mentioned poem is, technically speaking, a sentence fragment—but it is no less moving or dynamic for that.) In a given situation, the short, simple sentence can work as well as the most elongated and complex. But short and simple shouldn't be the default style simply because one cannot master the longer and more complex.

William Wenthe is the author of three books of poems: *Words Before Dawn* (LSU Press, forthcoming 2012), *Not Till We Are Lost* (LSU Press, 2004), and *Birds of Hoboken* (Orchises Press, 1995, reprint 2003). He has received poetry fellowships from the National Endowment for the Arts and the Texas Commission on the Arts, as well as two Pushcart Prizes. His poems have appeared in *Poetry, The Paris Review, The Georgia Review, TriQuarterly, Ninth Letter, The Southern Review, Shenandoah, Open City, Tin House,* and other journals and anthologies. Critical essays on the craft of poetry have appeared in *The Yale Review* and *Kenyon Review*. He received a Ph.D. in English from the University of Virginia; he now teaches creative writing and modern poetry at Texas Tech University.

David Kirby

The Braid and the Bits Journal

I began my career by writing and publishing a lot of what I call the Two by Four Poem, that is, a poem that's about two inches wide and four long and which, because it's relatively brief, deals only with one idea or image or theme. A lot of these appeared in decent magazines, and my first couple of books, one of which won a major prize, were composed largely of poems of this type.

Finally, though, I'd had enough. The Two by Four Poem had its satisfactions, but writing one was kind of like making a sandwich, and I was ready for dinner.

Now don't get me wrong: there are a lot of great short, one-note poems out there; in fact, that description probably fits most of the poems that have ever been written, and certainly it covers a lot of student poems. But why not try something new? What I propose is a type of poem I call the braid, which can be as simple as a camp lanyard or as colorful and textured as a Persian carpet. And yet this type of poem isn't that hard to write. All you need to do is assemble some parts, find a power source, and plug in.

Procedure

The assemble-some-parts aspect of the braid is the most important aspect, and it involves the maintenance of what I'll call your bits journal. And actually, your bits journal is going to be one of your most important tools as a poet; even if you never write a single braided poem, your bits journal is going to be a rich field of inspiration and practice for you.

A bits journal is where you write down all the bits you're going to make poems out of: ideas that come to you out of nowhere, quotes from your reading, bathroom graffiti, overheard conversations, childhood memories, stories you've told dozens of times, and so on. It's the warehouse where your treasures are stored. Sometimes you hear people say they have writer's block, but that's an imaginary ailment; what they're really saying is that they can't think of anything to write about. With your bits journal, that'll never be a problem. Another good thing about the bits journal is that you can write in it daily—I can't write a decent poem every day, but I can always top up my bits journal.

So open a new file and start jotting down your bits. Do this on your computer: some people still like to use paper notebooks, but you can combine your ideas more quickly if everything's digital. Don't censor yourself: nobody's going to see the bits journal but you, so never make the mistake of saying "Oh, this isn't important" or "This will never make a good poem." You don't know yet; at this stage, you're just accumulating bits.

Once you have five or six pages, you've probably got enough to write a poem. In fact, if your bits journal gets too long, it can get unwieldy, so when mine gets to, say, twenty pages, I figure it's harvest time.

That's when you find the power source for the bits you want to work with. Isolate two or three or twelve juicy bits and see what they have in common. Ask yourself what connects these random bits, but be prepared for a surprise. This is where the fun begins, because often a connection that appears to be obvious turns out to be misleading, and the poem finds its vitality elsewhere.

Examples
Take this poem of mine as an example:

My Favorite Foreign Language

"What's your favorite foreign language?" asks the cabby,
            and when I ask why, he says he knows "butterfly"
      in 241 of them, so I say, "Okay, French!" and he says,

"*Papillon*!" and I say, "German!"and he says, "*Schmetterling*!"
            and I'm running out of languages I know, so I say,
      "Uh, Wolof!" because I'm reading a short story

where a woman speaks Wolof, and he says something in Wolof,
            and the professor-y part of me wants
      to say, You shouldn't call them foreign languages, you know,

because that means there's only one real language, but
            I'd be saying that to him in our common
      tongue, so it really wouldn't make sense unless I were chiding

him in, say, Wolof, a language in which he knows only
            one word and I none. What's the best country?
      Heaven, probably: as everyone knows, the cooks are French,

the mechanics German, the police English, lovers Italian,
            and it's all organized by the Swiss, whereas
      in Hell, the cooks are English, mechanics French, police

Germans, lovers Swiss, and everything is organized by the Italians,
              which leaves out the Spanish,
        though perhaps not, for the ancients say a man should speak

French to his friends because of its vivacity,
              Italian to his mistress for its sweetness,
        German to his enemies because it is forceful, and Spanish

to his God, for it is the most majestic of languages.
              Hola, Señor! Okay if I put my suitcase
        over here? Thank you for having me! Yes, I *would*

like to hear what they're saying in the other place, like "Dictators
              over here" and "Corporate polluters
        in this area" and "Aw, come on—*another* boring poet?"

The five separate bits I use are obvious: the incident with the cabby, the story I'm reading in which a woman speaks Wolof (a language spoken in Senegal, Gambia, and Mauritania), the joke about different cultures, the part about which languages work best in different situations, and then the only bit I make up myself, the conversation with God.

I thought I was going to make a statement about the nature of language, but, while the poem starts out that way, towards the end it swerves toward a condemnation of boring poetry. To my way of thinking, there should be an eleventh commandment that says, "Thou shalt not write a boring poem." Otherwise, you're going to end up in Hell with the rest of the bad folks.

Let me give you a second example of a poem that's also a braid, one that's very different from mine. This one was written by a student of mine named W. P. Boyce, and it goes this way:

My Grandfather's Theology and Vinyl Collection

Beside a garage full of wooden golf clubs in faded glory—stiff 6-irons
        and Ping putter
carryovers from the days of culottes, sweaters, and argyle knee-high
        socks of sunset colors—
and instruction manuals from 1967 on the how-to's of humidifiers and
        Maytag
dryers, my grandfather in his small study thumped away at the roaring of
        the twenties.

Large in his leather recliner, his glasses slumped on his paling peregrine
     nose,
the vinyl player spinning like planets: yes, he was a king of sorts crooning
     in a resonant
baritone to the call and response of "Minnie the Moocher." And there
     throned
my grandfather, setting free the song that sleeps in the wounded flesh of
     humanity,

in antiphon with Cab Calloway: *Folk's here's the story 'bout Minnie the
     Moocher /*
she was a red hot hoochie coocher! The whole hallway echoed resonantly
with their entangled voices—*Hi Dee Hi Dee Hi Dee Hi*—soaking the
     walls like a fresh
coat of paint, which was badly needed. The soulful trumpeting and the
     rat-a-tat-tat

of the drums and Calloway's Orchestra returning his words like the ark's
     bird,
that symbol of the Holy Ghost, with an olive leaf in her beak, even
     returning like Jonah
to dry land and Nineveh: *O Minnie had a heart as big as a whale.* But
     something
haunting about Cab Calloway's love-girl lingered in the piercing notes, a
     tragedy or a comedy,
or a prophecy, more likely, that my grandfather divined long ago. Coffee
     still warm

in his hands, he was teaching me something almost mystical in this
     hymn. *She had a million*
dollars worth of nickels and dimes / and she sat around and counted them
     all
a million times, like the shining prophet whose shadow engulfed a po-
     dium in Moscow's
largest assembly hall, before 7,000 Russians, shortly after the Bolshevik
     Revolution.
Comrade Lunachatsky recited to his freed captives the psalm of the age
     and of progress,

how the Christian mysteries, the orthodoxy of the East, were now
        happily supplanted
by reason and modernity and those particular sciences, a substitution for
        the legends.
Like an opiate dream, conviction and sweat poured from his head as his
        hectic hands
conducted the sermon until nothing more echoed in the hall. With a
        final bark he bellowed,

Is there anything to be added? Near the end of a back row, one figure rose.
        Apologizing
first to the Commissar for his awkwardness and his weak knees, his
        stuttering tongue
and astigmatic eyes, bony elbows and murmuring heart, a twenty-six-
        year-old boy
stepped forward. Granted two minutes and no more to voice a refrain,
        he crossed

a creaking platform in silence and nodded to his comrade, *I won't take
        very long.* Sidling
to the podium and clearing his throat, and barely louder than his
        speaking voice, he eked
out his little song before the multitude, one for the ages, forever his call:
        "Christ is risen."
And as one man, the audience like a kiss roared in response: "He is risen
        indeed!"

A freshly ordained priest and a freshly brewed cup of black coffee, the
        way my grandfather
likes it, and a prophecy I learned to a tune I like to hum on days when
        everything is too much
going my way, counting my coins on the way to the bank or thinking I've
        figured out life,
that viscous jam with a head and a heart and a throat: *Ho Dee Ho Dee
        Ho Dee Ho!*

W. P. Boyce

You can imagine how much fun Boyce had making this braid, how excited he got when he realized the connection between his two king-sized bits, his grandfather's obsession with Cab Calloway's singing and the good news of the Gospel. Like all big poems, this one is simple at heart: it says that reason and science don't offer the satisfactions that music and religion do. Boyce just makes that point in a really crunchy, high-calorie way.

And it's all thanks to his bits journal. Well, his patience, his research skills, and, mainly, his ability as a writer as well.

Summing Up

- Since you can already write the poem based on a single subject, try using two or more subjects. Your poetry is going to be meaty, beaty, big and bouncy if you do.

- Start a bits journal. It'll provide the parts from which you'll make your poem.

- When your bits journal starts to fatten up, look through it for the bits you want to braid together.

- Decide on a sequence: line your bits up so that they march towards some kind of satisfying conclusion.

- Be prepared, though! You might end up saying something you didn't anticipate—something better, even.

- But whatever you do, start a bits journal. Start it today.

David Kirby is the author or co-author of twenty-nine books, including the poetry collections *The House on Boulevard St.: New and Selected Poems, The Ha-Ha, The House of Blue Light,* and *The Travelling Library,* in addition to the essay collection *Ultra-Talk: Johnny Cash, The Mafia, Shakespeare, Drum Music, St. Teresa Of Avila, and 17 Other Colossal Topics of Conversation.* His many awards include the Guy Owen Prize, the James Dickey Prize, the Brittingham Prize, and fellowships from the National Endowment of the Arts and the Guggenheim Foundation. Kirby's latest book, *Little Richard: The Birth of Rock 'n' Roll* (Continuum, 2009), has been hailed by the *Times Literary Supplement* of London as "a hymn of praise to the emancipatory power of nonsense."

Alternate Table of Contents

Voice or Persona

Incorporating Research

Nonlinear Approaches, Nonlinear Poems

Revision

For Beginning Poets

Note: These exercises would work especially well for students in the early stages of writing poetry, though we recommend them to all poetry writers, regardless of level of achievement. Please note, too, that many K–12 students would be capable of tackling even the most challenging exercises in *Wingbeats*.

For Poets Seeking a Challenge

Acknowledgments

The editors are grateful to the following authors, publishers, and journals for permission to reprint previously published work.

Allen, Paul, "A Tangle of Angels." From *Ground Forces* (Knockeven, Cliffs of Moher, County Clare, Ireland, Salmon Poetry, 2008). Reprinted by permission of the author and Salmon Poetry.

Bass, Ellen, "If You Knew." From *The Human Line*. Copyright © 2007 by Ellen Bass. Reprinted with the permission of Copper Canyon Press, www.coppercanyonpress.org.

Betts, Tara, "A Little Salt." From *e-poets.net,* Kurt Heintz, publisher, 02-01-11. Originally published in *Can I Hang?* (Tara Betts, 1999). Reprinted by permission of the author.

Beyer, Tamiko, "Setagaya-ku Haibun." From *Cheers to Muses: Contemporary Work by Asian American Women* (Asian American Women Artists Association, 2007). Reprinted by permission of the author.

Bly, Robert, translation of "Black Stone Lying on a White Stone" by César Vallejo. From *The Winged Energy of Delight: Selected Translations* (Harper Collins, 2004). Reprinted by permission of Robert Bly.

Boutté, Ann Reisfeld, "For the Ballerinas." From *Houston Poetry Fest Anthology* (2010). Reprinted by permission of the author.

Bridgforth, Sharon, from "love/rituals & rage." From *Kentecloth: Southwest Voices of the African Diaspora* (University of North Texas Press, 1998). Performed by The root wy'mn Theatre Company. Copyright © 1993 by Sharon Bridgforth. Reprinted by permission of the author.

Browne, Jenny, "Love Letter to a Stranger (Girl)" and "Love Letter to a Stranger (Suicide)." From *Sawbuck* (4.3, Fall 2010). Reprinted by permission of the author.

Castillo, Vangie, "As I walk in the moonlight." From *Salting the Ocean: 100 Poems by Young Poets,* edited by Naomi Shihab Nye (Greenwillow Books / HarperCollins, 2000). Text Copyright © 2000 by Naomi Shihab Nye. Used by permission of HarperCollins Publishers.

Cofell, Cathryn and Karla Huston, "Thigh Considers Her Heritage." From *MARGIE* (Vol. 4, 2005). Reprinted by permission of the authors.

Covey, Bruce, "Clytemnestra." From *Glass is Really a Liquid* (No Tell Books, 2010). Reprinted by permission of No Tell Books.

Dumitru, Cyra S., "Black Rock." From a poster produced and distributed by River Lily Press. Reprinted by permission of the author.

Ekiss, Keith, "Pima Road Notebook," two poems by the same title. From *Pima Road Notebook,* (New Issues Poetry and Prose, 2010). Reprinted by permission of New Issues Poetry and Prose.

Garner, Madelyn. "The Quantum Loom." From *Threaded Lives: Poems from the Fiber World,* October 3-5, 2009, RANE Gallery, Taos, NM. Curators Andrea L. Watson, Faith Welsh, and Carolyn Hinske. Reprinted by permission of the author.

Hamby, Barbara, "Zeus, It's Your Leda, Sweetie Pie." *From All-Night Lingo Tango,* by Barbara Hamby, © 2009 (Univ. of Pittsburgh Press, 2009). Originally appeared in *TriQuarterly* (125). Reprinted by permission of the University of Pittsburgh Press.

Hamilton, Carol, "Myself." *Hoosier Challenger* (Cincinnati, OH, Fall 1968). Reprinted by permission of the author.

Harter, Penny, "After the Blizzard." From *Frogpond* (Vol. 33, No. 2, Spring-Summer 2010). Reprinted by permission of the author. "Driving Home." From *Contemporary Haibun Online* (Vol. 6, No. 4). Originally published in *Modern Haiku & Haibun Prose* (No. 2, Winter, 2009). Reprinted by permission of the author. "Voices in the Rain." *Modern Haibun and Tanka Prose.* (Issue 2, Winter 2009). Reprinted by permission of the author.

Heinzelman, Kurt, "Bifocals." From *The Names They Found There* (Pecan Grove Press, 2011). Reprinted by permission of the author.

Hirsch, Edward, "For the Sleepwalkers." From *For the Sleepwalkers* (Knopf, 1981). Reprinted by permission of the author.

Huston, Karla, "Variations on a Text." From *The Chaffin Journal* (1999). Reprinted by permission of the author.

Huston, Karla and Cathryn Cofell, "Miracle Fish." From *qarrtsiluni,* Mutating the Signature, Dana Guthrie Martin and Nathan Moore, editors (January–April 2009) and a print volume of the same issue (March 2009). Reprinted by permission of the authors.

Lockie, Ellaraine, "An American Haibun." From *Ibbetson Street Magazine,* 2011. Reprinted by permission of the author.

Meyers, Bert, miscellaneous lines quoted from The *Wild Olive Tree* (West Coast Poetry Review, 1979) and *Sunlight on the Wall* (Kayak, 1976). Reprinted by permission of Daniel Meyers.

O'Donnell, Angela, "Other Mothers." From *Moving House* (WordTech Communications, 2010). Previously published in *Mine* (Finishing Line Press, 2007). Originally published online by *Die-Cast Garden.* Reprinted by permission of the author.

Oldmixon, Katherine Durham, "March Rites." From *Texas Poetry Calendar* (2011). Reprinted by permission of the author. "Poesis in Plato's Garden." From *qarrtsiluni,* Insecta, Marly Youmans and Ivy Alvarez, editors (12-15-07). Reprinted by permission of the author.

Popoff, Georgia A., "Ugly Duckling." From *Coaxing Nectar From Longing* (Hale Mary Press,1997). Reprinted by permission of the author.

Salamon, Russell, "She." From *Paren[thetical Pop]pies* (d. a. levy's Renegade Press, 1964). Reprinted by permission of the author.

Seyburn, Patty, "Red Level." From *Mechanical Cluster* (Ohio State University Press, 2002). Reprinted by permission of the author.

Shy, Shoshauna, "Unplanned Punctuation." From *The Los Angeles Review* (Vol. 7, Spring 2010). Reprinted by permission of the author.

Suzuki-Martinez, Sharon, "Desert Cicadas Haibun." From *BAP Quarterly* (Winter, 2009). Reprinted by permission of the author.

Terris, Susan, "Dry Heiligenschein." From *Black Rock and Sage* (2006). Reprinted by permission of the author. "The Horizon as Razor" and "Solstice Song." From *Double-Edged* (Finishing Line Press, 2009). Reprinted by permission of the author.

Turco, Lewis, "Time Goes Down in Mirrors." From *The Collected Lyrics of Lewis Turco / Wesli Court 1953-2004* (Star Cloud Press, 2004). Copyright © 2004 by Lewis Turco. Reprinted by permission of the author.

Watson, Andrea L., "Sleeping in the House of Saints." From *Nimrod International Journal* (Vol. 52, No. 2, Spring/Summer 2009). Reprinted by permission of the author.

Weaver, Afaa Michael, "BP." From *Three Coyotes* (1). Reprinted by permission of the author.

Wenthe, William, from "Goldsmith and Charity."From *Agni* online (2008). Forthcoming in *Words Before Dawn* (LSU Press, 2012). Reprinted by permission of the author.

Yates, Dillard, "I Sing Deep Songs." From *Salting the Ocean: 100 Poems by Young Poets,* edited by Naomi Shihab Nye (Greenwillow Books / HarperCollins, 2000). Text Copyright © 2000 by Naomi Shihab Nye. Used by permission of HarperCollins Publishers.

Zapruder, Matthew, "Poem for Happiness." From *Likestarlings* (September 2010). Reprinted by permission of the author.

Every effort has been made to trace the ownership of all copyrighted material in this book and to obtain permission for its use.

Additional Acknowledgments

The editors are grateful to the following individuals for permission to publish example poems and other work completed for the exercises in this book—appearing here for the first time.

Allen, Blaise, "Looting the Day." **Allen, Blaise,** and **Gretchen Fletcher,** "This, I must say, is the sum total of this day." **Alvarez, Amy,** personal Touchstones and Compass of Poetics. **Aronoff, Carol Alena,** "Willow Creek Road Notebook." **Barrett, Allison,** "Gretel" and "Distraught Moon." **Betts, Tara,** "Ways of Looking at a Blackwoman." **Blair, Travis,** "Fears." **Blair, Travis, Gretchen Fletcher,** and **Barbara Randalls Greg,** "This, then, is the sum total of the day." **Boyce, W. P.,** "My Grandfather's Theology and Vinyl Collection." **Briante, Susan,** "O BTYCF for spacious SKY." **Brown, Nathan,** "1965." **Brown, Nickole,** "Sweet Silver." **Budy, Andrea Hollander,** "Postcard from Taos." **Chen, Ching-In,** "An Ode to my Hair: A Haibun." **Cimino, Alison T.,** "After a Sudden Sorrow." **Cofell, Cathryn,** "I cling to a man who will not cling to me." **Cofell, Cathryn,** and **Karla Huston,** "I cling to" and "Thigh Worries about Friction." **Cohen-Burnell, Ashley,** "Summers in Charleston." **Dale, Brandon S.,** "It sounds like punching a punching bag." **Daviau, Monique,** "Ode to Meat Sticks." **DePalma, Katherine Morrow Jones,** "Lullaby." **Desrosiers, Lori,** "after leaving him" and "Herons." **Dye, William,** "Eight Ways of Looking at a Fallen Tree Trunk." **Feder, Rachel,** "Thing." **Fletcher, Gretchen,** "Measuring Time" and "The Sum Total of the Day." **Gardner, Mary L.,** excerpt from "What the Lilac Knew: A Memoir." **Geller, Allison,** "Self-Portrait as L.A." **Gregg, Barbara Randals,** "Angry Traces." **Harter, Penny,** "Estell Manor State Park." **Hilberry, Jane,** "Driving" and "My Muse Prefers." **Hook, Kathryn,** "The sizzle sounds like a snake hiss." **Hoppe, W. Joe,** "Freightliner West on I-40." **Huston, Karla,** "Miracle Fish," original draft version. **Huyser, Cindy,** "The Garden of Misunderstanding." **Jensen, Judy,** "Moon, Why Are You Following Me?" **Johnston, Logan,** Meeting Your Muse Collage. **Keller, Josh,** "Tons of balloons popping." **Kinga, Magdalena,** "Weeping Iris." **Kirby, David,** "My Favorite Foreign Language." **Luekhamhan, Phayvanh,** "Self-Portrait with Icarus." **McDougal, Jenny,** "Ursa Minor." **McDowell, Robert,** "Correcting the Big Mistake" and "How You Are." **Milton, Garret Lee,** "Gretel," the gluestick version. **Mirmow, Vic,** "Ten Ways of Looking at a Cedar Branch." **Morton, Karla K.,** "I *Am* the Other Mother." **Oldmixon, Katherine Durham,** "Bahía las Cabezas de San Juan." **Owens, Kaitlyn,** "At the Clinic." **Peak, Megan,** "Love Letter to a Stranger." **Randall, D'Arcy,** "A Walk between Worlds" and "Walk with New Vision." **Richardson, Laura,** "Armadillo Highway." **Robertson, Clint,** "love letter to a stranger." **Scanlon, Liz Garton,** "The Bowl." **Shankar, Ravi,** "Beyond the Pond House." **Sharif, Aisha,** line-finding exercise with *The Ideal Woman.* **Sickler, Michael A.,** "Bathing a Tiny Dog in a Very Large Bathroom." **Smith, Miranda,** "Paseo de las Luces." **Smyth, Jessamyn Johnston,** "Collage" and "Cove." **Spaar, Lisa Russ,** "Self-Portrait as Blue Boot" and "Self-Portrait in Summer with Grim Reaper, Glimpsed from a Bus." **Spriggs, Bianca,** "Pedicure." **Stephens, Rob,** "Ode to Old Testament Life." **Tetangco, Samantha,** "To Shannon, Upon News of Her Engagement (to Someone Else)." **Town, Kyla,** "Mom and Superman, circa 1972." **Turco, Lewis,** "Pines." **Wade, Sarah,** "Self-Portrait as Issa's Cabinets of Wonder." **Wallace, Christian,** line-finding exercise with *The Ideal Woman.* **Wiggerman, Scott,** "Afterward," "Because the Night," "Burnt Toast," "Coming Clean," "Introduction to Want," "Mortal Wounds," and "September 11." **Wong, Nicholas Y.B.,** "Foreign Exchange."

Index